SINDH THROUGH HISTORY AND REPRESENTATIONS

FRENCH CONTRIBUTIONS TO SINDHI STUDIES

SINDH THROUGH HISTORY AND REPRESENTATIONS

FRENCH CONTRIBUTIONS TO SINDHI STUDIES

EDITED BY
MICHEL BOIVIN

OXFORD
UNIVERSITY PRESS

OXFORD

UNIVERSITY PRESS

Great Clarendon Street, Oxford OX2 6DP

Oxford University Press is a department of the University of Oxford.
It furthers the University's objective of excellence in research, scholarship,
and education by publishing worldwide in

Oxford New York

Auckland Cape Town Dar es Salaam Hong Kong Karachi
Kuala Lumpur Madrid Melbourne Mexico City Nairobi
New Delhi Shanghai Taipei Toronto

with offices in

Argentina Austria Brazil Chile Czech Republic France Greece
Guatemala Hungary Italy Japan Poland Portugal Singapore
South Korea Switzerland Turkey Ukraine Vietnam

Oxford is a registered trade mark of Oxford University Press
in the UK and in certain other countries

ISBN 978-0-19-547503-6

Typeset in Times
Printed in Pakistan by
Kagzi Printers, Karachi.
Published by
Ameena Saiyid, Oxford University Press
No. 38, Sector 15, Korangi Industrial Area, PO Box 8214
Karachi-74900, Pakistan.

CONTENTS

ACKNOWLEDGEMENTS

The contributions to this volume were partly presented at a workshop held in Lyon in July 2004, under the supervision of Michel Boivin and Monik Kervran. This workshop was a part of the Annual Meeting of the AFEMAM (French Association for the Study of the Arab and Muslim World). It was obviously the first academic meeting to be devoted to Sindhi studies in France, and maybe in Europe. Since some scholars working on Sindhi studies could not attend the workshop, they were asked to write a paper which is included in the present volume.

Support from several persons and institutions facilitated the organization of the workshop and the preparation of this volume. We express our thanks to Sylvie Denoix, from AFEMAM, Ameena Saiyid and Rehana Khandwalla from Oxford University Press. We are also grateful to Nalini Delvoye. Her useful advice was always fruitful.

Monik Kervran is a world famous archaeologist. She devoted thirteen years to the study of several sites in Sindh. From 1989 to 1995, she worked in the delta of the Indus, and a number of articles were published on her achievements in academic journals. Then she shifted to Sehwan Sharif. With her team of Ph.D. students, she spent three months every year from 1996 to 2002 in the sacred city of the Qalandar. It is our pleasure to highlight the role she played in the French contributions to Sindhi studies. We would like to offer this volume to her as a token of gratitude.

INTRODUCTION
Michel Boivin

The Beginning of French Interest in South Asian Studies

South Asia, sometimes called the Indian subcontinent, is a very important area in today's world. French interest in South Asia and its culture can be traced back to the travels of French gentlemen in the empire of the Great Mughal.[1] Jean-Baptiste Tavernier (1605–1689) travelled six times to Turkia from 1623 to 1669, and to Persia and India from 1663 to 1669. In 1676, he published his memoirs in Paris. The data of this book, which was to see several new editions, is usually considered very reliable. It was translated into German (1681), Dutch (1682), and Italian in the same year. In the field of science, the French were the pioneers of South Asian studies. Antoine Hyacinthe Anquetil Duperron (1731–1805) published in 1776 the first translation of the Upanishads in a European language. Sanskrit was taught at the Collège de France from 1814 onwards; and between 1840 and 1847, Eugène Burnouf (1801–1852) published a translation of the *Bhagavata Purana*. in three volumes.

Pakistan is a young country but its history is 4000 years old. French interest in the study of languages spoken in present-day Pakistan is highlighted by the first Urdu grammar, published by a French missionary, Francision Maire de Tours (1680?), whose manuscript, copied by Anquetil Duperron, is still kept at the Bibliothèque Nationale. In 1830, Joseph Héliodore Garcin de Tassy (1794–1878) became the first professor of Hindustani at the Ecole Nationale des Langues Orientales, better known as Langues'O. Hindustani was at the time the *lingua franca* in northern India, as well as in some urbanised centres like Hyderabad Deccan, India. When Garcin de Tassy began to teach Hindustani, it was still a 'Persianized' language close to what is actually known as Urdu. It was only in 1850 that the word Hindi was designated to the language written in the Devanagari alphabet, while Urdu was used for the language written in the Arabo-Persian alphabet.[2]

From South Asian to Pakistan Studies

Today, Urdu is the national language of Pakistan, the official language of Kashmir, the second official language of Uttar Pradesh, Bihar, Delhi, and Andhra Pradesh. In 1886, the professorship in Hindustani was transformed into 'Hindustani and Tamil languages'. From 1920, it became 'the languages of India'. It was only in 1963 that a professorship in Urdu was created: the first Professor was André Guimbretière who did a Ph.D. on Muhammad Iqbal. Other Pakistani languages like Pashtu are taught at Langues'O. Although Punjabi is not taught, a well known scholar Denis Matringe is a specialist of Punjabi literature. He has devoted many studies to Sufi and Sikh literature in this language.

Other Pakistani languages were studied, and in 1984, Professor Gérard Fussman published an *Atlas des parlers dardes et kafirs* where he gave evidence that there was a linguistic group called *Kafir*, the only instance of an Aryan linguistic group whose language was more archaic than Vedic Sanskrit. French scholars also devoted attention to Pakistani languages which are not well known. The late Annette Frémont was a specialist of Burushaski, a language spoken in the Hunza valleys. Other scholars are specialists of languages like Khowar and Kalash.

In 1826, Masson, a French traveller, was the first to notice important ruins in Harappa, along the Ravi river. Excavations began at Harappa and Mohen-jo Daro in the 1920s. In 1924, the Louvre Museum received a seal made at Mohen-jo Daro from Lagash, in Mesopotamia. It was, however, in the 1950s after almost twenty years, that the first French Archaeological Mission arrived in Pakistan. Jean-Marie Casal was to be the man who in 1951 discovered an important site at Mundigak, near Kandahar in Afghanistan. While the British excavations were in progress at Mohen-jo Daro, Casal realized that Mundigak was a part of the Indus civilization. Later on, he decided to excavate in Pakistan. Casal began his investigations in Pakistan at Amri (1959–1962), before publishing in 1969 a reference book on the Indus Valley civilization. In 1973, Jean-François Jarrige was the head of the French Archaeological Mission in Pakistan. His main work was done at Mehrgarh. Roland Besenval worked in Balochistan while Monik Kervran focused on Sindh. A French mission was also sent to the Hindu Kush under the leadership of Anne Dambricourt-Malassé.

Social sciences related to Pakistan are more or less linked to Islamic studies of South Asia. Marc Gaborieau was trained in Arabic and philosophy before he specialized in anthropology. He went to work on the Muslim minority during a stay in Nepal. He also published chapters on Pakistan-related topics. There has been increasing attention paid to Pakistan by French scholars who were first Indianists. One can give the example of Christophe Jaffrelot, Max-Jean Zins or Jean-Luc Racine. All three have published books on Pakistan, mostly in French for French-speaking readers. In politics, the name of Mariam Abou Zahab, who teaches Pakistani studies at Langues'O is worth mentioning.

French Scholars and Sindhi Studies

When did Sindhi studies appear in France? One of the oldest scholarly works was written in French, though by a Sindhi gentleman. In the year 1926 he had defended a Ph.D. in French, at the University of Montpellier in the south of France.[3] The subject of Gopal Advani's research was rural life in Sindh. After 1926, it is not easy to find a work on Sindhi studies before Jean-Marie Casal's publication mentioned above. The political situation that has prevailed in Sindh over the last few decades has not encouraged French scholars, or other nationals, to choose Sindh for fieldwork. Nevertheless, a few students and scholars spend some time in Karachi and Sindh every year. Worthy of mention is Monik Kervran, a senior archaeologist who headed the French Archaeological Mission in Sindh from 1989 to 2002.[4]

The French Archaeological Mission in Sindh lasted no less than thirteen years. The mission's work was divided into two phases. The first phase, from 1989 to 1995, focused on the Delta area. The second mission was centred in the city of Sehwan Sharif. During the first phase, excavations of the important ports of Ratto Kot and Lahori Bandar gave evidence of the economic activities of this area in the Middle Ages. Other places, as well as regional capitals, were studied and a huge amount of data is now available on these places about which the mediaeval sources gave little information. Some methodological problems regarding these places were difficult to resolve due to lack of references in the medieval chronicles. Monik Kervran, therefore, decided to work in a place where it was possible to find remains of the different medieval periods.

The famous Alexander's Fort located in Sehwan Sharif was chosen. From 1996 to 2002, Monik Kervran spent several months every year on the tepe with a group of student archaeologists. Seven cultural phases were identified. They were particularly important because one knew almost nothing of the oldest. Digging up to twenty metres under the ground, the archaeologists were able to reach the level of Alexander's time (c.4 BC), although no remains related to the conqueror were found. The data found in the tepe is nevertheless very rich: *ostraca*, coins, ceramics. It will take some years to decipher all the implications of these pieces. Even though the French Mission is now over, Ph.D. candidates still work on Sehwan Sharif and other historical places of Sindh.

The most remarkable point is that neither French institutions nor French research groups appear in Sindh. Several projects have nevertheless been proposed by scholars like Roland Besenval, Monik Kervran or Michel Boivin. They were mostly conceived in connection with the Alliance Française de Karachi (AFK, French Cultural Centre). Although no French research group was created in Karachi, the successive directors of AFK always welcomed the students and scholars engaged in Sindhi studies. We remember Bernard Frontero, Jean-Marie Larose, Patrick Perez, and Nino Ciccarone, who hosted them most of the time and were helpful in many ways. We also have to name the cultural counsellors of the French Embassy in Islamabad, like Patrick Desseix, Alain Dhersigny, Frédéric Grare, and Marc de Grossouvre who tried their best to provide facilities.

One can count a substantial number of French students and scholars with an interest in Sindhi Studies, even if this is not the primary field of research for some of them. Among those whose work deals more or less with Sindhiyyat, we may list the following: Mariam Abou Zahab, Pierre-Alain Baud, Sophie Blanchy, Michel Boivin, Annabelle Collinet, Françoise Cousin, Chrystèle Dedebant, Reza Dehgan, Jean During, Jyoti Garin, Laurent Gayer, Pascaline Herrant, Christophe Jaffrelot, Gilles Kepel, Monik Kervran, Dominique-Sila Khan, Pierre Lachaier, Laurent Maheux, Françoise Mallison, Claude Markovits, Denis Matringe, Delphine Maucort, Audrey Péli, and Florence Toix-Giuliani.

Presentation of the Contributions

In 2004, a workshop on Sindh was organized in Lyon at the annual meeting of the French Association of Arabo-Muslim World Studies (AFEMAM). Some of the contributors of the present book attended: Michel Boivin, Annabelle Collinet, Pierre Lachaier, and Françoise Mallison. Other Ph.D. candidates and scholars could not attend but they contributed chapters to be published in the present volume. This volume, with its nine contributors, cannot encompass all the work done by French scholars in Sindh studies. Indeed, this volume presents only a small part of French contributions to Sindh Studies.[5]

The first part is devoted to historical insights. The authors study different periods of the history of Sindh, from several aspects like archaeology, medieval history, modern history, and contemporary history. Annabelle Collinet is an art historian. Her chapter gives an impressive survey of how Alexander's Fort can improve our knowledge of medieval times in Sehwan Sharif and in Sindh. The results of Collinet's work are numerous. They corroborate some facts and events which were previously doubtful, and above all, they provide new data that we had never heard about. Michel Boivin tries to point out the reasons why some Sufi centres were founded on previous Shivaite places. He observes that it is not always true that Sufi centres have visible relations with Shivaite places. On the other hand, those that were established in ancient Shivaite centres fall into specific categories. In this respect, it is interesting to look at the possibility of a reinterpretation achieved by some Sufis of ancient cults.

The two following chapters deal with urban society in Sindh. Claude Markovits studies how an urban class spread into nineteenth century Sindh. Members of this class were mainly Hindu, and the author examines how it is possible to explain this situation. While Claude Markovits focuses on colonial Sindh, and the role played by the British, Laurent Gayer chooses the post-partition period. His main interest covers the new migrants from India: the Mohajirs. He looks at the building of a 'divided city' and at the implications of this urban fragmentation on the populations living there. Even if the nationalist Mohajir party, the MQM, has lost its predominance in favour of the Jamaat-i Islami, the Mohajirs are still dominating the city of Karachi, though they cannot control entire fields of the economy.

The second part is composed of the chapters dealing with literature and society in a broader framework. Social features are studied from different approaches, like sociology or anthropology. The first one is Françoise Mallison's study on the Barmati Panth. She gives evidence that there are still devotional traditions to be found in Sindh, and also in Kutch and Saurashtra. Partition has not prevented the followers of the Barmati Panth from visiting the sanctuaries which are located in southern Sindh.

Dominique-Sila Khan and Pierre Lachaier focus on what is referred to as 'Outside Sindh'. Khan, a well-known author who has published on several Untouchable sects in Rajasthan, analyzes the role played by a Sindh Hindu divinity, Jhulelal, in the building of the Sindhi Hindus as a separate community in India. The cult of Jhulelal, reinvented by Ram Panjwani, was the nexus of the process by which a new Sindhi group appeared, knowing they will never go back to their motherland. Pierre Lachaier deals with a subgroup among the Hindu Sindhis in India, the Lohanas. The Lohanas are the most numerous group, but it is interesting to note that non-Sindhi Lohanas can be found in Gujarat. The Kutchi Lohanas are the most numerous. Lachaier observes that although they all agree they have a common origin, the Lohanas follow different rules and customs, be they Sindhis, Kutchis, or Kathiawaris.

The last two chapters deal with what is sometimes called folklore. It should be noted that in France, unlike in the United Kingdom or the USA, the term is considered somewhat pejorative. The fields under observation are nevertheless very important in anthropology. Françoise Cousin gives a survey of the different textiles as well as of the techniques used for printing them. She has travelled in southern Sindh, as far as Tharparkar, observing a great variety of practices mostly performed by specialist professionals. Finally, Delphine Maucourt tries to decipher the language expressed by the costumes and dressing techniques. Her paper makes clear that clothes are a social discourse by which the individuals give a lot of data on them, on their milieu, and on many other things.

Though rather eclectic in its range and coverage, this collection of essays is quite representative of the emerging trends in French studies on Sindhi culture. As the reader will observe, the aim of this collective volume is very modest. It wishes to give some samples of French research on Sindh. Most of the French scholars' works are published in French. The use of this language restricts readership somewhat, especially in Pakistan, India and world wide. Therefore, in order to make at least a selection of French scholarly work on relevant topics available to English language readers, we offer this contribution that also throws light on the variety of approaches made in order to achieve a greater understanding of the subject.

PART I

HISTORICAL INSIGHTS

1

CHRONOLOGY OF SEHWAN SHARIF THROUGH CERAMICS (THE ISLAMIC PERIOD)[1]

Annabelle Collinet

Abstract

Ceramics from Sindh during the Islamic period are hardly known. Some samples coming from the medieval sites of Banbhore/Daybul and al-Mansura have been published, and some glazed tiles from the 10th–12th/16th–18th centuries are also known. But the dating and typologies of glazed and unglazed contemporary ceramic types are widely unpublished: red wares with slip painted ornaments, stamped and moulded red wares, and grey and black wares are thus poorly known. The excavations in the old fort (Purana Qila) of Sehwan Sharif in central Sindh allow us to follow the history of ceramic, between the 2nd–12th cent. AH (8th–18th cent. AD), and the historical phases of the site. Five levels can be defined, linked with the Arab period of Sindh (Umayyad and then Abbasid governors, superseded by the local Habbarid emirate until the early 5th/11th century), the Ghaznawid and Ghurid periods (5th to early 7th cent. AH [11th to early 13th cent. AD]), the Delhi Sultanates and the Samma phases (7th–9th cent. AH [13th–15th cent. AD]), and finally Arghun, Tarkhan (10th cent. AH [16th cent. AD]), and Mughal periods (11th to early 12th cent. AH [17th to early 18th cent. AD]).

* * * *

This chapter aims to give the first results of the excavations of the so-called Alexander's fort in Sehwan Sharif. It will allow us to 're-construct', though not sequentially, the main phases of the medieval history of Sindh, after the advent of the Arabs. The stratigraphy of the Islamic period and how the site was occupied indicates what were the main activities of the neighbourhood, especially of the bazaars. The remains found here are a great variety of coins and ceramics. Finally, the study of the site will give a good bird's-eye view of the building of the composite culture of Sindh.

The identity of this province was framed by many different populations, arriving from the north, south, west, and east. Sindh was located at a crossroads, and like many maritime provinces, it showed a great capacity for integrating the many cultural items which were brought and used. On the other hand, the circulation of the pattern shows that every important change of ruler was accompanied by a change in the field of aesthetics. At a broader level, it could also give new evidence of the relations between the provinces and the central power.

The Archaeological Site and the Stratigraphy of the Islamic Period

The middle-sized city of Sehwan is situated in central Sindh and lies on the western bank of the Indus (FIG. 1). Near the western and southern sides of the town, the Kirthar and Lakki ranges close access to the valley, providing a passage between Upper and Lower Sindh, to which Sehwan is the key. Due to this situation Sehwan, the ancient Siwistan or Sadusan of the Islamic sources, has always been a strategic point in the Indus Valley. The site of the modern town was partly occupied by the ancient and lower city of Sehwan, around or near the Lal Shahbaz shrine. It is dominated by a huge tepe (17 ha, maximum height c.54 m) which is the ruined fort, Purana Qila (FIG. 2).

Between 1996 and 2002[2] the French Archaeological Mission in Sindh, headed by Dr Monik Kervran, worked for five seasons on this site. Several soundings were done to recognize the different phases of the fortifications and the whole period of the site's occupation. The widest excavation was done in the ravine called Asma, occupying the northern side of the tepe. This large sounding was done near the tepe centre in order to provide the site's whole stratigraphy (FIG. 3). The chronology and the ceramic ware presented here result from the study of this excavation,[3] which is the reference point for the dating of the other spots dug on the site. The team worked during three seasons in Asma ravine (1998–99, 1999–2000, and 2002) in order to provide a good stratification of all the occupation phases. In 2002 virgin soil was finally discovered (c.23.50 m).

The first three levels (c.24–30.50 m) are Pre-Islamic (c.4th century BC to the end of the 1st century AH/ 7th century AD) and the higher ones (Levels IV to VIII), up to the surface, are from the Islamic period (FIGS. 4 AND 5). This very long period of occupation is exceptional for Sindh, where the death of cities abandoned by the capricious flows of the Indus River is well known through historical texts and archaeological evidence. The Islamic levels of Sehwan's fort confirm the sources which mention its occupation from the Arab conquest to the reign of the Mughals.

The ceramic material, the stratigraphy, and the historical data defined five principal Islamic levels in the Asma sounding, corresponding to:

Level IV (c.30/31–35 m)	Arab period	2nd–4th cent. AH (8th–10th cent. AD)
Level V (c.35–38 m)	End of the Habbarid emirate, Ghaznawid, and Ghurid periods	5th–7th cent. AH (11th–13th cent. AD)
Level VI (c.38–40 m)	Delhi Sultanates and Samma periods	7th–9th cent. AH (13th–15th cent. AD)
Level VII (c.40–41 m)	Arghun and Tarkhan periods	10th cent. AH (16th cent. AD)
Level VIII (c.41–44 m)	Mughal period	11th to early 12th cent. AH (17th to early 18th cent. AD)

1. Sehwan during the Arab Period

The Arab Conquest

According to the *Chach Nama*,[4] the Arab conquest of Siwistan occurred in AH 93 (AD 711) after the seizure of Debal (Daybul, the site of Banbhore) and Nirun (modern Hyderabad). Sent to Sindh by his uncle al-Hajjaj bin Yusuf al-Thaqafi, the young conqueror Muhammad ibn Qasim took the fort after a one-week siege ended by the flight of the governor, Bachehra, and the surrender of its inhabitants after the intercession of the *Samaniyan*, or Buddhists.[5] Before AH 93 (AD 711) the fort was taken again by Massab (?) ibn Abd al-Rahman, sent with an army by Muhammad ibn Qasim to counter the installation of Chandram Halah, an ancient governor of the fort.[6] Al-Baladhuri mentions the conquest of *Sadusan* in connection with this second episode.[7]

The First Islamic Period in Sehwan (After AH 93 [AD 711–712])

The transition between the Pre-Islamic period and the Arabic one is not easy to see in stratigraphy. There is no trace of any battle which could be linked to the conquest in the Asma sounding. Nevertheless the area is almost abandoned at the beginning of Level IV (c.30.50–31m) as shown by the small quantity of pottery (9 sherds/m³), and the abandonment of the metal workshops discovered in the preceding Level (III). The ceramic material changes from this level onwards (typology differs from Level III); around 30–31m were found some Islamic coins, and a little higher (31.36m) appeared the first *ostraca* written in Arabic.[8] These elements indicate the Muslim presence, but the junction with the earlier conquest itself can hardly be seen.

Level IV: The Metal Workshops

The level (c.30.50–35 m) in which the earth was heterogeneous (mix of clay, ash, and charcoal) contained very few structures of mud and baked brick (**FIGS. 6/1–6/2**). The area was occupied by metal workshops, showing more or less intense activity. One workshop of mud brick with two ovens[9] was occupied for quite a long time, for three successive ground levels were cleared (at 31.50 m, 31.86 m and 32.20 m). A later oven was found higher up (c.33 m), and later on another workshop of mud brick (c.34.45–34.60 m) was erected and occupied in the same area.[10] Other signs of this metallurgical activity during the whole level are the numerous scorias of iron (around 300) and the crucibles found there (**FIGS. 8:41**).

Level IV can be divided into three sub-levels (IVa, b and c) corresponding to some significant changes in the ceramic material and in the site's political history. During the first phase (IVa, c.30.50–32.67 m), the density of occupation grew quite fast after the first layer described above (c.30.50–31.36 m) as shown by the number of sherds (73/m³). In Level IVb (c.32.67–34.13 m) the metallurgical activity seems to be less important, maybe like the occupation of the area (53 sherds/m³). The end of layer IVc (c.34.13–35.00 m) is marked by a reddened layer, which may be the sign of a battle. The metallurgical activity was more intense during this phase and the occupation more important as shown by the number of sherds found (89/m³).

Ceramic Material of Level IV

The ceramic material[11] of Level IV (**FIG. 8**) is characterized by the domination of cooking pots with everted rims and necked jar types. Numerous slip painted ornaments of a very good quality also define the level, along with the development of moulded and stamped wares adorned with mica particles on the surface. The grey wares are very few in the 2nd–3rd cent. AH (8th–9th cent. AD)[12] but they seem to be slightly more numerous during the 4th/10th century (**PL. 3:1–5**). Glazed wares are rare and the only imports occured between the 2nd/8th century and also c. AD 850. Sindhi production of glazed wares can be traced from the middle of the 3rd/9th century, with its development indicated during the 4th/10th century. It seems to have been linked with the Habbarid period.

1.1 Level IVa: The 2nd/8th Century (c.30.50-32.67 m)

The Period of the Umayyad and Abbasid Governors: Coin Data and Inscribed Sherds

The coins found in this sub-level confirm a datation of the 2nd century AH: one is dated AH 120 (AD 737–738).[13] In addition, other coins show the Umayyad and then Abbasid presence during this period. Three coins[14] in the name of Mansur ibn Jumhur al-Kalbi, the governor and adventurer of the end of the Umayyad period, were found. Two of them were minted in al-Mansura. According to al-Yaqubi, Mansur ibn Jumhur revolted against the caliphate, held Sindh for a while (c. AH 129–134 [AD 746–752]) and took the Sehwan fort when he arrived, before crossing the Indus.[15] Four coins[16] bearing the name of Umar b. Hafs Hazarmard (c. AH 142–151 [AD 759–767]) were found, and six others[17]—one of them minted in al-Mansura—from his successor, Hisham b. Amr (c. AH 151–157 [AD 767–773]). Both governors were sent to Sindh by the Abbasid caliph al-Mansur (r. AH 136–158 [AD 754–775]).[18]

Eight little sherds inscribed in Arabic with black ink on the fabric were discovered in the same layers, but also in the upper layers of occupation of Level IVa.[19] One of the first four sherds in stratigraphy (UF 407, 408, 409, 398) was associated with the coin dated AH 120 (AD 737-38) and with one of 'Umar b. Hafs Hazarmard (UF 407). Four other inscribed sherds came from the last occupation layers of Level IVa (UF 395, 338 and 339). One with a Kufic script bears an extract of the Quranic surat *al-Imran* (III, 103). The type of script suggests it is dated from the end of the 2nd century AH (8th century AD).

Ceramic Material

Painted Red Wares

The ceramic material is almost entirely composed of fine red and pinkish wares tempered with sand and mica but also quartz, and some contain white markings. The closed shapes often bear a layer of *barbotine* decoration on the body, and beautiful painted ornamentation on the shoulder, in black, red, and white slips. Motifs are geometrical and floral in the beginning of the level, and later represent big lotus flowers and birds (PL. 1 1-3:5). They are very similar to some painted wares associated with the first Islamic phases of Banbhore/Daybul[20]and al-Mansura.[21] The most common shapes in Sehwan are cooking pots (*handali* type) with elegant everted rims (FIG. 8: 11-12), jars with or without neck, (FIG. 8: 4, 6, 9), and numerous basins, all presenting the same truncated cone profile (FIG. 8: 34). Some jar shapes were present in the preceding level (III, Pre-Islamic) but they tend to disappear (FIG. 8: 1-3).

Stamped and Moulded Red Wares

Some rare red and pinkish wares found at the end of this level (c.31.86-32.67 m) are adorned with stamped and moulded motifs (PL. 2: 1, 7-8). More of these appear in the more recent layers of Level IV.

Imports

In the same layer were found some imported wares, probably coming from Mesopotamia, judging from their light buff clay paste. They included an unglazed handle of a pitcher[22] and a fragment of a jar with a turquoise glaze (PL. 4: 1-2).

1.2   Level IVb: The 3rd/9th Century (c.32.67-34.13 m)

The First Phase of the Habbarid Emirate

This phase is probably linked with the beginning of the independent Habbarid emirate, of Arab descent, who ruled Sindh from the capital of al-Mansura. The dynasty is not very well known, but their rule began in AH 240 (AD 854-855) according to al-Yaqubi, when their leader Umar ibn Abd al-Aziz al-Habbari asked the caliph al-Mutawakkil for nomination as governor.[23] Two illegible but Habbarid-type coins were found in these layers,[24] and may corroborate the relative dating of this sub-level.

Ceramic Material

Numerous puzzling ceramics (more than 250 fragments were found) appear in these layers and can be traced until the end of the Habbarid period in Sehwan (c. AH 416 [AD 1025]). They may be elements of camel necklaces (?)[25] and they are made of modelled and painted red clay (**FIG. 8: 40**)

Painted Red Wares

The ceramic colours like the temper materials do not change in this level, but one can observe some coarser pastes which did not exist earlier. Ceramic forms are more diversified than in Level IVa. Many of them are adorned with slip-painted motifs, of a very good quality. In addition to the flowers and birds described earlier, some new patterns are also found like dots and 'plumes' (**PL. 1: 4, 6-7, 9**). Some of the sherds mentioned above from Banbhore/Daybul are again similar. The *barbotine* layers on the cooking pots and jars are still numerous. The typology is now dominated by necked jars (**FIG. 8: 7**), and some *handali* with higher everted rims appear (**FIG. 8: 18, 20-21**). New shapes of little jars and water bottles are also seen (**FIG. 8: 28-29, 31**).

Stamped and Moulded Red Wares

The number of stamped and moulded wares increases, and these types of wares seem to characterize the Abbasid and Habbarid levels in al-Mansura.[26] As in these sites, the surfaces of the vessels (mostly little bowls and cooking pots or jars) are often embellished with mica particles (**PL. 2: 2-4, 9-10, 12-13**).

Imported and Sindhi Glazed Wares

The number of imported jars from Mesopotamia, with the same buff paste and turquoise glaze grows (**PL. 4: 3**). Some blue-green glazed jars of the same type were found in the early Islamic levels of Banbhore and al-Mansura.[27] At the end of this phase were found the first sherds of regional glazed wares ocurring on the site. They have a red clay paste tempered with sand, very similar to the unglazed material. One sherd is covered with a green glaze, another may be an imitation of the *faïences* produced in Mesopotamia during the Abbasid period: a green glaze fuses on a white slip ground, under a clear glaze (same type as **PL. 4: 7-8**). This second type of ceramic is also known in al-Mansura: describing some sherds of this kind coming from the site, Hobson says that the red paste is covered with a white slip, green and manganese ornaments under a clear glaze.[28] In Banbhore, the same type of glazed material is associated with the reconstruction of the curtain wall during what Khan calls the first Abbasid period (AD 750-892).[29] In Iraq (Samarra) and in the Persian Gulf (Siraf), the high-fired faïences decorated on a white glazed ground with other colours than cobalt blue seem to appear in the 3rd/9th century.[30]

1.3 Level IVc: The 4th/10th Century (c.34.13-35.00 m)

Sehwan and the Habbarid Kingdom of al-Mansura

Al-Masudi,[31] al-Istahri[32] and Ibn Hawkal[33] give information about the Habbarid emirate in the 4th/10th century, the other Islamic power being at that time centred in Multan in Punjab. The first author went to Sindh in AH 303 (AD 915), and the two others met there c. AD 951. They all write that the *qurays* Habbarid power extended from al-Mansura to al-Rur in Upper Sindh[34] which was on the boundary of their territories.[35] Their presence in Sehwan is confirmed by the five Habbarid coins found in this level.[36] Most of them are illegible but one[37] names Umar, who could be the Habbarid emir Umar b. Abdullah (c. AH 300-330 [AD 912-942]).[38]

Ceramic Material

Painted Red and Grey Wares

The wares do not really change in this level, but the majority are red in colour and the number of medium quality wares increases. The fine quality of the painted decorations continues, and we find the same beautiful motifs with some new animals, such as camels and an elephant (PL. 1: 8, 10-11). The ceramic forms, mostly in red but also in grey wares which are more commonly represented, do not dramatically change. The two dominating shapes are the *handali* with different types of more or less carinated rims (FIG. 8: 14, 17, 22, 24) and the necked jar (FIG. 8: 8). The type of open jars with pronounced lips is better represented in that phase (FIG. 8: 10).

Stamped and Moulded Red Wares

Moulded but overall stamped red wares are quite numerous and some cooking pots have stamped rims. Mica is abundant on the surfaces of these moulded and stamped wares (FIG. 8: 36; PL. 2: 5-6, 11, 14-15), certainly produced in the city as shown by a fragment of mould found during the excavation.[39]

Imported and Sindhi Glazed Wares

Imported glazed wares from Mesopotamia are of the same monochrome type as earlier, but one lustrous sherd shows that some more luxurious ceramics were also brought to Sehwan (FIG. 8: 39; PL. 4: 4). The same type of monochrome lustre wares from Iraq or western Iran was found in al-Mansura[40] and the description given by Hobson could be applied to the Sehwan sherd: 'soft buff faïence with opaque, greyish white glaze and decoration in olive-brown or golden brown lustre'.[41] The number of regional glazed wares grows and different types are now seen (FIG. 8: 37-38; PL. 4: 6-10): monochrome green and white glazes, imitations of faïences with green flows, splash wares with green and yellow colours, underglaze painted decoration and one *sgraffiato*. The same types of glazed wares are associated with the Abbasid period and late Abbasid period (from 750 to the 12th century AD) in Banbhore.[42]

2. Sehwan between the 5th and the Early 7th Century AH (11th to Early 13th Century AD)

Level V: The Bazaar Period

Level V (c.35-38 m) is the richest in the Islamic period of the fort as far as the ceramic material is concerned. The kind of occupation changes dramatically for in the Asma ravine a bazaar was discovered. Its existence can be traced for more than two centuries. It shows that at that time, the fort was occupied by a city. Several shops opening on little streets and sidewalks in baked brick, were cleared (FIG. 6/3-6/5). Six successive occupation phases of the market can be recognized (Level Va to f), which show the construction of the bazaar (Level Va, c.35.10-35.82 m), its first extension (Level Vb, c.35.57-36.17 m), and later a second (Level Vd, c.36.36-37.10 m) and a third extension (Level Vf, c.37.25-38.13 m) just before its violent destruction. The first layers of the market (Va to Vc, c.35.10-36.52 m) may be linked with the last period of the Habbarid rule over Sindh (c. AD 1000-1025). The higher ones (Vd to f, c.36.36-38.13 m) may correspond with the Ghaznawid and then Ghurid sultanates (c. 5th–early 7th cent. AH [11th–13th cent. AD]).

Ceramic Material from the Bazaar

This period shows great changes in all types of wares seen earlier on the site (FIG. 9-10). In the first two sub-levels of the market, we still find numerous 'necklace elements' which appeared in the middle 3rd/9th century, but they completely disappear later (PL. 1: 12). The imported ceramics also seem to disappear. The slip-painted red wares are less fine and the majority of the slip ornaments less precise, and during the first phase of the bazaar the motifs are only geometrical and rarely floral. The end of the second phase of the market is nevertheless characterized by new bird and animal motifs. The moulded and stamped red wares completely disappear, even if some rare sherds are still found in the first phase of the market. The grey and black polished wares, finer in the first phase, are very numerous and really define an important part of the bazaar ceramic material. The number of glazed wares, probably locally made, increases greatly and the wares are deeply influenced by the contemporary ceramics produced in Khurasan. Monochrome glazed wares, sgraffiato and underglazed painted types change throughout the long life of the bazaar. All the ceramic wares studied are earthenware; stone paste or fritware seems to be unknown in Sindh.

2.1 Level Va to Vc: The First Half of the 5th/11th Century (c.35.0-36.52 m)

The End of the Habbarid Kingdom in Sindh and the Coin Data

The end of the Habbarid kingdom of al-Mansura probably occurred with the arrival of Mahmud of Ghazna in Sindh c. AH 416 (AD 1025), after the seizure of Sumanat in Gujarat. The only contemporary source which mentions Mahmud's campaign in Sindh seems to be the *Diwan-i Farruhi* written by the Persian poet Abul-Hasan Ali b. Julug Farruhi (d. AH 429 [AD 1037–38]). He relates the attack on al-Mansura and the flight of Hafif, but does not say if this ruler was a Sumra or a Habbarid.[43]

All the coins found in the bazaar seem to be either Habbarid or of the Habbarid type. In the first levels of the market (Va to Vc), they may confirm the existence of the last emirs of the dynasty. Most of them are illegible, but two bear the name of Ahmad[44] and another one that of Umar.[45] In the same levels were found three coin moulds, suggesting that the city had a mint at that time.

The Bazaar at the End of the Habbarid Emirate: Stratigraphy

The first layers of the level (Va, c.35.10-35.82 m) show that the area was largely abandoned or poorly occupied as shown by the sherd density ($29/m^3$). The clayey earth mixed with ash and charcoal may be another trace of the battle (?) which ended Level IV, followed by a complete change in the occupation of the site. On this layer is erected the bazaar where a street and baked brick[46] shops have been cleared. A first extension of the bazaar quickly occurred (Level Vb, c.35.57-36.17 m), with the construction of new shops and sidewalks of baked brick.[47] The earth enclosed some broken baked bricks. The occupation is denser but remains middling judging from the number of sherds ($48/m^3$). A later layer of occupation in the same structures of the bazaar[48] (Vc, c.35.92-36.52 m) with ground levels[49] closes this first great phase of the bazaar and appears like a layer of transition as far as ceramics is concerned and may be dated c. AD 1025–1050. It can be linked with a change of power in the city. The rather medium occupation seen earlier is confirmed (46 sherds/m^3).

Ceramic Material

Painted Red Wares

The colours of the wares change slightly compared with Level IV: in Level Va they are red, from rather fine to coarse and tempered with sand and mica. In the successive layers (Vb and c) the wares are equally pinkish or red, rather fine to coarse in quality but tend to be mostly in-between. The painted ornaments are almost all geometrical (**Pl. 1: 13**); birds and other animals known before seem to disappear completely, as do the pointed dots. A new kind of flower with four petals replaces the more elaborate floral compositions of the past centuries (**Pl. 1: 14**). Types of necked or open jars change (**Fig. 9: 1-5**) like the cooking pot rims (**Fig. 9: 12-15, 17-18**). Some recall more ancient types (**Fig. 12: 16**) and others, with simple oblique (**Fig. 9: 20-21**) or hemmed rims (**Fig. 9: 22-23**), in red or black and grey wares, exist from the beginning to the end of the bazaar. Some new shapes also appear, such as lanterns or little beakers and coarse basins (**Fig. 10: 1-2, 6-7, 8**).

Moulded and Stamped Red Wares

Moulded red wares are very few and are only seen on closed shapes (**Pl. 2: 16-18**). The moulded ornaments enhanced with slip-painted motifs appear on the shoulder of cooking pots, which were made in two parts. The mica particles on the surface are not as common as before. Stamped red wares disappear also, for only three stamped sherds were found in the same layers (**Pl. 2: 19**).

Grey and Black Wares

Grey and black polished wares of very good quality, often bearing some engraved geometrical designs, characterize the bazaar period (**Pl. 3: 6-19**). They remain less numerous than the red wares, yet several hundred sherds were found in these layers. Their pastes are very fine to medium in quality and tempered with sand and mica. This production is a more luxurious one than the red wares, because the firing process is more complex and needs a reduced atmosphere and probably an oven with two rooms.[50] Types known in grey and black wares do not differ from the red: they are almost all cooking pots, sometimes with a barbotine layer on the body, but also with lids in the first phases of the bazaar (**Fig. 10: 4**). In al-Mansura, the grey polished wares seem to characterize the last phase of occupation, which ended c. 7th/13th century.[51]

Local (?) Glazed Wares
As with the grey and black ceramics, the glazed wares increase markedly in this period and are much more diversified. Pastes are all pinkish, tempered with sand and mica and of a rather fine quality. Two major types of cups are known, those with an open wall and rim, and those with a straight one (**Fig. 10: 15-20**). The bases are annular (**Fig. 10: 21-22**). A few samples of glazed pots were also found in the same layers. The glazes, opacified or not, are monochromes (green, turquoise blue, and yellow, **Pl. 4: 12-13**). Most of the glazed wares are painted on a white slip ground under a clear glaze (**Pl. 4: 23-26**), and slip painted in black or red on a white slip ground under a clear glaze (**Pl. 4: 29-32**). They are very close to the ceramics found in Khurasan (Nishapur,[52] Balkh,[53] Lashkar-i Bazaar, and Bust[54]), and are clearly influenced by these productions. We know from al-Masudi for instance, that a commercial traffic between Sindh, Khurasan, and India was well developed before that time.[55] The slip-painted and glazed wares are also very similar to some found in al-Mansura[56] and Banbhore.[57] The sgraffiato material (**Pl. 4: 15-18**) also increases and may give some dating elements: in Level Va are found some sgraffiato wares with false inscription motifs engraved in the slip ground, often enhanced with painted dots and a clear glaze. A second type of sgraffiato, the 'hatched type' appears as in Siraf slightly later, probably before AD 1050:[58] it was found from Level Vb to Vc (where it is more commonly represented) in the bazaar, and continues to exist later. The same kind of hatched sgraffiato was found in Banbhore. According to F.A. Khan, the engraved slip-painted wares was introduced in Banbhore[59] between the 10th and 12th centuries AD and were characterized by the ceramic material of that phase of the city. The hatched type is dated from the 11th century AD and later.[60]

2.2   Level Vd to Vf: c. AD 1050–1220 (c.36.36-38.13 m)

The Ghaznawid and Ghurid Power in Central Sindh and Sehwan
From the 5th/11th century onwards, it is difficult to know how Sindh was divided between the local Sumra dynasty and the Ghaznawid and later Ghurid empires. It seems that the Sumra were centred on Lower Sindh and the strategic city of Sehwan may have escaped their rule, being on the boundary of the Ghaznawid and Ghurid dynasties.

According to C.E. Bosworth, the Ghaznawid empire at the death of Mahmud of Ghazna (AH 421 [AD 1030]) extended over the Punjab and a part of Sindh.[61] It seems that their power in Central Sindh, in fact down to Sehwan, was still exerted under Ibrahim Sultan (r. AH 451–492 [AD 1059–1099]) according to al-Mervarrudi,[62] who says that his emir (?) Abul Faraj inspected a great part of the Ghaznawid territories once a year, and mentions Siwastan in this context.[63] The situation remains obscure in the Ghurid period, for if Muizz al-Din (r. AH 569–602 [AD 1173–1206]) took Multan and Uchch in AD 1175–76 and Daybul in AD 1182, the events in Sehwan are not mentioned.[64] The troubled period of Sehwan and the whole of Sindh in the period AH 607–625 (AD 1210–1228), is probably the time of the destruction of the bazaar. In AH 607/1210,[65] Nasir al-Din Qubacha seized Multan, Sindustan, and Diwal according to the *Tabaqat-i Nasiri*.[66] It also says that the city of Sehwan at the arrival of Qubacha was ruled by his deputy Fahr al-Din Salari, who gave him the place. Qubacha stayed for one month in Sindustan and then marched on Dibal.[67] In AH 618 (AD 1221) Jalal al-Din Kwarizm Shah attacked Shiwistan/Siwastan and for a second time in AH 620 (AD 1223) according to the same source.[68] The *Tabaqat-i Nasiri* also states that in AH 623 (AD 1226), 'a body of the tribe of Khalj, a part of the Khwarazmi forces, acquired supremacy over the district of Mansurah, which is one of the cities of Siwastan, and their head was Malik Khan, the Khalj'. Malik Khan Khalji took Siwistan the same year according to Juzjani.[69] He was finally defeated by Qubacha.[70] Malik Khan Khalji was linked with Jalal al-Din Khwarizm Shah and protected by Iletmish, hence the reprisals on Qubacha who died in AH 625 (AD 1228) when Iletmish had taken the whole of Sindh.[71]

The coins coming from this second phase of the bazaar are very numerous (c.200) but are illegible. Some seem to be of the Habbarid type[72] and none can actually be linked with the dynasties mentioned above.

The Second Phase of the Bazaar: Stratigraphy

This phase (Level Vd to Vf, c.36.36-38.13 m) begins with a new extension of the bazaar (Level Vd, c.36.36-37.10 m) where new shops and sidewalks of baked brick are constructed[73] along the streets.[74] Some ground levels were cleared c.36.50 m in the shops and at 36.95 m for some landings. The density of occupation increases considerably as shown by the number of sherds (185/m³). It stays the same in Level Ve (c.36.80-37.62 m), corresponding with a later occupation of the same structures,[75] where some ground levels were found c.37.13 m. A last extension of the bazaar characterizes the above layer (Vf, c.37.25-38.13 m) which was destroyed at the end of this phase (c.38 m). Some new shops and a street appear,[76] beside the occupation of more ancient structures. Some floor levels with fireplaces were cleared at c.37.80 m. The occupation is still dense although less than in the preceding layers judging from the sherd numbers (122/m³).

Ceramic Material

Painted Red Wares

The wares are mostly red in Level Vd, and then tend to be pinkish in the majority (Level Vf). They are fine to coarse in quality and are always tempered with sand and mica. The types of closed shapes change significantly: the more common shapes are large water jars with a short rim opening (FIG. 9: 7-11), and cooking pots with frequently an engraved hemmed rim (FIG. 9: 24-27). Some common or painted bowls (FIG. 10: 13-14) appear in the last two layers. Barbotine layers covering the cooking pot bodies are common, as well as some slip-painted ornaments in black and red slip. The four-petal flowers are still known (Pl. 1: 15), in addition to geometrical patterns also known in the first phase of the market. But some new birds (waders) appear with other animals (goats?). They are always depicted on dotted grounds (Pl. 1: 16-17). They become more numerous during the last level of the bazaar. The use of mica particles to enhance some parts of the painted ornaments becomes common in the same layer.

Grey and Black Wares

They are still very numerous, but the wares are medium and coarser than in the first part of the bazaar. The temper materials are unchanged (sand and mica). The shapes are usually cooking pots (Pl. 3: 15-19) and cups or bowls (FIG. 10: 10-12), close to the red wares in typology and chronology. Some black wares also characterize the ceramic material dated before the 13th century AD at Cambay in Gujarat, according to Mehta.[77]

Local Glazed Wares

The production of glazed ware at Sehwan is quite certain for this period, for an oven rod with trickles of green glaze was found in another sounding of the site, in contemporary layers.[78] The wares, always tempered with mica and sand, are rather fine to rather coarse in quality. Their colours are red in general, but also pinkish. The cups (FIG. 10: 23-25) present an oblique rim and stand on flat bases. Other bases are flat or annular (FIG. 10: 29-32) and are coarser at the end of the level. A new type of bowl also characterizes the end of the bazaar (FIG. 10: 26-28; PL. 4: 21), as also some plates found in the same layers (FIG. 10: 34-35; PL. 4: 20). One spouted water or milk jar belongs to the same period and bears an inscription painted in brown under a green glaze (FIG. 10: 36).

The glazed wares present the same techniques of decoration as in the first phase of the bazaar: monochrome glazes (mostly green, but also yellow and turquoise blue), sgraffiato or combed decoration (PL. 4: 20-21), painted motifs (mostly in green and brown, or with red and black slips, PL. 4: 27-28) on a white slip ground and under clear glaze. In Level Vd were still found some painted wares which recall the 'buff ware' group of Nishapur.[79] Underglaze painted and slip-painted motifs are still produced but tend to disappear at the end of the level. The same changes in the glazed material were observed in Bust and Lashkar-i Bazaar,[80] Ghazna,[81] and Balkh[82] between the Ghaznawid and the Ghurid period.

The most common type of this bazaar phase is a kind of splash ware, with green and yellow flows on a cream or white slip ground and under a clear glaze (FIG. 10: 25, 32; PL. 4: 33). This type is represented during all the bazaar levels but it grows from Level Vd onwards. In Level Vf, it has become the most common glazed type. Some close ceramic types were picked out in Bust and Balkh for the 12th century AD.[83] The second characteristic type of this period is the sgraffiato. Engraved motifs are seen under clear glaze, under green and yellow solash glaze, under monochrome green glaze (FIG. 10: 34-35), and under black glaze (Level Vf, PL. 4: 19). This important presence of sgraffiato types also characterizes the above mentioned sites in Khurasan.[84] Some rare monochrome black glazes coming from the last layer of the bazaar (PL. 4: 14) recall the brown-black glazed tiles from Ghazna and are linked with the Ghurid period of the site, and thus dated c. AD 1150–1210.[85]

3   Sehwan during the Delhi Sultanates and the Samma Period (7th–9th/ 13th–15th centuries)

Level VI: The Fort Garrison Structures

Above the bazaar level, the occupation mode of the fort changed profoundly, for it became a well-built garrison site in Level VI (c.38-39.60 m, FIG. 7/1-7/2). Ibn Battuta bears witness to that fact, for, when he came to Sehwan in c. AH 734 (AD 1333–1334), he saw the large cavalry garrison in the citadel, and his lodging was in the lower city.[86] Some broken iron weapons and tools found in this level corroborate this military occupation.

The level can be divided into two major phases, with two layers in each. The first phase (Level VIa and VIb, c.38-39 m), is linked with the Delhi Sultanate period and datable to the 13th–14th centuries AD. After the destruction of the bazaar, some baked brick structures were built. The soil is clayey in this level, and the area much less occupied and rich than in Level V, as shown by the number of sherds (VIa: $56/m^3$ and VIb: $30/m^3$) and the quality of the ceramic material. The second phase (Level VIc and VId, c.38.80-39.60 m) may be related to the Samma dynasty and dated c.15th century AD. The occupation is very loose judging from the sherd numbers (Level VIc: 12/m3 and VId: $22/m^3$). The baked brick structures are reworked and iron metalworking is well attested (Level VIc, c.38.80-39.35 m). The last layer of the level (VId, c.39.30-39.60 m) may have been quite short in duration. The same baked brick structures are occupied, and iron metalworking is still visible. The level is ended by a very thick black layer, visible in the whole sounding and one metre high in spots. This easily visible trace of battle and fire fits in with the destruction of the structures.

Ceramics from Level VI

The new type of occupation of the area can be linked with some deep changes in the ceramic material (**FIG. 11**), whose quantity and quality fall. The most represented type is red—common, painted ware, and the most common shape is a rather big cooking pot with oblique and engraved rim. Some moulded red wares may have also been produced, but this type is rare. The level is also characterized by the concomitant decrease of the black and grey wares and of the glazed ceramics. They almost disappear in the last layer of the level. Lastly, imported wares are totally unknown in the first phase of the level, but a Chinese *dusun* jar and a porcelain sherd were found in the last layers of Level VI.[87]

3.1 The Delhi Sultanate Citadel

The Delhi Sultans and Sehwan: Historical and Numismatic Data

In AH 625 (AD 1228), Shams al-Din Iletmish (r. AH 607–633 [AD 1211–1236]) had seized Nasir al-Din Qubacha and conquered the whole of Sindh according to the *Tabaqat-i Nasiri*[88] in which it is said that the fort of Siwastan is one of twelve famous forts taken by the sultan.[89] Sindustan appears again in the text, when some Mongol incursions, under the reign of Ala al-Din Masud Shah (AH 639–644 [AD 1242–1246]), brought the Delhi governor from Multan to the city.[90]

According to a much later source, in AH 659 (AD 1251) the sultan Nasir al-Din Mahmud Shah (r. AH 644–664 [AD 1246–1266]) marched with an army from Delhi to the Punjab and went as far as Sehwan, where he named Kalich Khan governor of the place.[91]

The most remote and legible coins bearing names of Delhi Sultans were found in the first layers of the level (VIa, EU 260). One is inscribed with the name of Ghiyas-ud-din Balban (r. AH 664–686 [AD 1266–1287]). The other names Ala al-Din Muhammad Shah (r. AH 695–715 [AD 1296–1316]). Under his reign, the territories of the Delhi sultanate witnessed their greatest extension, and the same source says that in AH 696 (AD 1296) the sultan sent Nusrat Khan with an army to the principal cities of Punjab and Sindh, among them Sehwan, in order to subdue the revolting tribes and name trustworthy governors.[92] But in AH 697 (AD 1297–98) according to Barani and Mir Masum,[93] Sehwan was attacked by the Mongols and the governor of Multan, Nusrat Khan, came to Sehwan for the defence of the city and seized them. At that time, c. AH 720 (AD 1320), the Sehwan governor was Taj al-Din Kafur according to Barani.[94] He was replaced the same year by Ghiyas-ud-din Tughluq (r. AH 720–725 [AD 1320–1325]), for Mir Masum says that the sultan named Malik Ali Sher in charge of the city.[95] In AH 728 (AD 1327), a new governor was sent to Sehwan by the sultan Ghiyas-ud-din Muhammad Shah II (r. AH 725–752 [AD 1325–51]).[96] Ibn Battuta came to *Siwecitan* a few years later (c. AH 734 [AD 1333–1334]) and recounted the revolt which had occurred in the city just before his arrival. The future Samma Jam Unnar had killed Malak Ratan, the Delhi governor of the fort. One army under command of the Delhi governor of Multan came and led the siege, seized the fort and carried out bloody reprisals, but Unnar escaped.[97] The power of Delhi in Sehwan is demonstrated at the accession of Firuz Shah Tughluq (r. AH 752–790 [AD 1351–1388]), who was at Sehwan in AH 752 (AD 1351), where the *khutba* was for the first time read in his name according to Isami.[98]

An inscription in the shrine of Lal Shahbaz Qalandar also indicates that in AH 756 (AD 1356), domes were erected in the monument, under the patronage of the local Delhi governor, Ihtiyar al-Dan Malik.[99] In addition, a coin in the name of Firuz Shah, minted in Delhi and dated AH 789 (AD 1387) was found in the Mughal level (VIIIa) of the sounding.[100]

Level VIa and VIb: Stratigraphy

During the first phase (c.38-39 m, Levels VIa and VIb), some baked brick structures[101] erected above the rubble of the bazaar are seen clearly in the northern area of the sounding (Level VIa, c.38-38.50 m). But the ancient street layout is reused, and also perhaps some structures dating from the preceding level. The same street is still in use during the later occupation layer of the buildings, which probably housed some members of the garrison. This second level is clearly visible (Level VIb, c.38.40-39 m) with some surface levels which were cleared and a new structure built in baked brick on a stone base.[102] The northern part of the sounding is devoid of construction.

Ceramic Material

Painted Red Wares

The rather fine to medium red wares, tempered with sand and mica, are adorned with animal motifs, four-petaled flowers and geometrical patterns similar to the painted ornaments seen in the last phase of the bazaar (**PL. 1: 18-19, 22**). Mica particles enhancing the painted bands are common. But shapes change, for, if some types of jars without neck and small jars (**FIG. 11: 1-2, 6**) recall some more ancient ones, new kinds of cooking pots with engraved rims (**FIG. 11: 8**) are now the characteristic and more common type. They can be seen until the end of Level VI (**FIG. 11: 12-13**). Their rims are often inlaid with little stones. Some water pots (*kuza*) with fine painted decoration are also seen (**FIG. 11: 9; PL. 1: 18**), beside new shapes of painted plates (**FIG. 11: 14-15**), cups, and bowls (**FIG. 11: 18-20**) generally bearing slip-painted motifs which also characterize this period.

Moulded Red Wares

A new production of moulded cups and cooking pots seems to begin at this period and can be found from the beginning of the level (VIa). Mica particles illumine the surfaces of these moulded wares (**PL. 2: 20**).

Black and Grey Wares

This type of ceramic (**PL. 3: 20-23**) is less numerous than in the bazaar level but is still well represented in Level VIa. The proportion is much lower in the second sub-level (VIb). The almost contemporary material from the fort of Adilabad in Delhi[103] includes a few black and grey wares. On the contrary, the most common type of unglazed ware in Baroda (Gujarat) is the black ware. It is associated with levels from the 14th century AD onwards according to Mehta: the shapes are almost handali with an oblique rim and a globular body, with engraved designs on the shoulder.[104]

Glazed Wares

Their number and quality diminish a great deal in Level VIb. Great changes are observed even from the beginning of the level, for the glazed wares are henceforth essentially monochrome: almost green, with some yellow and turquoise blue, though there are also some instances of white wares (**PL. 4: 34-35**). The great majority of shapes seem to be of cups and bowls. Much less represented are the underglaze painted wares, always on a white or cream slip ground (**PL. 4: 36-39**). The underglaze painted wares seem to be more common in Adilabad, the fort built by Muhammad b. Tughluq c. AD 1325 near Tughluqabad in Delhi.[105] They are essentially adorned with floral patterns, and the monochrome wares of the site are, on the contrary, rare and always green. In Sehwan, the sgraffiato types are also much less numerous and the engraved motifs are only found under monochrome glazes. Besides, the green and yellow splash wares tend to disappear.

3.2 The Samma Phase of the Citadel c. 15th to the beginning of the 16th century AD

The Samma in Sehwan under Control of Delhi Sultans

From AD 1351 to 1520, the local dynasty of the Sammas held a part of Sindh. Their struggle for power is mentioned by Ibn Battuta c. AD 1333–1334, but if they seized Lower Sindh c. AD 1351, their power in Sehwan can be detected slightly later. They may have tried to take the fort again during the second half of the 14th century AD, but in AH 795 (AD 1393) according to Mir Masum, Jam Tamachi was seized by the army of the Delhi Sultan, Ala al-Din Sikandar Shah and made prisoner in the Sehwan fort.[106] According to Mir Masum, Jam Taghlak Samma, who must have ruled during the first part of the 9th/15th century,[107] named one of his brothers in Sehwan as his successor.[108] Succession was troubled after the death of the Jam and the same author says that Sehwan and Bakkhar refused the nomination of Jam Sikandar, who then marched against Sehwan.[109] The *Ta'rikh-i Mubarak Shahi*[110] mentions the Timurid incursion in Sehwan, headed by the Kabul governor Shaykh Ali, during the year AH 826 (AD 1423). In the early 10th/16th century, the inhabitants of Sehwan gathered under the flag of Jam Firuz Samma (c. AD 1508–1524) according to Mir Masum.[111]

Some illegible coins found in the surface layers of the site relate this period to the Delhi Sultans; one (EU 233), which was minted in Delhi, is inscribed in the name of Mahmud Shah (r. AH 837–849 [AD 1434–1445]) and is dated AH 846 (AD 1442). Other coins found on the surface or in the Mughal level come from the Sultans of Gujarat, whose matrimonial and political links with the Samma were very important during the 15th century AD.[112] One coin (EU 118) names the sultan Mahmud Shah Begra (r. AH 862–917 [AD 1458–1511]), who was born from a daughter of the Samma Jam Tughluq and the Gujarati sultan Muhammad Karim (r. AH 846–855 [AD 1442–1451]).[113]

Level VIc and VId: Stratigraphy

Level VIc (c.38.80-39.35 m) corresponds with a phase of reworking in the structures built during the first phase on Level VI.[114] This occupation layer is clearly defined by several ground levels, cleared at c.39.20 m in two structures.[115] An iron metalworking is attested in Levels VIc and VId by some slags. The last and loose occupation of the baked brick structures (Level VId, c.39.30-39.60 m) is associated with some floor levels (c.39.35 m), and a pillar was erected in the largest structure.[116] Then the walls collapsed and the level is terminated by the thick black layer already mentioned (c.39.60 m).

Ceramic Material

Painted Red Wares

The rather fine to medium wares are mostly pinkish in colour, and temper materials are always sand and mica. The closed shapes are adorned with animals, 'snakes', and geometrical patterns (**PL. 1: 21, 23**). In the last layer of the level, birds no longer appear as motif. Besides some jars with little oblique rims (**FIG. 11: 3-4**), the most common type is always the cooking pot with oblique and engraved rim (**FIG. 11: 12-13**). Compared with the first phase of Level VI, their number is higher. Some small water and cooking pots are also represented (**FIG. 11: 10-11**). A new kind of rather coarse plate (**FIG. 11: 16-17**) appears, and continues to be seen later. Some samples of painted bowls (**FIG. 11: 21**) are also known. Some of the jars (**FIG. 11: 3**) and plates (**FIG. 11: 16**) are close to the 14th century AD types found in Adilabad.[117]

Glazed Wares

As with the black and grey wares, the glazed material is still represented in Level VIc, but in a much lower proportion. They tend to disappear completely in Level VId. The glazes show the same characteristics as in the first phase of Level VI: mostly monochrome (the majority green; occasionally yellow, turquoise blue, and white) cups and bowls on heavy bases (**FIG. 11: 22-23**) can also be underglaze painted. The splash wares (**PL. 4: 40**) and sgraffiato almost disappear.

In the site of Baroda in Gujarat, the first glazed material seems to appear with the regional sultanate, and according to Mehta cannot be dated before the end of the 14th century AD but is well attested in the 15th century.[118] Mehta's dating of the glazed ceramics seems to fit with the hypothesis of T. Hasan, who describes the development of glazed tiles in the Indian sultanates from the end of the 14th to the 15th century AD.[119] The major types of glazed wares from Baroda are monochrome cups and plates (green, blue, white, and red), and the same types are to be found in the 16th century AD:[120] they recall the Sehwan monochrome wares. But some underglazed painted wares contemporary with the monochrome types according to Mehta, and bearing some geometrical and lotus patterns,[121] are quite different from the presumably contemporary Sehwan material.

4   Sehwan during the Arghun and Tarkhan Period (10th century AH [16th century AD])

The Arghun and Tarkhan Dynasties in Sehwan

The destruction of the fort signalled by the thick black layer visible in the whole Asma sounding, and elsewhere on the site (c.39.60 m), may be linked with the seizure of the place by Shah Beg Arghun in AH 928 (AD 1521–1522). Knowledge of the Arghun and Tarkhan periods in Sindh is mostly derived from the *Ta'rikh-i Masumi*.[122] When peace was made with the last Samma ruler, Jam Firuz, Shah Beg marched on Siwistan with a powerful army and took the fort in AD 1521. He then named some Arghun and Tarkhan officers in charge of the place.[123] Shah Beg came again to Sehwan in AD 1522 and inspected the fort's defences. He appointed some trustworthy men in the fort, in which he ordered the harvest to be gathered, and told his officers to build their houses.[124] During the reign of his heir and successor Shah Hasan Arghun, Sehwan was threatened by Humayun in AH 948 (AD 1541).[125] Shah Hasan prepared for the siege by gathering all the reserves in the fort. The armies of Humayun conducted a siege of seven months according to Mir Masum, but the fort resisted and the Mughal, finally overtaken by the monsoon and starvation of his troops, left in AH 949 (AD 1542).[126] Shah Hasan came back to Siwistan two months later in order to organize the repairs of the fort.[127] After the accession of Mirza Isa Tarkhan in AH 962 (AD 1554), the possession of Sehwan led to several conflicts between the Arghuns and Tarkhans, but in AD 1555 Isa Tarkhan took the place.[128] In AH 970 (AD 1562–63) his son Mirza Muhammad Baqi received Siwistan as *jagir*, and had to face an Arghun rebellion which led to a four-or five-month siege of the fort in AD 973 (AD 1565–66).[129] But Sehwan stayed in Tarkhan hands until its conquest by the Mughal army under the reign of Mirza Jani Beg Tarkhan. Between AH 994 (AD 1586) and AH 996 (AD 1588), the Mughal Nawab Muhammad b. Sadiq Khan attacked the fort and destroyed a part of the curtain walls and a gate of the fort, but the garrison resisted and the nawab lifted the siege.[130] In AH 999 (AD 1591), Mir Masum took part in the Mughal campaign to seize Siwistan. After the siege of the place, Jani Beg finally handed it over to Khan-i Khanan Abd al-Rahim Khan who had been sent by Akbar.[131]

Level VII: Stratigraphy

The citadel, and the Asma sounding in particular, shows a very loose occupation during this period (c.38.80/39.60 m-40.90 m, **FIG. 7/3**) with a sherd number of c.5/m^3. A rubbish pit (38.80-39.60 m) nevertheless yielded a great quantity of sherds. The earth was clayey with charcoal and ash above the black layer of destruction, and the ancient structures were destroyed (c.40-40.41 m) after a last ground level paved with baked bricks at 40.15 m.[132] A new structure of baked brick was also erected (c.40.13-40.68 m).[133] Another baked brick wall was cleared c.40.35-41.20 m. At the end of this level, the earth was compact, clayey with some green parts perhaps from water flows. Iron metallurgy in the citadel is attested during all of that phase by numerous scorial and fragments of crucibles.

Ceramic Material

The fabrics of unglazed and glazed wares are rather fine to medium in the beginning of Level VII (c.40 m), and tend to become coarser at its end (before 41 m). The wares are mostly red and tempered with mica and sand.

Painted Red Wares

Motifs of birds and ducks are present in the first layer of the level, but seem to disappear later (**PL. 1: 25-26**). Layers of barbotine on the jars and cooking pot bodies are quite common.

A few jars with or without collars were found (**FIG. 12: 1-2**), but the most common type of red wares is the cooking pot, of a more or less large size, with an oblique and often engraved rim (**FIG. 12: 3-9**). These types are very close to the cooking pot shapes known in Level VI. The heavy and unadorned plate type originating in the preceding level also becomes more common.

Moulded Red Wares

The finest types of ceramics from this period are the moulded water bottles and pots (**FIG. 12: 10-11**), which present rather fine fabrics with many mica particles on the surface. Their ornamental designs are always floral and geometrical (**PL. 2: 21-24**). These wares begin to appear at this level and their number increases later, during the Mughal period.

Glazed Wares

Of the few glazed bowls found, most are covered by a thick and quite poor whitish opaque glaze (**PL. 4: 41**). The other monochrome glazes are occasionally turquoise blue (**PL. 4: 42-43**;

Fig. 12: 17) and green. Some white-glazed wares bear a sgraffiato design (Fig. 12: 16). In Baroda, the majority of underglaze painted wares are attributed to the 16th century AD. They are mostly painted in black under a blue glaze and bear some vegetal and geometrical designs. Mehta noted that during the same period, sgraffiato completely disappeared.[134]

5   Sehwan During the Mughal Period (11th to Early 12th century AH [17th to Early 18th century AD])

Sehwan as *Khalisa-i Sharifa* (Imperial Property) and Its Decline Under the Mughals
After its conquest by the Mughal armies in AH 1000 (AD 1592), the citadel kept its strategic importance, as shown by its very particular status, known from several sources of the Mughal period, such as the *Akbar Nama* of Abu'l Fazl and the *Mazar-i Shahjahani* of Yusuf Mirak (AH 1044 [AD 1634–35]).[135] But it may have lost this status with the reign of Jahangir (AH 1014–1037 [AD 1605–1627]).[136] Probably as early as AH 1001 (AD 1593), Siwistan was ruled by Bakhtiyar Beg and other Mughal officers named by Akbar.[137] For the first part of the 17th century AD, Sehwan's administration is well documented by the testimony of Yusuf Mirak, who lived in the city. The succession of governors was rapid during this period, which saw constant troubles with the local tribes of the area. This led to the erection of a wall around the lower city of Sehwan c. AH 1044 (AD 1634–35).[138] Yusuf Mirak notes that Sehwan 'is the name of an old, dilapidated mud-built fort which is perched on a mound' and that '11 parganahs are attached to this fort'.[139] The poor state of the fort suggests that it declined in this period. Some later Mughal officers who ruled Sehwan from c. AH 1047 (AD 1657) to the 18th century AD are also known from Mir Ali Shir Qani Tattawi.[140] The last Mughal governor mentioned is Asrshad Khan (appointed in AH 1114 [AD 1702]),[141] before the arrival of Nadir Shah in AH 1151 (AD 1738) and the nomination of Mian Nur Muhammad Kalhora as governor of the place.[142]

Level VIII: Stratigraphy
This level (c.40.90-43.50 m, Fig. 7/4) is rather poor in the Asma ravine but better represented in other soundings of the site, where a Mughal residence was discovered. Nevertheless, it seems that the citadel declined from this period on: some areas, as in the Asma ravine, are not really occupied. At the beginning of the level, the compact and clayey earth contained ash and charcoal (c.40.90-41.20 m). This layer (VIIIa) of occupation is associated with a ground level with fireplaces cleared (c.40.90 m) in a mud brick structure.[143] The upper layer (VIIIb, c.41.20-41.91 m) is a very loose occupation of the same area. An iron metalworking, indicated by the scoriae and crucibles found, is attested in these layers but disappears later. This spot was actually almost abandoned as indicated by the sherd numbers (10/m³). Three later layers of very poor occupation were recognized (Level VIIIc to VIIId, c.42-43.30 m), but in a disturbed stratigraphy, because of the erosion of the ravine.

Ceramic Material
The most common wares of this last level are red painted utensils of common use. As in Level VII, some finely moulded red wares were found, but there were no black and grey wares.

The glazed wares are only monochrome. But other types of underpainted wares were found elsewhere on the site, as some painted glazed tiles associated with the governor's residence and a bath. These tiles, painted in cobalt and turquoise blue on a white ground, can be dated c. AD 1590-1650.[144] Their presence, in addition to quite numerous Chinese wares found in stratified locations (c.40.90-41.90 m) and on the surface of the sounding, seems to characterize the Mughal period.

Painted Red Wares

In the first layer (VIIIa) the wares are mostly red and of fine to medium quality, but tend to be coarser from Level VIIIb to the surface. The painted motifs are less common and of a very mediocre quality. The bird and animal motifs seem to have totally disappeared and the patterns are geometrical (**PL. 1: 29**). Some new types of jars with a round rim, short collar, or oblique top characterize the level (**FIG. 13: 1-5**), such as globular or rounded cooking pots with often engraved rims (**PL. 1: 28**). The rims are oblique and quite long (**FIG. 13: 6-10**). Other shapes of little pots and water bottles are much less common (**FIG. 13: 13-15**), while some generally unpainted lids and little cups are present (**FIG. 13: 16-21**).

Moulded Red Wares

Fragments of moulded cooking pots and *gargoulettes* (water-jars) also characterize the ceramic material of that Mughal phase (**FIG. 13: 11-12**). They may be enhanced with painted motifs, while mica particles generally cover the surface of the vessels (**PL. 2: 25-28**). The same types of moulded wares were found in Lahori Bandar, the port city of the Indus Delta,[145] where their production is attested by some mould fragments. The moulded wares are linked with the Mughal period of Lahori.

Glazed Wares

The wares are red, and their quality varies between fine and coarse. Some rare examples of sgraffiato under a white glaze were found (**FIG. 13: 23-26**), as in Level VII. But the glazed ceramics coming from the Asma ravine are mostly monochrome and of a rather poor quality. The shapes are bowls and cups standing on rings or higher bases (**FIG. 13: 22-26**), and sometimes footed lamps (**FIG. 13: 27**). The glazed colours are white in the main, but also green and turquoise blue (**PL. 4: 44-45**). The Mughal levels in Lahori Bandar produced many glazed wares, probably locally made. Thanks to this site we know that besides the monochrome wares, quantities of underglaze painted and sgraffiato ceramics in a wider range of colours were also produced in Sindh.

Conclusion

Sehwan's Purana Qila is the first site studied in Sindh which shows the sequence of the ceramic wares without any gap between the 2nd/8th and the 12th/18th centuries. It tells us which kinds of wares co-existed during the different phases and allows us to date the appearance, development and disappearance of the different types of ceramics made in Sindh during ten centuries. Thanks to this site the regional characteristics of the ceramic wares from Sindh, as well as the influences of other areas, like Khurasan and north-western India are adequately identified.

The different Islamic periods of Sehwan's fortified city and later citadel have been defined by the stratigraphy of the large sounding in the Asma ravine, but other soundings and excavations made at the site also helped to facilitate richer documentation concerning the history of Sehwan's ceramic material from the Arab to the Mughal period. One sounding made in the northern part of the Asma ravine enriched the typologies for the 3rd/9th and 4th/10th centuries and corroborated the appearance of a Sindhi glazed material during this period, as

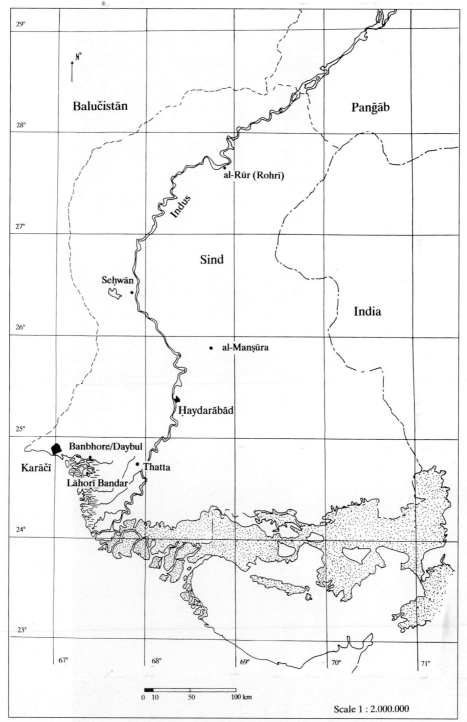

Figure 1: Map of Sindh with localization of Sehwan

Figure 2: Sehwan, Purana Qil'a (M. Kervran)

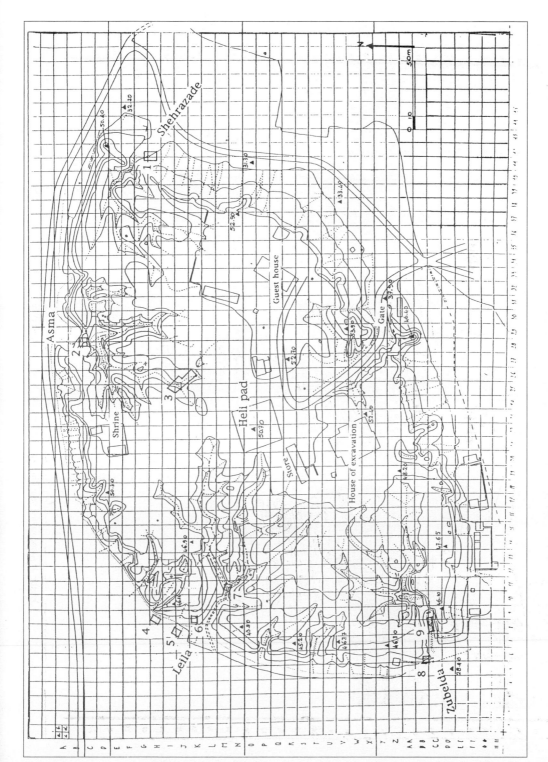

Figure 3: Sehwan, Purana Qil'a, topography and localization of the Asma big sounding (n°3). (R. Saupin)

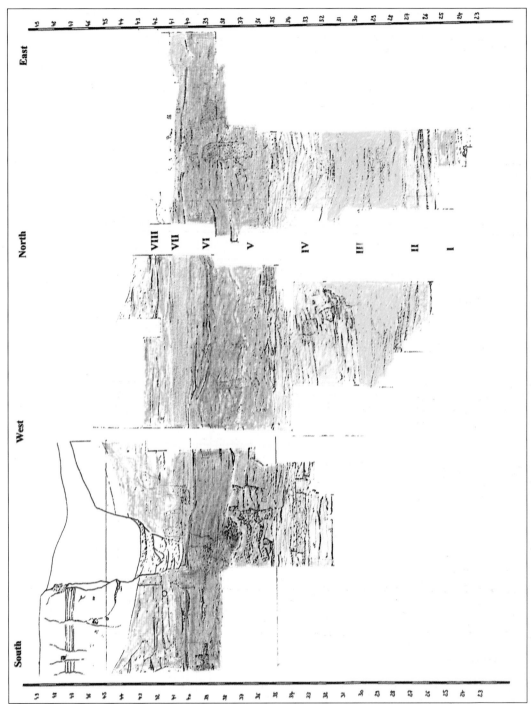

Figure 4: Asma ravine sounding and stratigraphy (based on M. Kervan's sections and stratigraphy)

Interpretation	Date	Levels' Description
Citadel occupied by a garrison and the governor's palace	Mugal Period 11th–12th cent. AH./ 17th–18th cent. AD.	Abandon above loose occupation in mud brick structures. Iron metalworking.
Citadel occupied by a garrison Refection of the fort	Tarkhan period Argun period 10th cent. AH/ 16th cent. AD.	Iron metallurgy Loose occupation above a thick black layer of destruction c.39.60 m.
Citadel occupied by a garrison Refection of the fort	Samma period Delhi Sultanates period 7th–9th cent. AH/ 13th–15th cent. AD	Iron metallurgy Medium occupation in baked brick structures.
Fortified city: Bazar phase	Gurid period Gaznawid period 5th–7th cent. AH/ 11th–13th AD.	The bazar destroyed c.38 m had a very dense occupation.
Fortified city? Metal workshops	Habbarid emirate Abbasid governors Umayyad governors from 93 AH/711–712 AD to the end of 4th cent. AH/10th cent. AD.	Rubified level c. 35 m. Iron metallurgy Occupation growing in baked and mud brick structures. (workshops) First Islamic level from c.30–31 m?
Dense occupation	↑ Pre Islamic levels from c.4th cent. BC to the end of 1st cent. AH/ 7th cent AD?	Green and sandy layers Brown layers.
Occupation?	↓	Sticky layers of clay, with sand.
Occupation?		Sand and clay layers.
Virgin Soil.		

Figure 4 (continued)

Level	Layer	Z	Excavation Units	Datation
VIII	Surf.	c.45,75/43,10	101-102-233	
	d	c.43,10/42,50	103	12th cent. AH/18th cent. AD?
	c	c.42,50/42,00	104-106	
	b	c.41,90/41,20	108-112-122-114-120-111-113-121-234	11th cent. AH/17th cent. AD
	a	c.41,20/40,90	156-157-159-131-129-133-127-147-148-124-235	After 1000 AH/1592 AD.
VII	c	c.40,90/40,20	158-160-143 bis-145-144-146-142-143-137-141-135-140-150-151-152-149-134-138-139-238-236	2nd 1/2 10th cent. AH/16th cent. AD.
	b	c,40,41/40,00	154-165-153-155-161-162-163-164-239-240	
	a	c.40,00/39,60	166-167-168-170-169-242-241-246-248	After 928 AH/1521-1522 AD.
VI	d	c.39,60/39,30	175-174-173-172-171-245-247-244	Late 9th cent. AH/15th cent. AD
	c	c.39,35/38,80	203-204-205-177-176-180-179-178-249-251-256	
	b	c.39,00/38,40	209-211-192-197-184-181-182-183-250-252-255-259-262-258-268	
	a	c.38,50/37,75	220-206-212-187-185-186-267-265-272-273-260-261-263-264-266-213-188-189	7th cent. AH/13th cent. AD.
V	f	c.38,13/37,25	219-190-191-305-269-270-277-278-279-280-288-289-286-290-281-275-274-282	Early 7th cent. AH/13th AD.
	e	c.37,62/36,80	229-193-194-195-196-198-201-202-271-295-294-300-291-292-287-353-343	6th cent. AH/12th cent. AD.
	d	c.37,10/36,36	228-227-200-208-207-217-215-222-225-218-307-308-302-303-309-299-296-297-293-298-350-348-358-346-352-347-351-365-354-355-344-349	2nd 1/2 5th cent. AH/11th cent. AD.
	c	c,36,52/35,92	230-214-216-314-301-311-312-361-362-366-356-357-360-359	c.416-441 AH. /1025-1050 AD?
	b	c.36,17/35,57	221-315-310-306-318-320-323-316-364-368-369-372-371-363-379-367-345	
	a	c.35,82/35,10	224-228-319-321-324-325-322-313-317-326-370-374-375-373-376	Early 5th cent. AH/11th AD.
IV	c	c.35,00/34,13	231-327-328-330-333-334-377-378-380-381-476-382-384-386	4th cent. AH/10th AD.
	b	c.34,13/32,67	232-343-332-331-385-387-388-389-475-335-337-336-390-391-392-426-427	3rd cent. AH/9th cent. AD?
	a	c.32,67/30,50	338-339-393-397-394 341-340-342-395-396 398-406-407-399-400-408-401-409-404-410-405-439-417-416-415-414-413-411-412-403-428	After 93 AH/711-712 AD.

Figure 5 : Asma ravine chart (Islamic levels)

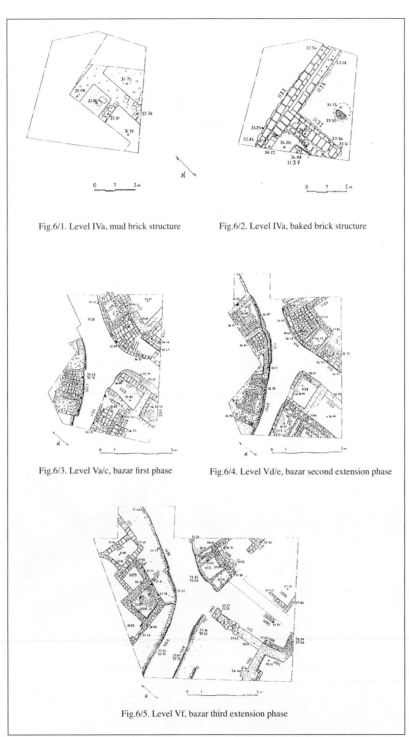

Fig.6/1. Level IVa, mud brick structure

Fig.6/2. Level IVa, baked brick structure

Fig.6/3. Level Va/c, bazar first phase

Fig.6/4. Level Vd/e, bazar second extension phase

Fig.6/5. Level Vf, bazar third extension phase

Figure 6: Sehwan, Asma ravine — structures from level IV to V (V. Bernard)

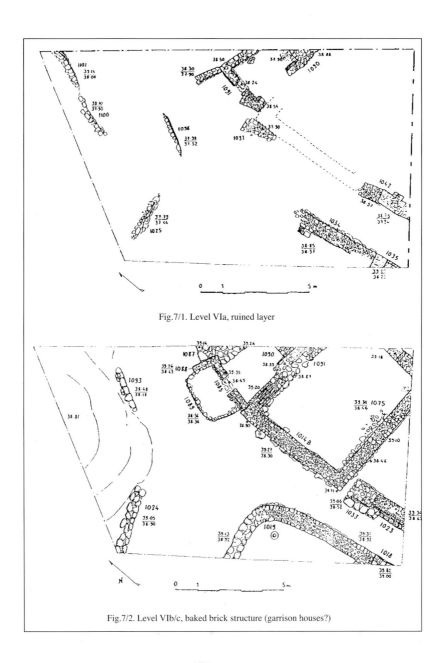

Fig.7/1. Level VIa, ruined layer

Fig.7/2. Level VIb/c, baked brick structure (garrison houses?)

Figure 7: Sehwan, Asma ravine—structures from level VI to VIII (V. Bernard)

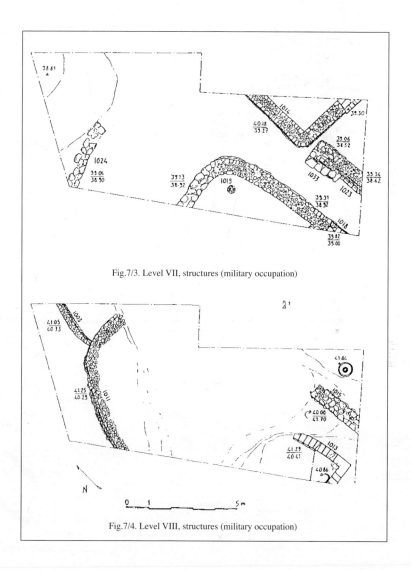

Fig.7/3. Level VII, structures (military occupation)

Fig.7/4. Level VIII, structures (military occupation)

0   1   5 m

Figure 7: Sehwan, Asma ravine—structures from level VI to VIII (V. Bernard)

Common and painted red wares

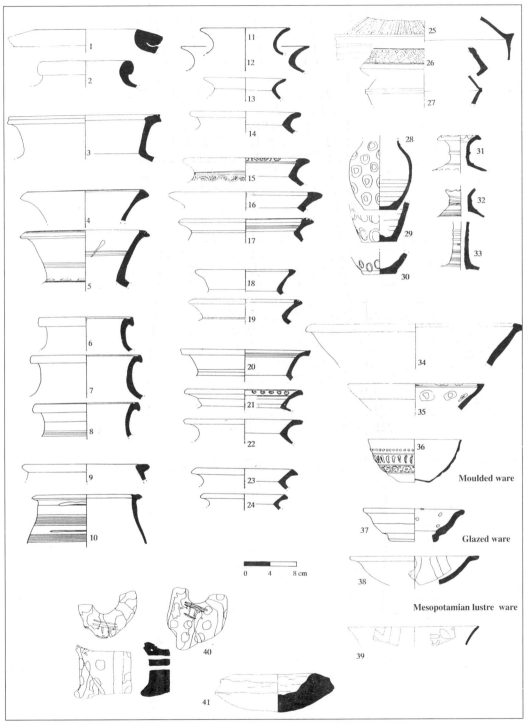

Figure 8: Ceramics of level IV (2nd–4th cent. AH/8th–10th cent. AD)

N°	Find n°	Level	Sector	Description
1	410-2	IVa	Asma	Jar rim. Pinkish red ware with mica, sand, quartz, white inclusions.
2	406-2	IVa	Asma	Jar rim. Fine red ware with mica and sand.
3	410-1	IVa	Asma	Jar collar. Rather fine reddish ware with mica, sand, white inclusions. Black slip on red ground.
4	399-3	IVa	Asma	Jar collar. Dark red ware with mica, sand, white inclusions. Black and red slips.
5	328-6	IVc	Asma	Jar high collar. Slip painted ornament.
6	401-2	IVa	Asma	Jar collar. Fine reddish orange ware with mica, sand, white inclusions. Dark red slip.
7	385-4	IVb	Asma	Jar collar. Very fine red ware with mica and sand. Black and red slips on a buff ground.
8	328-25	IVc	Asma	Jar collar. Slip painted ornament.
9	399-2	IVa	Asma	Jar rim. Very fine pinkish ware with mica and sand, white inclusions.
10	231-6	IVc	Asma	Jar rim. Medium red ware with mica and sand. Black and red slips on a cream ground.
11	411	IVa	Asma	Cooking pot rim.
12	413-1	IVa	Asma	Cooking pot rim.
13	392-1	IVb	Asma	Cooking pot rim. Pink ware with mica, sand and quartz. Black, red and white slips.
14	382-19	IVc	Asma	Cooking pot rim. Pinkish ware with mica and sand, white spots. Slip painted.
15	401-1	IVa	Asma	Cooking pot rim. Fine pinkish orange ware. Black and dark red slips.
16	385-5	IVb	Asma	Cooking pot rim. Fine red-orange ware with mica and sand, white spots. Black and red slips.
17	328-28	IVc	Asma	Cooking pot rim. Slip painted and engraved ornaments.
18	392-4	IVb	Asma	Cooking pot rim. Pinkish ware with mica, sand, quartz. White spots. Black and red slips.
19	328-7	IVc	Asma	Cooking pot rim. Engraved ornament.
20	332-5	IVb	Asma	Cooking pot rim. Medium red ware. Black and red slips on a cream ground.
21	391-2	IVb	Asma	Cooking pot rim. Rather fine ware with mica and sand. Red slip on the fabric.
22	381-15	IVc	Asma	Cooking pot rim. Red ware with mica and sand, white spots. Black, red and white slips.
23	385-3	IVb	Asma	Cooking pot rim. Rather fine red ware with mica, sand. Black slip.
24	380-1	IVc	Asma	Cooking pot rim. Very fine pinkish ware with mica, sand. Black slip on a red ground.
25	328-12	IVc	Asma	Cooking pot fragment. Medium pinkish ware with mica, sand. Barbotine, black, red and cream slips.
26	328-10	IVc	Asma	Cooking pot fragment. Medium pinkish ware with mica, sand. Black, red and cream slips.
27	377-1	IVc	Asma	Cooking pot fragment.
28	392-5	IVb	Asma	Little jar (rim missing). Wheel traces inside the body. Slip painted ornament.
29	331-4	IVb	Asma	little jar base. Rather fine pinkish ware with mica, sand. Black, white and red slips.
30	328-18	IVc	Asma	Little jar base. Rather coarse red ware with mica, sand. Black, white and red slips.
31	335-1	IVb	Asma	Bottle rim and collar. Pinkish ware with mica and sand. Black slip on a red ground.
32	231-11	IVc	Asma	Bottle collar. Medium red ware. Black and red slips on a pinkish cream ground.
33	328-27	IVc	Asma	Bottle collar. Slip painted ornament.
34	406-1	IVa	Asma	Basin rim. Medium pinkish brown ware.
35	331-5	IVb	Asma	Cup rim. Rather coarse pinkish ware with mica and sand. Black, white and red slips.
36	328-1	IVc	Asma	Little moulded bowl. Pinkish ware with mica and sand.
37	231-2	IVc	Asma	Little glazed cup fragment. Coarse pinkish cream ware, bluish white glaze with spots.
38	328-31	IVc	Asma	Cup fragment. Medium red orange ware with sand, white spots. Green glaze on white slip.
39	328-33	IVc	Asma	Cup fragment (Mesopotamia). Fine yellow cream ware, lustre on a white opaque glaze.
40	387-1	IVb	Asma	Element of an animal necklace? Black and red slips on a cream pinkish ground.
41	328-32	IVc	Asma	Crucible base. Very coarse red ware with mica, sand. Fire traces outside the base.

Figure 8 (continued)

Common and painted red wares

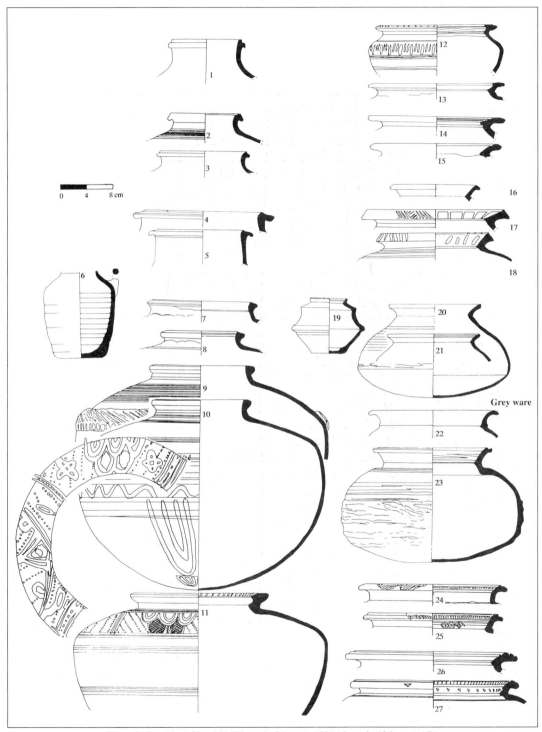

Figure 9: Ceramics of level V (5th–early 7th cent. AH/11th–early 13th cent. AD)

Nº	Find nº	Level	Sector	Description
1	370-1	Va	Asma	Jar collar. Red orange ware with mica, sand, white inclusions.
2	228-1	Va	Asma	Jar rim. Medium red ware, black and red slips.
3	349-2	Vd	Asma	Jar rim. Medium red ware tempered with mica, sand, white inclusions.
4	346-6	Vd	Asma	Jar rim. Medium red ware with mica and sand. Black and red slips on a buff ground.
5	344-1	Vd	Asma	Jar rim. Medium red ware with mica and sand, white inclusions.
6	280-1	Vf	Asma	Little jar (rim missing). Medium pinkish paste with mica, sand. Wheel traces inside.
7	349-1	Vd	Asma	Jar rim. Medium pinkish paste with mica, sand. Black and red slips on a buff ground.
8	346-4	Vd	Asma	Jar rim. Medium red ware with mica and sand. Black and red slips on a buff ground.
9	296-1	Vd	Asma	Jar fragment. Fine pinkish ware with mica, sand. Black and red slips on a buff ground, barbotine.
10	288-1	Vf	Asma	Jar. Medium pinkish ware with mica and sand. Black and red slips on a cream ground.
11	269-2	Vf	Asma	Jar fragment. Medium pinkish ware with sand. Black and red slips on a buff ground.
12	221-3	Vb	Asma	Cooking pot fragment. Rather coarse red ware with mica. Black, red slips on a white ground.
13	350-10	Vd	Asma	Cooking pot rim. Medium pinkish ware with mica, cand. Black, red slips on a buff ground.
14	359-2	Vc	Asma	Cooking pot rim. Medium pinkish ware with mica, sand. Black, red slips on a buff ground.
15	349-6	Vd	Asma	Cooking pot rim. Medium red ware with mica, sand. Black slip on a red ground.
16	360-1	Vc	Asma	Cooking pot rim.
17	214-3	Vc	Asma	Cooking pot rim. Medium red ware. Black slip on a red ground.
18	350-5	Vd	Asma	Cooking pot rim. Medium red ware with mica, sand. Black, red slips on a buff ground(?)
19	229-1	Vc	Asma	Little cooking pot. Fabric not visible. Pinkish cream slip.
20	312-2	Vc	Asma	Cooking pot. Medium pinkish ware with mica. Black and red slips on a buff ground.
21	190-2	Vf	Asma	Cooking pot rim. Medium ware.
22	351-8	Vd	Asma	Cooking pot rim. Medium dark grey ware with mica, white spots.
23	269-3	Vf	Asma	Cooking pot. Rather fine pinkish ware with sand. Black, red and buff slips, barbotine.
24	350-3	Vd	Asma	Cooking pot rim. Medium red ware with mica, sand. Black, red, buff slips, engraved design.
25	208-1	Vd	Asma	Cooking pot rim. Black and red slips, engraved ornament.
26	194-3	Ve	Asma	Cooking pot rim. Engraved ornament.
27	190-3	Vf	Asma	Cooking pot rim. Rather fine pinkish ware, engraved ornament.

Figure 9 (continued)

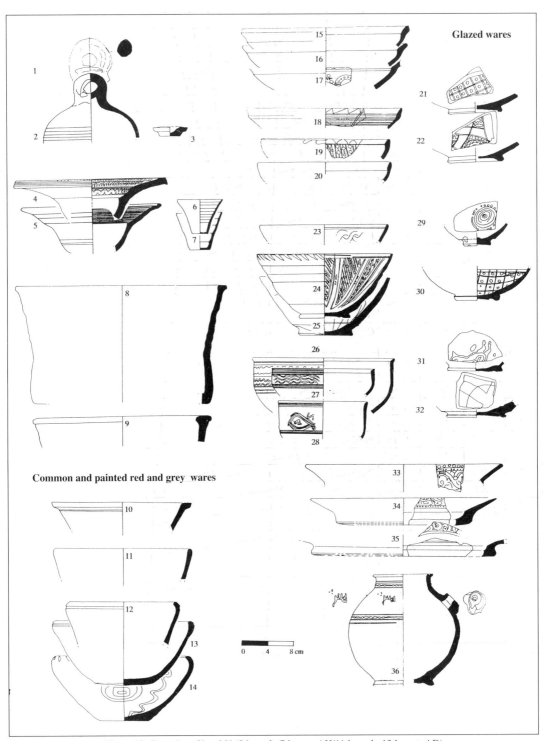

Glazed wares

Common and painted red and grey wares

0   4   8 cm

Figure 10: Ceramics of level V (5th–early 7th cent. AH/11th–early 13th cent. AD)

Nº	Find nº	Level	Sector	Description
1	301-1	Vc	Asma	Lantern prehension ring. Rather coarse pinkish ware with mica and sand.
2	350-3	Vd	Asma	Lantern top. Medium red ware with mica and sand. Wheel traces outside.
3	320-1	Vb	Asma	Little oil lamp or lid? Rather coarse pinkish paste with sand and mica.
4	301-3	Vc	Asma	Lid fragment. Grey ware, engraved ornament.
5	208-3	Vd	Asma	Lid fragment. Medium red ware. engraved ornament.
6	315-2	Vb	Asma	Beaker. Fine pinkish ware. Wheel traces inside.
7	315-1	Vb	Asma	Beaker. Fine pinkish ware. Wheel traces inside.
8	374-1	Va	Asma	Basin fragment. Rather fine red orange ware with mica, sand and white spots.
9	343-1	Ve	Asma	Basin rim. Coarse pinkish ware.
10	208-4	Vd	Asma	Cup rim. Rather coarse grey ware with mica.
11	196-1	Ve	Asma	Cup rim. Rather coarse dark grey ware.
12	193-2	Ve	Asma	Cup rim. Rather coarse grey ware.
13	270-1	Vf	Asma	Bowl. Medium grey ware with mineral temper.
14	280-2	Vf	Asma	Bowl. Rather fine pinkish ware with sand and mica. Black and red slips on the fabric.
15	306-2	Vb	Asma	Cup rim. Medium pinkish ware with sand. Green glaze.
16	301-10	Vc	Asma	Cup rim. Pinkish ware with sand and mica. Green glaze on a white slip ground.
17	301-12	Vc	Asma	Cup fragment. Pinkish ware with sand and mica. Underglaze painted (green, brown) on slip.
18	301-11	Vc	Asma	Cup rim. Rather fine pinkish ware with sand and mica. Underglaze slip painted (black, red)
19	306-4	Vb	Asma	Cup rim. Rather fine pinkish ware with sand and mica. Underglaze slip painted (black, red).
20	362-3	Vc	Asma	Cup rim. Fine pinkish ware with mica and sand. Underglaze slip painted (black, red)
21	306-1	Vb	Asma	Cup base. Pinkish ware with sand and mica. Underglaze painted (green, brown) on slip.
22	301-5	Vc	Asma	Cup base. Pinkish ware with sand and mica. Underglaze painted (green, brown) on slip.
23	201-3	Ve	Asma	Bowl rim. Medium red ware. Sgraffiato under green glaze.
24	229-3	Ve	Asma	Bowl. Medium red ware. Underglaze painted (green, brown) on slip.
25	280-3	Vf	Asma	Bowl (rim missing). Coarse red ware. Sphash ware type. Green and yellow glazes.
26	229-5	Ve	Asma	Bowl (base missing). Medium red ware. Sgraffiato under green glaze.
27	195-2	Ve	Asma	Bowl (base missing). Rather fine red ware. Sgraffiato on white slip, under green glaze.
28	201-2	Ve	Asma	Bowl (base missing). Rather fine pinkish ware. Sgraffiato under green glaze.
29	207-1	Vd	Asma	Bowl base. Medium red ware. Brown design under green glaze.
30	194-1	Ve	Asma	Bowl base. Medium red ware with mica. Underglaze painted (yellow, green, brown) on slip.
31	190-1	Vf	Asma	Bowl base. Rather fine pinkish ware. Underglaze painted (green, brown) on slip.
32	219-1	Vf	Asma	Bowl base. Rather fine red ware. Underglaze painted (green) on slip.
33	207-3	Vd	Asma	Plate rim. Medium pinkish ware. Sgraffiato and painted (brown) under green glaze.
34	291-1	Ve	Asma	Plate fragment. Medium red ware with sand. Sgraffiato and painted (brown) under glaze.
35	270-2	Vf	Asma	Plate base. Medium red ware with sand. Sgraffiato under dark green glaze.
36	280-4	Vf	Asma	Little jar with a spout. Rather coarse red ware, with sand and mica. Sgraffiato and painted (brown) under green glaze.

Figure 10 (continued)

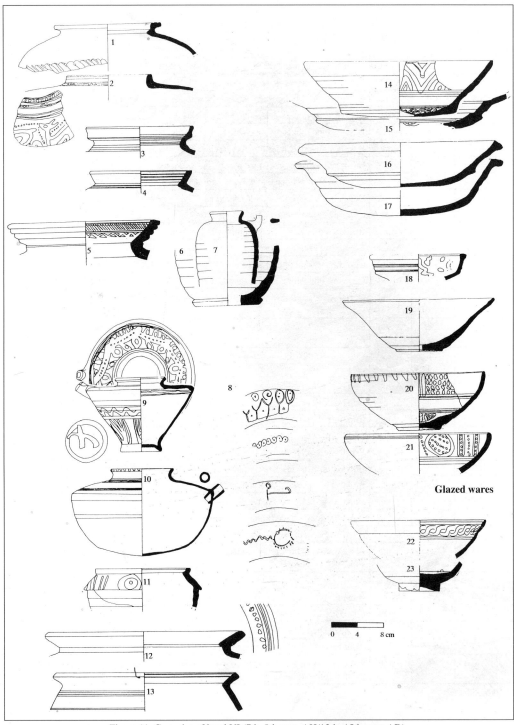

Glazed wares

Figure 11: Ceramics of level VI (7th–9th cent. AH/13th–15th cent. AD)

N°	Find n°	Level	Sector	Description
1	209-1	VIa	Asma	Jar rim and shoulder. Fine red paste with mica (numecrous inside). Slip and barbotine.
2	244-1	VId	Asma	Jar rim. Rather coarse pinkish ware with sand and mica. Black and red slips on a buff ground, mica on the red slip band between rim and shoulder.
3	171-1	VId	Asma	Jar rim. Slip painted.
4	175-6	VId	Asma	Jar rim. Rather fine red ware. Black and red slips on a buff ground.
5	175-5	VId	Asma	Jar rim. Medium pinkish cream ware. Engraved decoration.
6	259-1	VIb	Asma	Little jar base. Medium ware with sand, mica. Wheel traces.
7	245-2	VId	Asma	Little jar (base missing). Pinkish ware with sand and mica. Wheel traces.
8		VIa/d	Asma	Engraved designs on cooking pots rims.
9	262-1	VIb	Asma	Water pot. Medium pinkish ware with sand, mica. Black and red slips on a buff ground, mica on the red slip band between shoulder and body.
10	243-2	VId	Asma	Water pot. Rather fine pinkish ware with sand, mica. Black and red slips on pinkish ground, mica on the shoulder and the base.
11	179-3	VIc	Asma	Cooking pot (base missing). Medium red ware. Black and red slips.
12	179-1	VIc	Asma	Cooking pot rim. Medium red ware. Black and red slips, little stones inlaid in the rim.
13	179-2	VIc	Asma	Cooking pot rim. Rather fine red ware. Black and red slips.
14	258-3	VIb	Asma	Plate. Medium red ware with sand and mica. Black and red slips.
15	258-6	VIb	Asma	Plate fragment. Medium pinkish ware with sand, mica. Black and red slips.
16	245-4	VId	Asma	Plate.
17	245-3	VId	Asma	Plate. Rather coarse pinkish ware.
18	267-1	VIa	Asma	Little cup (base missing). Rather fine red ware with sand, mica. Black and red slips.
19	262-2	VIb	Asma	Cup with a hole in the base. Rather fine pinkish ware with sand and mica.
20	258-4	VIb	Asma	Bowl. Medium pinkish ware with sand. Black and red slips on a buff ground.
21	175-1	VId	Asma	Bowl. Rather coarse red ware. Black and red slips.
22	254-1	VIc	Asma	Cup (base missing). Medium pinkih ware with sand. Sgraffiato under green glaze.
23	245-1	VId	Asma	Cup base. Very heavy pinkish buff ware with sand, mica. Turquoise blue glaze, stilt trace.

Figure 11 (continued)

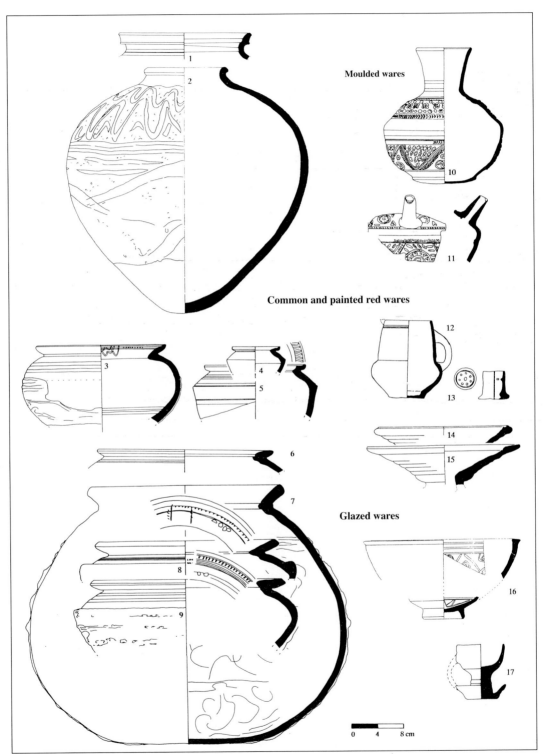

Moulded wares

Common and painted red wares

Glazed wares

0   4   8 cm

Figure 12: Ceramics of level VII (10th cent. AH/16th cent. AD)

N°	Find n°	Level	Sector	Description
1	166-2	VIIa	Asma	Jar rim. Red and black slips.
2	241-1	VIIa	Asma	Jar. Medium pinkish ware with sand and mica. Barbotine.
3	164-2	VIIb	Asma	Cooking pot (base missing). Medium pinkish ware with sand and mica. Mica particles inside the body. Black slip designs.
4	165-3	VIIb	Asma	Little pot (base missing). Medium red ware.
5	135-2	VIIc	Asma	Cooking pot (base missing). Medium pinkish ware with sand and mica.
6	153-2	VIIb	Asma	Cooking pot rim. Rather fine red ware. Black slip on a buff ground.
7	142-1	VIIc	Asma	Cooking pot. Red ware with sand. Slip painted design (rim) and barbotine.
8	135-1	VIIc	Asma	Cooking pot rim and shoulder. Red ware. Little stones inlaid and engraved design (rim), black and red slips, barbotine (shoulder).
9	140-1	VIIc	Asma	Cooking pot rim and shoulder. Medium red ware. Little stones inlaid and engraved design (rim). Black and red slips and barbotine (shoulder and body).
10	165-1/2	VIIb	Asma	Moulded water jar. Medium red ware with sand, mica. Mica particles on the moulded ornaments, black and red slips.
11	240-1	VIIb	Asma	Moulded water pot with a spout. Medium pinkish ware with sand and mica.
12	236-6	VIIc	Asma	Little pitcher. Rather fine pinkish ware with sand and mica.
13	240-2	VIIb	Asma	Spout with filter. Rather coarse ware with sand, mica. Covered with red slip and mica.
14	242-1	VIIa	Asma	Lid fragment. Rather fine pinkish ware with sand and mica.
15	236-8	VIIc	Asma	Lid (top missing). Medium pinkish ware with sand. Wheel traces.
16	236-9	VIIc	Asma	Bowl fragments. Rather coarse pinkish ware with sand and mica. Sgraffiato under thick white glaze.
17	165-4	VIIb	Asma	Oil lamp. Rather coarse red ware. Blue glaze.

Figure 12 (continued)

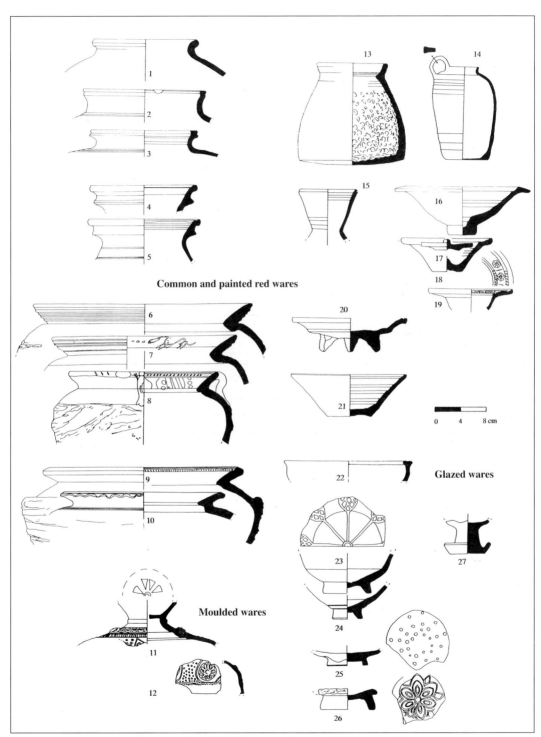

Common and painted red wares

Moulded wares

Glazed wares

0 4 8 cm

Figure 13: Ceramics of level VIII (11th–early 12th cent. AH/17th–early 18th cent. AD)

N°	Find n°	Level	Sector	Description
1	159-7	VIIIa	Asma	Jar rim. Rather fine red ware.
2	159-8	VIIa	Asma	Jar rim. Medium red ware. Black and red slips.
3	159-6	VIIIa	Asma	Jar rim. Medium red ware. Black and red slips on a slip ground.
4	120-3	VIIIb	Asma	Jar rim. Medium red ware. Black and red slips.
5	124-2	VIIIa	Asma	Jar rim. Rather fine pinkish ware with sand and mica. Black and red slips.
6	133-1	VIIIa	Asma	Cooking pot rim. Rather coarse red ware.
7	233-2	Surf.	Asma	Cooking pot rim. Rather coarse red ware with sand, mica and baked clay. Engraved design and little stones inlaid (rim).
8	120-2/ 114-1	VIIIb	Asma	Cooking pot fragment. Rather coarse red ware. Engraved band and black and white slips (rim), barbotine.
9	233-5	Surf.	Asma	Cooking pot fragment. Rather coarse pinkish ware with sand, mica and baked clay. Engraved design, slip painted and barbotine.
10	159-9	VIIIa	Asma	Cooking pot rim. Engraved design (rim), black and red slips (rim and shoulder).
11	104-1	VIIIc	Asma	Moulded water jar with filter (gargoulette). Medium red ware, surface covered with mica.
12	108-1	VIIIc	Asma	Moulded jar sherd. Grey ware, surface covered with mica.
13	233-4	Surf.	Asma	Little pot. Rather fine pinkish ware with sand.
14	159-1	VIIIa	Asma	Little pitcher. Medium red ware with sand.
15	120-4	VIIIb	Asma	Water jar collar. Medium ware with mica. Black and red slips.
16	159-10	VIIIa	Asma	Lid. Medium red ware.
17	159-14	VIIIa	Asma	Lid. Red ware.
18	159-13	VIIIa	Asma	Lid. Medium red ware.
19	234-1	VIIIa	Asma	Lid (base missing). Medium pinkish ware with sand, mica. Stamped ornament on the rim.
20	106-1	VIIIc	Asma	Little basin. Medium red ware. Black and red slips.
21	159-2	VIIIa	Asma	Little cup. Medium pinkish ware.
22	108-3	VIIIb	Asma	Bowl rim. Rather coarse red ware. Turquoise blue glaze.
23	106-3	VIIIc	Asma	Bowl base. Rather coarse red ware. Sgraffiato under white yellowish glaze.
24	104-2	VIIIc	Asma	Bowl base. Red ware. White glaze.
25	159-3	VIIIa	Asma	Cup base. Medium red ware with sand. Sgraffiato and dark blue dots on a white ground, under a clear glaze. Stilt trace.
26	103-1	VIIId	Asma	Cup base. Medium red ware. Sgraffiato under white glaze.
27	111-3	VIIIb	Asma	Oil lamp base. Fine red ware. Yellowish white glaze.

Figure 13 (continued)

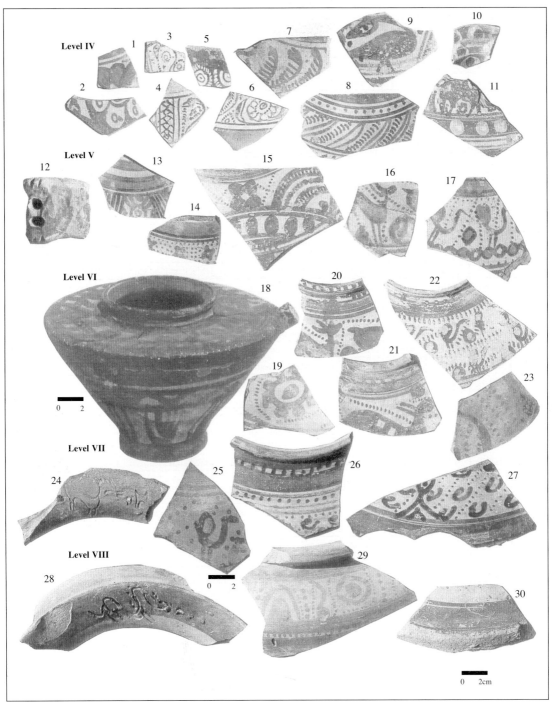

Level IV

1

3

5

7

9

10

2

4

6

8

11

Level V

12

13

15

16

17

14

Level VI

18

20

22

19

21

23

0   2

Level VII

24

25

26

27

Level VIII

28

29

30

0   2

0   2cm

Plate 1: Sehwan, Asma ravine. Red painted wares.

N°	Exc. Unit	Level	Sector	Description
1	340	IVa	Asma	Cooking pot sherd with lotus design in black and red slips on a cream ground.
2	338	IVa	Asma	Cooking pot sherd with lotus design in black and red slips on a cream ground.
3	339	IVa	Asma	Cooking pot sherd with bird design in black slip on a cream ground.
4	331	IVb	Asma	Cooking pot sherd with bird and geometrical design in black slip on a cream ground.
5	338	IVa	Asma	Cooking pot sherd with « sun » design in white slip on a red ground.
6	335	IVb	Asma	Cooking pot sherd with lotus design in black and red slips on a cream ground.
7	335	IVb	Asma	Cooking pot sherd with leaves or plumes design in black and red slips on a cream ground.
8	334	IVc	Asma	Cooking pot sherd with plumes design in black and red slips on a cream ground.
9	335	IVb	Asma	Cooking pot sherd with bird design in black and red slips on a cream ground.
10	334	IVc	Asma	Lid rim with plumes dots design in black and white slips on a red groud.
11	327	IVc	Asma	Cooking pot sherd with elephant design in black and red slips on a cream ground.
12	321	Va	Asma	Necklace element? Modeled red ware with red and black slips.
13	322	Va	Asma	Cooking pot sherd with geometrical pattern in black and red slips on a cream ground.
14	306	Vb	Asma	Cooking pot sherd with floral design in black and red slips on a cream ground.
15	293	Vd	Asma	Cooking pot sherd with floral and geometrical design, black and red slips on a cream ground.
16	274	Vf	Asma	Cooking pot sherd with goats? design, black and red slips on a cream ground.
17	274	Vf	Asma	Cooking pot sherd with birds design, black and red slips on a cream ground.
18	262-1	VIb	Asma	Figure 11:9.
19	259	VIb	Asma	Cooking pot sherd with lotus? design, black slip on a cream ground.
20	244-1	VId	Asma	Figure 11:2.
21	256	VIc	Asma	Jar rim with goats? design, black and red slips on a cream ground.
22	259	VIb	Asma	Jar rim with birds design, black and red slips on a cream ground.
23	243	VId	Asma	Sherd with « snakes » design, black slip on the fabric.
24	248	VIIa	Asma	Cooking pot rim with engraved animal and inlaid stones, black slip on the fabric.
25	242	VIIa	Asma	Cooking pot sherd with bird, black slip on the fabric.
26	242	VIIa	Asma	Jar rim with birds? black and red slips on a cream ground, mica particles.
27	242	VIIa	Asma	Sherd painted with black and red slips on a cream ground, mica particles.
28	233	Surf.	Asma	Figure 13:7.
29	233	Surf.	Asma	Jar top with geometrical pattern in black and red slips, on a pinkish buff ground.
30	234	VIIIb	Asma	Jar sherd with barbotine and black and red slips on a cream ground.

Plate 1: (continued)

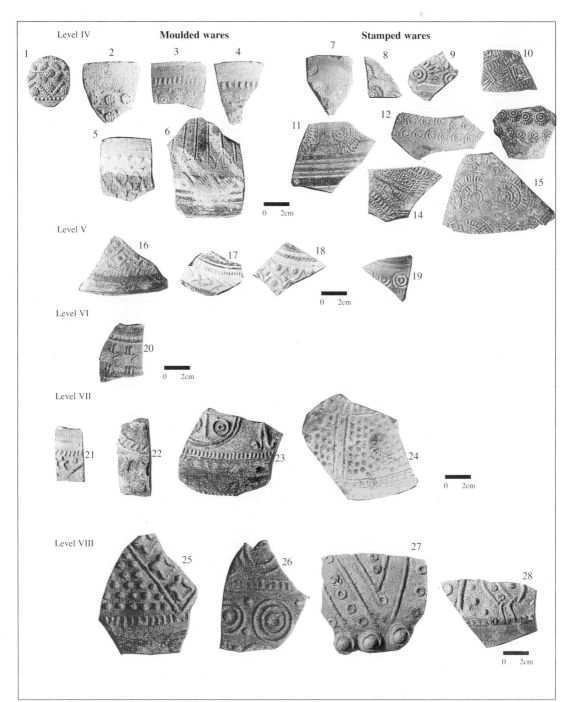

Plate 2: Sehwan, Asma ravine. Red moulded and stamped wares.

N°	Exc. Unit	Level	Sector	Description
1	338	IVa	Asma	Bowl sherd? with moulded flower designs, mica particles.
2	335	IVb	Asma	Cup rim with moulded flower designs, mica particles.
3	331	IVb	Asma	Cup rim with moulded flower designs, mica particles.
4	331	IVb	Asma	Cup rim with moulded flower designs, mica particles.
5	328	IVc	Asma	Cup rim with moulded geometrical designs, mica particles.
6	328	IVc	Asma	Pot sherd with moulded geometrical designs, red and black slips, mica particles.
7	338	IVa	Asma	Bowl rim with stamped « sun » designs.
8	338	IVa	Asma	Sherd with stamped « sun » designs.
9	335	IVb	Asma	Pot sherd with stamped lotus designs, black slip, mica particles.
10	331	IVb	Asma	Pot sherd with stamped square designs, mica particles.
11	328	IVc	Asma	Pot sherd with stamped lotus designs, black and red slip, mica particles.
12	331	IVb	Asma	Pot sherd with stamped « sun » designs.
13	331	IVb	Asma	Pot sherd with stamped « sun » designs.
14	328	IVc	Asma	Pot sherd with stamped square designs, mica particles.
15	328	IVc	Asma	Pot sherd with stamped lotus designs, mica particles.
16	312	Vc	Asma	Pot sherd with moulded geometrical designs, black and red slips.
17	312	Vc	Asma	Pot sherd with moulded geometrical designs, black and red slips.
18	293	Vd	Asma	Pot sherd with moulded geometrical designs, black and red slips.
19	322	Va	Asma	Pot sherd with stamped circles designs, black and red slips.
20	187	VIa	Asma	Pot sherd with moulded geometrical designs, black and red slips, mica particles.
21	246	VIIa	Asma	Pot sherd with star and geometrical designs.
22	246	VIIa	Asma	Pot sherd with stars and flowers designs.
23	246	VIIa	Asma	Pot sherd with geometrical designs.
24	160	VIIc	Asma	Pot fragment with floral and dots designs.
25	159	VIIIa	Asma	Pot fragment with stars and dots designs, mica particles.
26	159	VIIIa	Asma	Pot fragment with circles and dots designs, mica particles.
27	233	Surf.	Asma	Pot fragment with geometrical designs, mica particles.
28	233	Surf.	Asma	Pot fragment with bird design, black and red slips, mica particles.

Plate 2: (continued)

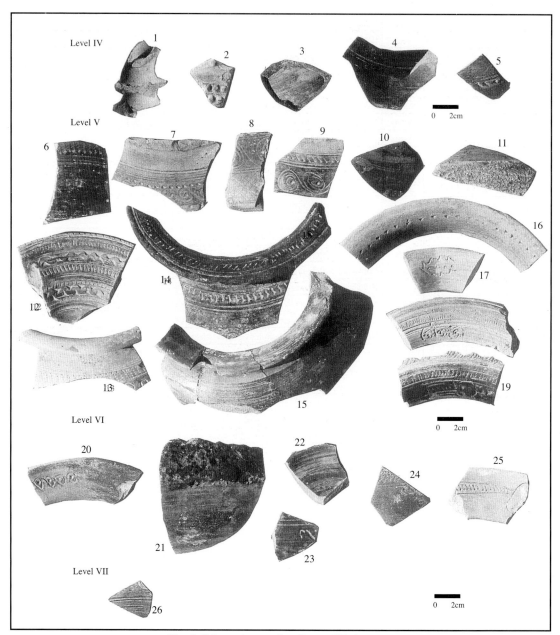

Level IV

Level V

Level VI

Level VII

Plate 3: Sehwan, Asma ravine. Grey and black wares.

Nº	Exc. Unit	Level	Sector	Description
1	339	IVa	Asma	Bottle collar, grey ware.
2	338	IVa	Asma	Moulded sherd, grey ware.
3	331	IVb	Asma	Bowl sherd? grey ware.
4	331	IVb	Asma	Cooking pot rim, grey fabric with black polished surface.
5	334	IVc	Asma	Cooking pot sherd, grey fabric with black polished surface, engraved design.
6	317	Va	Asma	Cooking pot sherd, grey fabric with black polished surface, wheel engraved.
7	311	Vc	Asma	Cooking pot sherd, grey fabric and surface, engraved design.
8	311	Vc	Asma	Cooking pot sherd, grey fabric and surface, engraved design.
9	293	Vd	Asma	Cooking pot sherd, grey fabric and dark grey polished surface. Engraved design.
10	291	Ve	Asma	Cooking pot sherd, black polished surface.
11	296	Vd	Asma	Cooking pot sherd, dark grey ware and barbotine.
12	301-3	Vc	Asma	Figure 10:4
13	301	Vc	Asma	Cooking pot fragment, grey fabric and surface, engraved design.
14	306	Vb	Asma	Cooking pot fragment, black polished ware, engraved design.
15	269	Vf	Asma	Cooking pot fragment, black polished ware.
16	271	Ve	Asma	Cooking pot rim, grey ware, engraved design.
17	292	Ve	Asma	Cooking pot rim, grey ware, engraved design.
18	296	Vd	Asma	Cooking pot rim, grey ware, engraved design.
19	280	Vf	Asma	Cooking pot rim, dark grey polished ware, engraved design.
20	264	VIa	Asma	Cooking pot rim, grey ware, engraved design.
21	264	VIa	Asma	Cooking pot sherd, black ware and barbotine.
22	268	VIb	Asma	Cup sherd, grey fabric and dark grey surface.
23	268	VIb	Asma	Cooking pot sherd, grey fabric and black polished surface, engraved design.
24	253	VIc	Asma	Cooking pot sherd, black polished ware, engraved design.
25	253	VIc	Asma	Cooking pot rim, grey ware, engraved design.
26	241	VIIa	Asma	Cooking pot sherd, dark grey ware, engraved design.

Plate 3: (continued) .

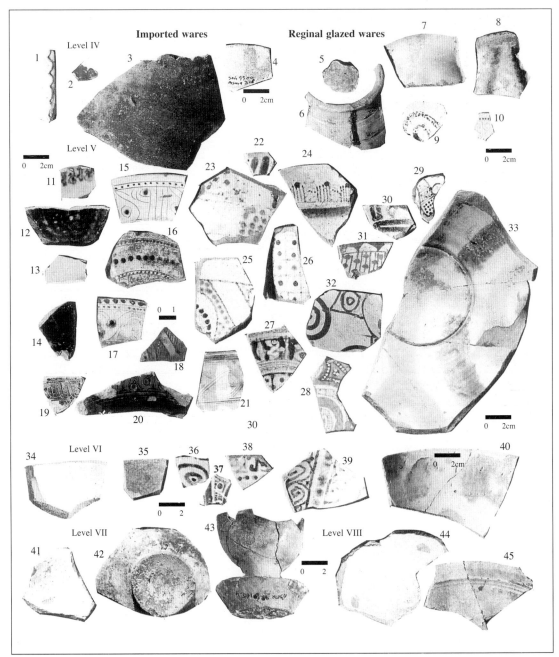

Plate 4: Sehwan, Asma ravine. Imported and glazed wares.

N°	Exc. Unit	Level	Sector	Description
1	339	IVa	Asma	Pitcher handle (import from Mesopotamia), white ware, applied ornament.
2	338	IVa	Asma	Sherd (import from Mesopotamia), clear buff ware, blue glaze.
3	331	IVb	Asma	Jar sherd (import from Mesopotamia), clear buff ware, blue glaze.
4	328-33	IVc	Asma	Figure 8:39.
5	334	IVc	Asma	Sherd, red ware, green glaze.
6	384	IVc	Asma	Pot fragment, red ware, splash ware.
7	330	IVc	Asma	Cup rim, pinkish ware, falence imitation.
8	328-31	IVc	Asma	Figure 8:38.
9	328	IVc	Asma	Cup sherd, underglaze painted in brown, on a cream slip ground.
10	327	IVc	Asma	Cup rim, sgraffiato and underglaze painted in brown on a cream slip ground.
11	317	Va	Asma	Cup sherd, underglaze painted in brown on a cream slip ground.
12	301	Vc	Asma	Cup base, dark green glaze on a cream slip ground.
13	293	Vd	Asma	Cup sherd, yellow glaze.
14	290	Vf	Asma	Cup sherd, black glaze.
15	317	Va	Asma	Cup rim, sgraffiato and underglaze painted (brown and green) on a cream slip ground.
16	301	Vc	Asma	Cup sherd, sgraffiato and underglaze painted (brown) on a cream slip ground.
17	207-3	Vd	Asma	Figure 10:33.
18	216	Vc	Asma	Cup sherd, hatched sgraffiato under yellow glaze.
19	286	Vf	Asma	Bowl rim, sgraffiato under black glaze.
20	270-2	Vf	Asma	Figure 10:35.
21	201-2	Ve	Asma	Figure 10:28.
22	316	Vb	Asma	Cup rim, underglaze painted (brown) on a cream slip ground (lustre imitation).
23	317	Va	Asma	Cup base, underglaze painted (yellow brown, green) on a cream slip ground.
24	316	Vb	Asma	Cup sherd, underglaze painted (yellow brown, green) on a cream slip ground.
25	301-5	Vc	Asma	Figure 10:22.
26	306-1	Vb	Asma	Figure 10:21.
27	293	Vd	Asma	Cup sherd, underglaze painted (brown) on a cream slip ground.
28	207	Vd	Asma	Cup sherd, underglaze painted (brown, orange and white slip) on a cream slip ground.
29	316	Vb	Asma	Cup base, underglaze painted (brown slip) on a white slip ground.
30	316	Vb	Asma	Cup base, underglaze painted (black slip) on a white slip ground.
31	316	Vb	Asma	Cup rim, underglaze painted (red slip) on a white slip ground.
32	301	Vc	Asma	Cup base, underglaze painted (red and black slip) on a white slip ground.
33	280-3	Vf	Asma	Figure 10:25.
34	188-189	VIa	Asma	Cup base, red orange ware, white glaze.
35	265	VIa	Asma	Cup base, red orange ware, green glaze.
36	265	VIa	Asma	Cup sherd, underglaze painted (brown) on a cream slip ground.
37	265	VIa	Asma	Cup sherd, underglaze painted (brown, red slip) on a cream slip ground (lustre imitation?)
38	265	VIa	Asma	Cup rim, underglaze painted (brown, green) on a cream slip ground.
39	262	VIb	Asma	Cup base, underglaze painted (brown, green, orange) on a cream slip ground.
40	257	VIc	Asma	Cup rim, splash ware type on a cream slip ground.
41	248	VIIa	Asma	Cup rim, white glaze.
42	246	VIIa	Asma	Cup base, turquoise blue glaze.
43	165-4	VIIb	Asma	Figure 12:17
44	233	Surf.	Asma	Cup base, white glaze.
45	233	Surf.	Asma	Cup rim, turquoise blue glaze.

Plate 4: (continued)

already seen in the large sounding in Asma. Several soundings and larger excavations made close to some fortifications (in the Leila and the Zubeida ravines) and out of the tepe, completed the ceramic data and typologies of the richest phase of the city, during the 'bazaar period'. Shapes and surface treatments were the most diversified during this period, which was also characterized by the numerous grey or black polished and glazed wares. Ceramics of the Mughal period were more common in the Leila area, where a residence and a bath were found.

The entire study of the ceramic material discovered in Sehwan's fort will be included in a wider publication of the site. The phases between the Delhi Sultanates and the Tarkhan period (7th/13th–10th/16th centuries) are in fact less well represented in the areas excavated, and a more extensive excavation of these levels in the fort would be very useful in enriching their corpus. The last occupation of the site did not really end with the fall of the Mughal power in Sindh. Some signs of the Kalhoras were also found, besides the textual data mentioned in this chapter, as a glazed tile discovered in Sehwan's Purana Qila and which can be dated from this period has been identified by Audrey Péli.[146] It would be interesting to compare further work on the latest ceramic material—wares and tiles—present in the fort with the tile ornaments covering some of the shrines in Sehwan Sharif.

An important issue is that Sehwan, as well as Sindh as a whole, was located at a crossroads between China and Mesopotamia. Like all cultures, the Sindhi identity was formed during many centuries through an integrative process. Turning back to the Purana Qila, the excavation highlights the process by which Sindhi identity was built as a composite culture. A detailed and incisive study of the appearance, development, transformation and disappearance of the animals and geometrical patterns should be very significant in this field.

2

SHIVAITE CULTS AND SUFI CENTRES A REAPPRAISAL OF THE MEDIEVAL LEGACY IN SINDH

Michel Boivin

Abstract

In Sindh, it is well known that some of the main Sufi centres are associated with Shivaite figures like Gopichand or Bhartrhari, and others. The aim of this study is to highlight how these associations arose, and their meaning. The chapter proposes the hypothesis that the answers lie in the religious legacy of medieval Sindh. In the first part, it surveys the main religious movements that were deeply rooted in Sindh, especially Shivaism and Sufism. The second part investigates three main areas where the association between Shivaism and Sufism can be deciphered. The conclusion states that Sufis deliberately tried to locate their religious message in a continuum with Shivaism, while at the same time a new orientation and understanding was given according to Sufi spirituality.

* * * *

In my research on Sufism in contemporary Sindh, I often encountered elements related to the Hindu god Shiva. The role played by Shiva's cult in the province has been highlighted by Derryl MacLean (MacLean, 1989), and before him George Briggs had noted that Sindh was an important place for the Shivaite sect of the Kanphatas (Briggs, 1938). At a broader level, S.A.A. Rizvi devoted some pages to the relations between Sufis and Naths in the Indian subcontinent (Rizvi 1978, vol. 1: 331-341). Other studies were devoted to regional contexts like Bengal (Tarafdar 1992), Punjab (Matringe, 1992), or to more literary approaches to the question.[1] Despite this, one can find no study on the relations between Shiva's cult and the Shivaite sects, and the specificity of Sufism in Sindh. Several among the most venerated Sufis are nevertheless associated with dominant figures of Shivaite devotion, and some Sufi centres were previously Shivaite shrines. It could, therefore, be of some use to take stock of the available material on the question.

Since the ultimate aim of this study is to reappraise the medieval spiritual legacy in Sindh, it is important to point out that the present day religious situation arose through a very complex process which had lasted centuries. Consequently, the study does not try to prove that local Sufism was shaped by Shivaism, nor any other attractive but simplistic theory. There is no doubt that Sufism is based on Quranic injunctions, and that it was shaped by Islamic values. Carl Ernst has discussed at length the role played by Christian, and especially Protestant, concepts of Orientalist understanding of the Sufi-Yoga relationship. While using different kinds of data, this study wishes to understand how, and to what extent, Sufism was historically a continuum of the Shivaite legacy.

Although the present contribution refers to the medieval spiritual legacy of Sindh, it is beyond its scope to encompass all the religious figures and sects which have spread in the province. Today, two categories of charismatic figures are still prevalent: the Shivaites and the Sufis. Even if Buddhism left important remains in Sindh, there is actually not a single worshipped figure that can confidentally be linked to Buddhism. This is the reason why Buddhism is not included in this study. On the other hand, some Shiite schools are included because their followers are still present in Sindh today, even if they are few. Moreover, they can sometimes hardly be distinguished from the Sufi *tariqas*.

The first part of the chapter is devoted to the pre-Islamic cult of Shiva and the medieval sects devoted to his worship. The data related to 'proto-Shiva' and the so-called Shiva Pashupati of Mohen-jo Daro, as well as other remains related to the god are examined. The second part analyses how Sufism arrived in Sindh. It was through a slow process and two periods can be distinguished, as elsewhere in the Muslim world; first, the time of the ascetics, and second, the Sufi orders. The three following parts are devoted to the problem of the correlation between Shivaite cults and Sufi centres in different regions in southern Sindh: Thatta, Sehwan, and Hyderabad.

Shiva's Cult in the Pre-Islamic Period and Shivaite Sects in Medieval Times

Shiva's Cult in Ancient Sindh

Huien Tsang's narrative is the most useful source regarding the religious situation of Sindh before the advent of the Muslims in 711. Hinduism was then predominant in Upper Sindh, while Buddhism and Hinduism were balanced in Lower Sindh (Huien Tsang 1884, II: 272-81). The question is, therefore, why only a few Hindu remains were found in Upper Sindh, while many were discovered in Lower Sindh, knowing that Sindh at the time, sometimes called Great Sindh, was, including the Multan area, actually located in Punjab. The Chinese pilgrim Huien Tsang stated in 642 that 273 Hindu temples were to be found in Great Sindh. Of these, one was the famous sun-temple of Multan, thirty-seven were inter-sectarian, and the remaining 235 belonged to the Pashupata Shivaites.

Archaeology gives evidence of the flourishing of Hinduism. One of the most beautiful brass images of Brahma was discovered in the neighbourhood of Mirpurkhas. It can be dated to the late 6th or 7th centuries. Measuring not less than 3 feet 2 inches, it is one of the largest metal images we possess from any period. It is unique because it has only two arms. According to J.E. van Lohuizen, one of the hands is held in the attitude typical of an ascetic carrying a water pot (Lohuizen, 1981, 51). At Brahmanabad many fragments of stone images were discovered. One of them was an image of Surya, the sun god, whose most important temple was at Multan. Stylistically, the frame dates to the 10th century, and J.E. van Lohuizen concluded that Hinduism was still flourishing under Arab rule.

Despite these remains of Brahma and Surya, Shiva was obviously the most important god in pre-Muslim Sindh. The *Shiva Purana* refers to the Indus River as a place where the holy ascetics can divest themselves of all their impurities (MacLean, 1989, 15). The only Hindu monument dating from the early historical period was discovered at Banbhore, which in all possibility represents the ancient city of Debul. Although fragments of a Vishnu image were found there, two *linga*s were standing in the pre-Muslim layers. One of them was still standing on its *yoni*. It is possible that this structure was described in the *Chach Nama* as the large Shiva temple 'surmounted by a dome and lofty spire, over which flew a green silken flag with four streamers' (quoted by Lohuizen, 1981, 51). The veneration of the *linga* is confirmed at a later date by Muslim travellers. Al Beruni stated that Shiva is most frequently venerated in the south of Sindh.

If deltaic Sindh was a stronghold of his cult, Shiva was also worshipped in the north of the province. A number of terracotta seals were discovered at Jhukar, near Larkana, and Vijnot. In Brahmanabad too, several statues of Ganapati (Ganesh, Shiva's son), Shiva and consort, and a large trident have been found (Cousens, 1929, 51). Last but not least is the numismatic evidence. Although they were discovered in the Buddhist monastery at Mohen-jo Daro, several coins undoubtedly show the image of Shiva. They are usually dated between 500 and 800. One side shows a standing figure with a nimbus around his head and a trident in his hand or next to him (Lohuizen, 1981, 52). The same type of coins were found at Jhukar. It is possible that these coins were produced by the Hindu dynasty of the Rai, who ruled Sindh before the usurper Chach, whose son Raja Dahir was the king of Sindh when the Arabs conquered the province in 712.

The Pashupatas

The cult of Shiva is, therefore, well attested in pre-Muslim Sindh and several archaeological remains show that Shivaism was flourishing up to the 10th century. Different indices give evidence of the Shivaite sects which were predominant at the time. First is the famous small seal first identified by Marshall as a proto-Pashupati form of Shiva (Marshall, 1931, vol. 1: 52-56). In this aspect, Shiva is worshipped as the Lord (*pati*) of the animals (*pashu*), namely as the 'Herdsman'.

Huien Tsang firmly stated that the Shiva temple of Debul was managed by the Pashupata heretics (Huien Tsang 1884, II: 276). Several accounts quoted by Lorenzen show that Lakulisha, the founder of the Pashupata school, was born and settled in present-day Gujarat, in a region between Broach and Baroda, maybe in the 2nd century (Lorenzen, 1972, 177). Lakulisha's cult seems to have shifted from north to south India at the beginning of the 11th century. It is quite possible that Mahmud of Ghazni's attacks was one of the reasons for this move. Mahmud raided Somnath, a place where Pashupatas were still attested in 1289 (Lorenzen, 1972, 109). The Pashupatas were declared to be outside of the Vedas and to be one of the divisions of the Tantras. Thus, the Pashupatas were seen as heretics by the main schools of Brahmanism. The custom of courting dishonour by disreputable behaviour is the most distinctive feature of the Pashupata cult of Shiva (Lorenzen, 1972, 187).

The Pashupatas were also located in Sehwan Sharif, and in Koteshwar. This place located on the edge of the Rann of Kutch was previously included in Sindh proper, while today it is in Kutch. There was an important temple of Mahadev, and the pilgrims coming back from Hinglaj had to stop there. In 1894, Haig wrote that the pilgrimage centre was still managed by the heretic Pashupatas (Haig, 1894, 37). According to Briggs, the Gorakhnathis lost control of the pilgrimage centre in the 16th century in favour of the Atits, another order of Shivaite ascetics (Briggs, 1938, 110).

Different Muslim sources, including the *Chach Nama*, state that several hundred women were devoted to the service of the temple of Debul. The reference is clearly to the professional temple prostitutes, known as *devadasis* (literally 'god's slaves'). The tradition of women attached to sanctuaries is very common all over the world. In South Asia, they were professional dancers and worked in Shivaite temples because Shiva was the 'Lord of Dance' (*Nataraja*).[2]

In Shivaite mythology, dance is a kind of magical instrument used by Shiva in different contexts. First, it is through the cosmic dance (*tandava*) that all earthly creatures sprang into existence. Second, it was by dancing that Shiva defeated the demon of ignorance, Mauyalka (Walker, 1968, I: 263-5).

For the *devadasis*, singing and dancing were like a prayer to the god. Interestingly, the *devadasi* was 'married' to the deity: a marriage badge was tied around her neck in a ceremony. After that, the girl was 'ritually deflowered by the temple priest, or by being made to sit atride a stone *linga*, or on the member of an ithyphallic deity representing the god Baleshvara, a form of Shiva' (Walker, 1968, II: 247). Thereafter, the girls were trained by Brahmans in dancing and in the erotic arts, and served as temple prostitutes available to the public, their earnings being kept by the priests. The *devadasi* was often envied her freedom and prestige, and being wedded to the god, her presence at weddings was considered auspicious.

The Kapalikas

Other interesting artefacts are the terracotta seals found at Jhukar with the inscription of 'Hara (Shiva), the wearer of skulls' (*shri karpari harasya*) (Majumdar, 1934, 9, 17 and plate 14). This is a clear reference to a famous heretic sect, the Kapalikas, usually seen as an offspring of the Pashupatas. Lorenzen clearly stated that the Kapalikas have served as the archetype of an immoral and heretical ascetic (Lorenzen, 1972, 215). They carried a skull as a begging bowl and they worshipped Shiva as Bhairava (Lorenzen, 1972, 20).

The ultimate aim of the Kapalikas was a mystical communion with Shiva as Bhairava, based on personal devotion (*bhakti*). The rewards were two-fold: on the mundane level, the devotee gained supernatural magical powers, and on the spiritual level he attained final liberation. As a tantric Shivaite sect, they used to eat meat and drink wine, and they were addicted to sex. Lorenzen has pointed out that the tantric practice of partaking of wine and meat had both hedonistic and eucharistic aspects but 'is in no way connected with materialism' (Lorenzen, 1972, 89). Several tantric texts state that wine, meat, fish, and also grains possess aphrodisiac qualities to prepare for the final sexual union (*maithuna*). Shiva is associated with meat while Shakti is wine. Finally, the communicant becomes the god himself in eating the products which symbolize him.

The Kanphatas and the Problem of Udero Lal as Daryanath

Many of the tantric practices attributed to the Kapalikas resemble those of the Kanphatas (Lorenzen, 1972, 35). According to the *Shabara-tantra*, several names of the sages to whom the Kapalika doctrine was revealed are also found in the traditional Kanphata lists of the eighty-four Siddhas and nine Nathas. Due to these different clues, modern authorities think that the Kanphatas were a later 'transformation' of the Kapalikas.[3] In his book devoted to Gorakhnath and the Kanphatas, George Briggs quotes Sindh as one of the strongholds of the sect. The Kanphatas got their name, which means the split ears, from the initiatory ritual when the ear was split for big earrings. They were also known as the Gorakhnathi Jogis.

The greatest poet of Sindh, Shah Abdul Latif Bhittai (d.1752), sees in the Kanphata the pattern of the renunciant. He mentions once the name of Gorakhnath himself (*Shah-jo-Risalo*, 1951, Sur Ramkali, II, III, and VII). It is well known that he spent three years with them, visiting different Hindu pilgrimages like Girnar, Hinglaj, and Dwarka. In the middle of the 19th century, Richard Burton described the renunciants of Sindh as Nathpanthis of the Kanphata branch. He also calls them Gorakhnath Jogis, whose local patron is one Bhabaknath (Burton, 1851, 322-3). He is probably Balaknath, a follower of Gorakhnath. According to the *Gazetteer* of 1907, the Kanphatas of Sindh were followers of Shiva and their patron saint was

Gorakhnath (Aitken, 1907, 184). Undoubtedly, the Kanphatas were a main Shivaite group in Sindh, from the Middle Ages to the British time.

There is another tradition related to Gorakhnath, especially among the Hindu Sindhis who migrated to India in 1947 and after. Udero Lal, the river god venerated by the Hindu Sindhis, should have been initiated by Gorakhnath, who gave him the *guru-mantra* called *alakh niranjan*.[4] As far as I know, the devotional poetry of Udero Lal, known as *panjra*s, never mentions such a reference. The Kanphata affiliation of Udero Lal is nevertheless stated by George Briggs (Briggs, 1938, 64-5). Briggs's thesis is that Udero Lal, better known here as Daryanath, created the Daryapanth, which is a branch of the Kanphatas, even if it was later separated from the main branches, and subsequently became independent. Briggs argues that the Daryapanth belongs to the Heth *panth* of the original Gorakhpanthis. The Heth *panth* or Hethnathpanth, was founded by Laksmannath, who succeeded Gorakhnath at Tilla, in Punjab.

There are, however, several points which need to be discussed since they look dubious. The first is that Briggs never quotes a source, which suggests he takes it from the oral tradition of the Naths. In the eleven lists of the sub-divisions of Gorakhnathis that he gives, the name of Daryanath occurs only twice in oral lists given to the author. The second one, given to the author in Srinagar, gives the name Darya instead of Daryanath, though it is possible to add a third one, recited in Devi Patan. But the main name is that of Natesri, which is finally a name of Laksmannath (Briggs, 1938, chart A). Without further explanation, Briggs adds that 'Ratannathis are counted as Daryanathis as well' (Briggs, 1938, 66). Ratannath was a famous disciple of Bharrhari and he stayed in Peshawar.[5]

From a scholar's point of view, it is therefore very difficult to follow Briggs' thesis. What is more interesting is to understand how this identification came about. Obviously, some informants really gave the name Daryanath. My conviction is that Briggs was inclined to see him as Darya Shah, the Indus river god. Later on, the Hindu Sindhis could have read Briggs and then concluded that he was initiated by Gorakhnath. This is in any case untrue, because in Briggs's version, Darya Shah was the disciple of Laksmannath, himself Gorakhnath's follower.

The second point is related to an unclear identification between Daryanath, namely Udero Lal, and one Dayanath. The mention of the town of Udero Lal, where Udero Lal's main sanctuary stands, as a main Nath centre will be discussed later. According to Briggs, Dayanath was a *sadhu* who used to stay in a cave (Briggs, 1938, 118). This Dayanath is connected with Gorakhnath but the episode of the narrative places their meeting in the south of Thatta, while Udero Lal's place is north of Hyderabad. The similarity of the two names is, however, confusing, especially when no Dayalal or Daryalal is mentioned in other parts of South Asia in relation with Gorakhnath and the Kanphatas. Consequently, this Dayanath has probably been confused with Daryanath. Briggs may have got these stories from two different sources, and this could be what prevents him from understanding it as a single figure.

Although the remains of the place are unfortunately not helpful, the chronology can help to understand the event. There is obviously a focus on the 10th century. It is the period when Udero Lal is said to have lived, and he created the Daryapanth at the beginning of the 11th century. It is also in the 10th century that we find the last known evidence of the activity of the Shivaite temple at Banbhore. At the regional level, a new local dynasty, the Sumras, began to rule Sindh at the beginning of the 11th century while at the subcontinent level, Mahmud of Ghazni raided India many times. It is well known that when coming back from Gujarat, he travelled through Sindh on the way to Afghanistan. In any case, a new balance appeared between military forces and religious ones at the turning point of the 10th-11th centuries.

The problem of a supposed correlation between Shiva's cult and Sufism in Sindh can be seen as the main hypothesis of this chapter. In the first part, the importance of Shiva's cult as well as of Shivaite sects was to be attested. This goal was obviously reached. In South Sindh, it was possible to give evidence that Shiva's cult was prevalent. Interestingly, archaeological evidence as well as textual sources are concordant in showing that there were different Shivaite sects: the Pashupatas, maybe the Kapalikas, and finally the Kanphatas. Moreover, these sects pointed to the main features of Shivaite Sindh. The first is that the main Hindu sects were heretical Shivaite sects. The second is that of asceticism which belonged to Tantrism, as the role played by sex and eroticism indicates. The third are specific rituals like dance understood as a prayer, and the fourth, is a very special social behaviour where the rejection of social codes was to be considered as a path to salvation. These four main features were to give a unique colour to Shivaism in Sindh. In British times, this unique Shivaism was also well attested: the sources agree in stating that all the Hindu ascetics were related to the Kanphatas or to the Gorakhnathis.

Interestingly, the legend of Udero Lal as given by Muslim traditional sources is quite different. According to a recent *tazkira*, Udero Lal was also known as Shaykh Tahir. The story is that one Udero Lal was a Hindu beggar. He went to meet the great saint of Multan, Bahauddin Zakariyya, and was so impressed by his teachings that he converted to Islam and became a Sufi with the name of Shaykh Tahir. The *tazkira's* author even quoted a *qasida* written by Mowla Ali Thattawi in praise of the great Sufi Shaykh Tahir (Naimi, 1997, 182).

Messianism and the Diversity of Shiite Movements in Medieval Sindh

The Coming of the Messianic Alids

Derryl MacLean has devoted several pages to the messianic Alids and Shiism in medieval Sindh (MacLean, 1989, 126-130), and there is consequently no need for a detailed analysis here. Suffice it to highlight two points with regard to Messianic Shiism. Firstly, Shiism reached Sindh very early, and secondly, the Shiism reaching Sindh first was a heterodox form. It is nevertheless necessary to examine the thesis according to which the importance of charismatic figures' cult in Sindh is due to the spread of Shiism in the province. Among others, this study is presented by Sarah Ansari and most scholars take it as proven (Ansari, 1992, 17).

The most important Shiite revolt having some consequences for Sindh was that of Muhammad al-Nafs al-Zakiyyah (d.762). He took refuge there for a while with his brother Ibrahim b. Abdullah. The Arab historians agree that even after the departure of the Shiite leader, they had a number of followers in Sindh. The Arab authors do not quote them any more after a few years. One has to note that Sindh, due to its strategic geographical position on the frontier of the Muslim empire, was frequently used as a refuge for leaders of heterodox Muslim schools.

Another important trend of early Shiism was that of the followers of Muhammad b. al-Hanafiyya. In 915, Masudi met some of his descendants in Multan. In the first half of the 10th century, Abdullah al-Umari, a leader of the Kaysaniyyah, was executed in the city (MacLean, 1989, 130). The Kaysaniyyah was a branch of early Shiism claiming Muhammad b. al-Hanafiyya to be the *mahdi*. It is not known whether the Kaysaniyyah sect was powerful in Sindh. Some of them openly claimed incarnationism (*hulul*) and metempsychosis (*tanasukh*). Abdullah al-Umari was one of the Umari Alids who, according to MacLean who does not unfortunately propose evidence, were to convert to Ismailism after some decades.

From Messianism to Devotionalism: The Ismailis as Mediators

The first messianic movement of Shiism to be well documented is undoubtedly Ismailism. The first missionary, named al-Haytham, was sent from Yemen in 883. Ismaili authors like al-Qadi al-Numan state that the Ismaili missionaries won many converts in Sindh. The first phase of the spread of Ismailism looks however to have been in vain due to two reasons. First, are the Ghaznavid raids from 1005. The Ismaili state of Multan was eventually annexed in 1010 to the Ghaznavid empire. The second cause is the internal divisions of the Ismaili movements: the Qarmat challenge as early as the middle of the 10th century, followed by the Druze split at the beginning of the 11th century, and the Nizari split at the end of the same century. Historical evidence shows that these contests would have had the effect of weakening Ismailism in Sindh and elsewhere.

Interestingly, the second phase of the spread of Ismailism to Sindh occurred after the 13th century. The first historical missionary (*dai*) of this period is Pir Shams al-Din. He is said to have travelled in the region of Multan and Uchch in the first half of the 13th century. It is well known that this was the time of the Sufi renaissance of Multan. Pir Shams was contemporaneous with the great Suhrawardy *pir*s like Bahauddin Zakariyya and with the more controversial figure of Lal Shahbaz Qalandar. The real founder of the Nizari Ismaili community of India, commonly known as Khojas, was nevertheless Pir Sadr al-Din, who lived in the 14th century. Pir Sadr al-Din is said to have given the two pillars of the community: the *jamaat-khana* (house of meeting) and the *mukhi* (local leader).

The 14th century was a time of challenge for the Nizari community. In Persia where the *imam*s stayed, a contest occurred between two pretenders resulting in a new split. In the 15th century, some missionaries like Imam Shah and Ramdeo Pir claimed the imamate for themselves and broke their allegiance to the Persian imam. The consequence was the appearance of many sects more or less related to the imam. This situation makes it difficult to state firmly that Ismailism could have been a deciding factor in the cult of charismatic figures in Sindh. Many other religious sects or schools in the Islamic milieu highlighted the importance of human guidance on the way of spiritual knowledge. Twelver Shiism and Sufism were among the most influential. There is a great lack of scholarly work on the spread of Twelver Shiism in Sindh and in other parts of the Indus valley.

Sayyid Muhammad Jaunpuri and the Mahdawis in Sindh

The last messianic movement which achieved some favour in Sindh was the movement launched by Sayyid Muhammad of Jaunpur (1443-1505). Affiliated to the Chishtiyya, Sayyid Muhammad Jaunpuri proclaimed himself to be the *mahdi* in 1495 while he was in Ahmedabad, Gujarat. He was then compelled to leave Ahmedabad and settled in Patan. The *ulamas* expelled him from Gujarat and he reached Sindh where he stayed for a while. He finally settled in Qandahar where he died in 1505. Even if his stay in Sindh was of short duration, he succeeded in converting a number of followers.

The stay of the *mahdi* in Sindh occurred under the Samma dynasty. It is not known how the Samma rulers welcomed him. In any case, prominent officials in the army and in the administration became his followers, including Shaykh Sadr al-Din, the spiritual mentor of the sovereign (MacLean, 2000, 244). The most famous of his followers was Qadi Qadan (1463-1561), a famous poet to whom is attributed the oldest poetry in Sindhi. According to some authors, the Arghun dynasty was also influenced by the *mahdi* of Jaunpur. Later on, the Kalhora dynasty was also said to have Mahdawi affiliation but this is a controversial question. Ali Sher Qani in his *Tuhfat al-kiram* stated that Adam Shah Kalhora was a follower of the *mahdi*.

Sindh is nowadays one of the few places in the Indian subcontinent where Mahdawis can still be found. According to Derryl MacLean, who has worked on the topic for several years, the Sindhi Mahdawis are different from those of Balochistan, locally known as Zikris, Gujarat or Deccan. The Sindhi Mahdawis (unlike the Gujaratis or the Deccanis) have developed a distinct tradition quite separate from that in India. Mahdism in Sindh does not become a *firqah* but simply a *tariqah*, and in a very Sindhi way becomes a mystical choice, increasingly of *majzubs*. The Sindhis would have been attracted by the Ibn Arabism, the *Insan-i kamil* concept, and especially the original Mahdawi sense of a literary apocalyptic, where Mahdawis play language games unleashed by the approach of the end time.[6]

The Spread of Sufism in Medieval Sindh

The Time of Ascetics (8th–12th Century)

During the Arab rule, the first Sufis to appear in Sindh were ascetics, as in other parts of the Muslim world. Here again, sources are very scarce. Between 767 and 1106, MacLean could estimate the rate of mystics/ascetics to be 18.6 per cent of all Sindhi Muslims. This is the second category after the traditionists (72.86 per cent) and before the Shiites (18.57 per cent) (MacLean, 1989, 96). They started appearing in the 9th century, one century after the Arab conquest (712). They gradually declined during the 10th century and disappeared in the last half of the 11th century (MacLean, 1989, 110).

It is interesting to contextualize this evolution in the light of the local political and religious context, and the larger Sufi context. The two centuries between the 9th and 11th saw the appearance of the first important characters in Sufism. Some of them had a direct or indirect connection with Sindh. The first to be mentioned is Abu Yazid al-Bistami (d. 874 or 877). Some scholars state that it was one Abu Ali al-Sindi, his mystical master, who introduced Bistami to some Hindu concepts. Bistami is known for being the first exponent of the concept of *fana'*, an 'Islamised' version of the Hindu concept of *nirvana*.[7]

The most notable Sufi to visit Arab Sindh was undoubtedly al-Husayn al-Mansur al-Hallaj (858–921). He is said to have travelled in Sindh in 896–97. Most of the scholars generally agree with this. Annemarie Schimmel has devoted an article to the figure of al-Hallaj in Sindhi folk poetry from the 16th century, which is a much later period.[8] Such devotion does not appear to be a specific feature of Sindh. Notwithstanding, many legends on al-Hallaj are related to Sindh but there is no place devoted to him.

Among the early places related to ascetic figures, Hajji Turabi is the most famous. His shrine is located in the deltaic Sindh, close to the medieval city of Thatta and to the ancient town of Banbhore. As usual, it is very difficult to know who this figure was: a mystic, a warrior, a governor? His tomb (*mazar*) is associated with the oldest date of Muslim Sindh, 787, seventy-five years after the Arab conquest. The legend describes Hajji Turabi as both an ascetic and a military commander. He is said to have transmuted a hostile Hindu army into a hill through his miraculous powers. MacLean is inclined to think he was an ordinary soldier, named Turab al-Hanzali, who died in 711, drowned while fording the Indus River somewhere in the Delta (MacLean, 1989, 111). The date of the tomb would therefore refer to the erection of the monument.

The second oldest dated monument is not located in southern Sindh. It is in a shrine on a small island off Bhakkar, in northern Sindh. It is devoted to Khwajah Khizr, an enigmatic Quranic figure. Patron saint of sailors, the guardian of the fountain of life, the different roles he played are obviously linked to water. In Sindh, he is also venerated by the name of Zindah Pir by the Hindus, who is a form of the Indus river god, Udero Lal. The date is 952.

A third place could be related to the period of ascetics in Sindhi Sufism. Pir Patho is, by a metonymic process, the place where a saint named Pir Patho lived. The site is composed of two parts: (1) the cemetery where Pir Patho's tomb stands, and (2) the so-called mosque of Muhammad bin Qasim.[9] The most striking thing is the minaret which is quite separate from the mosque. Even if datation work is still going on, this part of the site probably refers to the period of the ascetics. In any case, the complex figure of Pir Patho is related to the Sumra rule in Sindhi context. Sumra power apparently rises just after the first attacks of Mahmud of Ghazni, in 1010 or 1026. This was a time when many Sufis reached the Indian subcontinent. It is well known that al-Hujwiri, well known as Data Ganj Bakhsh, was himself born at Ghazna and he died between 1063 and 1076.

It is usually agreed that the Sumras, at least some of them, were converted to Ismailism. There is a letter from the Fatimid caliph which gives evidence, and the Sumras are frequently called 'Qarmatians' by the Arab and Muslim travellers of this period. Interestingly, the modern Ismaili Sindhi authors see Pir Patho as an Ismaili (Allana, 1984, 34). Multan was controlled by the Fatimid Ismailis from 943. After Mahmud razed the city in 1005, the Ismailis are said to have taken refuge in Mansurah in 1010. It was probably the same year that the first Sumra ruler, named Khafif I, rose to power after the death of the last Habbarid governor. Mahmud invaded Multan again in 1010 and 1011. Finally, Mahmud invaded Mansurah on his way back from Somnath in 1025 and the next winter, he came back once more to destroy the flourishing trade developed by the Ismailis. Khafif I was drowned in the Indus River (Lari, 1994, 45-6).

The Time of the Suhrawardys (from the 13th Century)
It is quite possible that the first Sufis came to Sindh to challenge the Ismaili power. Shihab al-Din Suhrawardy, the founder of the Suhrawardy order, died in 1234. At the same time, the first Suhrawardy Sufis reached the Indian subcontinent. The Suhrawardy order was introduced by Bahauddin Zakariyya (d. ca.1274). The many legends and traditions related to him in different religious communities of the Indus Valley show how important was the role played by this Sufi. The coming of Bahauddin Zakariyya is a turning point in the religious history of the area. Some Sufis belonging to Zakariyya's house even settled in Sindh, especially in Thatta and Nasarpur (Khan, 1980, 280-1). It is nevertheless very difficult to state the real influence of the Suhrawardys in the most troubled time of the Mongol invasions. Despite this, oral tradition as well as textual sources unanimously affiliate most of the famous Sindhi Sufis of the period to the Suhrawardy order if not to Zakariyya himself. The influence of the Suhrawardys grew under the Sammas when the king asked Makhdum-i Jahaniyyan to arrange peace with the sultan of Delhi, Firuz Tughluq.

Moreover, the Sufis who are worshipped by Muslims and Hindus, though by different names, were allegedly Suhrawardys. Lal Shahbaz Qalandar is Raja Bhartrhari, Pir Patho is Raja Gopichand, and Mangho Pir is Lalu Lasraj. Their sanctuaries are located in places possessing strong pre-Islamic connections, as will be shown below. The sources are very clear that at the time, the Muslims, who were in a minority in Sindh, were Ismailis, Sunnis or Shiites. The coming of the Suhrawardys must, therefore, be understood as a proselytising mission, both to reject the Ismaili heresy, and to convert Hindus and other non-Muslims to Islam.[10]

In the 14th century, a new wave of Sufis arrived in Sindh. It was composed of a variety of *silsila*s but the Suhrawardys continued to be drawn to the region 'largely by the existence of a network through which to work' (Ansari, 1992, 20). The rise of the Arghuns also changed the scene. It is said that the Suhrawardy leaders allied with the local population against the

Arghuns, the new rulers of Sindh. As punishment, some Suhrawardys had to leave Sindh and went to Gujarat and Burhanpur where they finally settled. In the meantime, the small town of Hala, located a few kilometres north of present Hyderabad, became the leading centre of the Suhrawardys. This was due to a prominent family who produced the great Sufi Makhdum Nuh (d. ca.1592).

The Coming of the Qadiris and the Naqshbandis (15th Century)

Shah Beg, the Arghun ruler, welcomed a number of Sufis of the Qadiri and the Naqshbandi orders. Some Qadiri Sufis had already settled in Sindh in the ascetic times. Two disciples of Abd al-Qadir al-Jilani (d.1166) were buried at Makli near Thatta. It was not until the 15th century, however, that the Qadiri order really took firm root in the province. Ansar Zahid Khan notes it is perhaps not a coincidence that this new wave of Sufis meets a renewal of the Ismaili proselytising in the Indus valley (Khan, 1980, 284). It is, therefore, probable that the Qadiris came to Sindh to fight the new Ismaili mission. They apparently succeeded because the last Ismaili pir, Pir Dadu, left Sindh after his two brothers were beheaded at Fateh Bagh in the 16th century.

In this regard, the few Qadiri Sufis whose accounts are available generally concentrated around the Thatta region. They were very active in the course of the 15th century. The first notable Qadiri, Sayyid Muhammad, was the ancestor of two very important Sufi lineages of Sindh: the Lakyaris and the Matyaris, who were controlling numbers of prevalent shrines (Khan, 1980, 285). The main centres of the Qadiris were Bhakkar, Sehwan, Nasarpur, and above all Thatta. But there was no rivalry between the Suhrawardys and the Qadiris and many Sufis were initiated in both *tariqas*.

In the beginning of Mughal rule, the Qadiris increased their activity to counteract the growth of the Mahdawi movement in Sindh. The Naqshbandis had been welcomed by Shah Beg, the Arghun ruler, like the Qadiris. But their rise as a leading *tariqa* in Sindh coincided with Mughal power in the Indian subcontinent. In Thatta, a group of Naqshbandis was deeply influenced by the thought of Shaykh Ahmad Sirhindi (1563–1626?), who refuted the *wahdat-e wujud*, and also counteracted the Mahdi movement of Sayyid Ali Jaunpuri. In the meantime, the Naqshbandis finally replaced the Suhrawardys as the most influential *tariqa* in Sindh. Their main centre was Thatta, the capital of the Sammas, then the provincial capital under the Mughals. While they were very influential in other parts of the Indian subcontinent, the Chishti order was not very powerful in Sindh.

The Sufi Renunciants

Traditional records like *tazkiras* give very structured narratives of the *tariqa* affiliations of the most prominent Sufi *shaykh*s. The reality could not have been so clear. Many Sufis were affiliated to several *tariqas*. Heads of some local branches could finally claim their independence or some Sufis could create their own regional or local *tariqa*. The very 'normative' Sufism depicted in classical literature has, therefore, to be moderated. Ansar Zahid Khan rightly states: 'Besides these Sufis there is a host of other Sufis whose affiliations to regular Sufi orders is difficult to trace due to lack of information ...' (Khan, 1980, 294). Finally, the affiliation of the vast majority of the Sufis is not known.

It is not certain, however, that this is due to a lack of information. I prefer to put forward the hypothesis that many of these Sufis had no affiliation with the orthodox orders. For instance, the classic *tazkiras* and Sindhi narratives in Persian give but little information on the *be-shar* Sufis. It is nevertheless well known that the coming of Sayyid Jalal Makhdum-i Jahaniyyan induced the spread of the Jalali *faqir*s. Different signs show that these Sufis were also influential in Sindh. Several sanctuaries are for instance devoted to Juman Jati. Juman Jati was the founder of a famous heterodox Sufi order named the Malang order. Juman Jati also has a tomb in Makli, south of Jam Nizam al-Din's. The name *qalandar* is quite common as can be seen later on.

The evolution of Sufism in Sindh follows the same path as in other parts of the Muslim world. The first period was dominated by the ascetics, and the second by the Sufi orders like the Suhrawardiya or the Qadiriyya. But the specificity of Sindh is linked to two main features. First is the place devoted to the *be-shar* Sufi groups. The most famous is Lal Shahbaz Qalandar, but there are other *qalandars* who have reached fame in the province, as for instance Pir Qaim al-Din Qalandar (Naimi, 1997, 264). Second is the role played by the institutionalised *tariqas*, based in Multan or elsewhere. According to Naimi's *tazkira*, there are only 21 Sufis who bear the *tariqa* affiliation in their names, from a total of 383 Sufis. Qadiris are sixteen, Naqshbandis are four and only three are Chishtis, while three are both Qadiris and Chishtis (Naimi, 1997, 5-20). This feature highlights the autonomy the Sufis had acquired and leads one to think that the regional context was predominant, instead of the centres of the *tariqas* at the subcontinent level. Last but not least, the lack of nominal identification related to institutionalised *tariqas* makes it obvious that the Sindhi Sufis were embedded into the local context.

Pir Patho Alias Gopichand and the Devi in the Thatta Area

Pir Patho/Gopichand at Pir Patho

There are three main areas where some materials allow the hypothesis of a correlation between Shivaite cults and Sufi centres. Interestingly, they are located on the Indus River, in the southern part of Sindh. It reveals how important the river god was and the chronology of these different sites show that they succeeded each other. The oldest one is the complex of Thatta. Archaeological remains, textual sources, and oral traditions, namely legends, give evidence that it was a very active sacred place for the Shivaites and also for the Sufis. The correlation of these two religious movements is highly symbolized by the fact that some of the most important charismatic figures are venerated under two names: one is Sufi, and is used by the Muslims; the second is Shivaite and is used by the Hindus. The Pir Patho area is the place where the Kanphata influence was the more powerful, as is reflected by legends, and by the local toponymy which can be understood as a symbolic discourse.

The question of the correlation between Sindhi Shivaism and Sindhi Sufism can be studied through the topos of the location. A quick survey shows that some of the Sufi centres in Sindh were created in the same locations where Shivaite centres were already established, or very close to them. It is nevertheless important to point out that this was not always the case. The first aim is therefore to identify the nature of the Sufi centres located in Shivaite territories, and also the nature of those which were totally independent of these territories. The area covered here will be restricted to southern Sindh for two reasons. First, my own fieldwork was mainly limited to this part of Sindh; and second, which is a more scholarly explanation, most of the Shivaite sites are located there.

The region of Thatta is formed by the area which stands south of the town. It is more or less the western branch of the old course of the Indus River. This region can be subdivided into three areas: (1) Banbhore/Debul, (2) Pir Patho, with the adjacent places of Kalankot and Pir Ar (the Protector Saint), and (3) Thatta/Makli. It was previously noted that Banbhore was where the most important Hindu temple of Sindh was located at the time of the Arab conquest. Suffice it to repeat that as the *linga*s found there attest, it was a Shivaite temple. This temple was still in use in the 10th century. Unfortunately, it is not possible to know how it disappeared. Was it destroyed by the raids of the Ghaznawids or the Ghurids? No historical chronicle can help in giving an answer.

All the sources obviously point out the importance of Pir Patho and its surroundings as an area where several Shivaite cults and early Sufi centres were concentrated. The area between Thatta and Pir Patho, known as the Makli Hill, is scattered with places devoted to the Devi and to different figures related to the Nathpanth. Despite this, the figure of Pir Patho is a very mysterious one. Richard Burton himself is not very helpful. At the beginning of the 20th century, Pir Patho was still the second pilgrimage centre (*ziyaratgah*) in Sindh, after Lal Shahbaz Qalandar's at Sehwan. According to some sources, Pir Patho was living during Saadi's time, in the 14th century. He is supposed to have taken the tomb of a Hindu saint. Under the Talpur dynasty, which ruled Sindh from 1783 to the British conquest in 1843, there was a store always full of grains for nourishing the pilgrims, patronized by the local governor. During British times, Pir Patho was declining and it was apparently mainly visited by Kutchis (Smyth, 1919-1920, vol. 1: 77).

As is the case for most of the saints of Sindh, Pir Patho has not yet received attention from scholars. The only sources are the short notices from the traditional Islamic literature like the *tazkira*s, and oral tradition, to which Carter's short papers must be added. Interestingly, the first two sources are perfectly contradictory and it is possible to see inside these contradictory representations the expression of two different milieus. The first, which I will call 'intellectual Sufism', is linked with normative Islamic religion. It focuses on legalistic and exoteric understanding and practices of Islam. The second, which I will call 'devotional Sufism', is based on the cult of the intercessors. The situation is so confused with Pir Patho that it is not possible yet to state firmly what his real name was. Some mention Pir Husayn Shah (Hughes, 1876, 320), others Pir Alim Shah (Burton, 1851, 326), while some oral traditions mention Sayyid Firuz Shah.

In his *Tuhfat al-kiram*, an 18th century Sindhi narrative in Persian, Ali Sher Qani is more prolix. Pir Patho's real name was Hasan bin Rajpar bin Lako bin Sakhirah and his most common *laqab* was Shah Alim. According to the *Tuhfat al-kiram*, Shaykh Patho was a scion of the Arplan tribe settled near Mirpur Bathoro, on the eastern shore of the Indus River (quoted in Khan, 1980, 280). In the classical sources, Pir Patho is usually associated with the early influence of the Suhrawardys in Sindh, like Lal Shahbaz Qalandar in Sehwan Sharif. Both are credited with having converted many Hindus to Islam.

The most interesting narration regarding Pir Patho can be found in the *Tarikh-i Tahiri*, composed in 1621 by Mir Tahir Muhammad Nasyani. Nasyani only speaks of Pir Patho after the foundation of Thatta by Jam Nanda, the new Samma ruler of Sindh. Born in Thatta, the author called Pir Patho the 'Shaykh of Shaykhs' and he describes some of the traditions which are performed at his shrine. The people of Thatta celebrate many fairs (*id*s) every month. There is one which is held on the first Friday after the new moon, called in Sindhi *mah-pahra jum'a*, and another one on the first Monday in each month, called in Sindhi *mah-pahra somar*. Pir Patho's shrine is surrounded by ten or twelve places where dervishes perform an ecstatic dance. Nasyani comments that although this custom is much opposed to the laws of Islam, ulamas and governors have never succeeded in putting a stop to it (quoted in Elliott & Dowson, 1867, 274).

In these conditions, the date of Pir Patho's death is highly conjectural. The *Tuhfat al-kiram* gives the date of 1248 but other sources give 1300 (Lari, 1994, 51). Pir Patho's tomb is located in a mosque which is said to be his mosque. Archaeologists have only found one date on the *mihrab* which is in the mosque: AH 547/AD 1152 (Kervran, 1989 and 1994, 19). The date of his fair, which is the commemoration of his death and understood as his union with god is also uncertain. The annual fair was held from the 11th to the 14th Rabiul Awwal (Smyth, 1919-20, vol. 1, 77). In the *Gazetteer* of 1876, Hughes mentions three different fairs: one in January, one in April, and one in July, each of them lasting only one day. The first two were visited by 2000 pilgrims each, and the latter by 4000. The Hindus were supposed to attend Pir Patho's shrine on the 1st of Vaisakh (April–May), that is on the same day they also visited the shrine of Darya Pir in Tali Makan, east of Mirpur Sakhro (Carter, 1932, 87).

Several authors mention that Pir Patho is worshipped by the Hindus under the name of Raja Gopichand. Here again, the first source in which this association appears is not traceable. Gopichand is a very popular character who usually appears in relation with Gorakhnath and the Nathpanthis (Grodzins Gold, 1992). Gopichand was the nephew of Bhartrhari who renounced the throne of Ujjain to become an ascetic. There are several legends and traditions which are related to the activities of Gopichand/Pir Patho in Sindh. In one of them, it is said that Gopichand wanted to gain possession of a cave in the hill of Pir Ar, which was held by one Dayanath. Dayanath was a very powerful ascetic who could keep alight sufficient fires for the 125,000 *faqir*s who used to live on the hill. He asked Gorakhnath, who was in Girnar, to come to his aid.

A kind of magical fight took place between Dayanath and Gorakhnath. The latter was finally victorious and Dayanath was obliged to leave the place for Dhinodhar in Kutch. But Gorakhnath knew that after taking all the austerity measures, Dayanath could, by breathing thrice, blast all Sindh. Gorakhnath extended his hand and seizing Dayanath by the ear, brought him back to Pir Ar. Finally he made Dayanath his follower, by cutting his ears and putting ivory ornaments in them, and placing a black turban on his head (Briggs, 1938, 192-3). Then Dayanath went back to Dhinodhar. This legend could allude to a rivalry between two schools of Shivaism or two ascetic orders. Was it the arrival of the Kanphatas? A rivalry between the Gorakhnathis and the Daryapanthis? If one agrees that Dayanath is a form of Daryanath, it is quite possible.

Carter was, as a matter of fact, the first to highlight an old presence of the Kanphatas in Sindh.[11] He based his assertion on a description given by Ibn Battuta (c.1333–4), although the evidence is not very convincing (Carter, 1932, 89-90). More surprising is his statement that Pir Patho is Guru Gorakhnath, since elsewhere he says he is Gopichand (Carter, 1917, 206). He also gives the name of three other spots which are related to Pir Patho through toponymy. Similarly, it is difficult to understand which sources are used by Carter for stating that Pir Patho is 'also equated with pre-Islamic Raja Gopichand of Sehwan, of whom a purely Buddhist story of a great renunciation is told' (Carter, 1932, note 22, p. 90).

Jamil Shah Datar/Gorakhnath at Pir Ar

Jamil Shah Datar is also known as Jamil Shah Girnari. His mausoleum stands in the village of Pir Patho, also known as Pir Ar. His *nisba* relates him to Girnar, a very important pilgrimage centre located in Kathiawar (or Saurashtra), Gujarat, near the town of Junagadh. On the Girnar mountain, there are a number of temples, Hindu as well as Jain. Two of the Hindu temples are devoted to Gorakhnath, and the other to Amba, a figure of the Devi. In Sindh legends, Girnar was a favourite place of Gorakhnath. Shah Abdul Latif mentions the place in Sur Sorath. Briggs is, however, the only one to state that Gorakhnath is worshipped in Sindh under the name of Datar Jamil Shah (Briggs, 1938, 181).

Jamil Shah Datar is probably one of the Sufis of Sindh whose *tazkira* version, which I have called intellectual Sufism, is the most opposed to oral tradition, or devotional religion. In his book on the Sufis of Sindh published in 1997, Mawlana Naimi gives his complete name as

Sayyid Abd al-Hadi Taha or Jamil Shah Girnari. He was born in AD 1185 in Mashhad and soon became a prominent Hafiz-e-Quran. Although well versed in exoteric (*zahiri*) knowledge, he went to perform *ziyarat* in Surat and Girnar. He is said to have composed *qasidas* in Persian, and was more or less a disciple of Pir Patho (Naimi, 1997, 124-5). He was affiliated to both Chishtiyya and Naqshbandiyya and died in Rabiul Awwal AD 642. It is to be noted that usually these two orders are antagonistic. For instance, the first one is inclined to use music as a path, while the second bans it.

It is very interesting to see how the *tazkiras'* authors wish to affiliate the great Sufis to one or the other dominant South Asian *tariqas*. It shows that they cannot conceive Sufism without the institutional level embodied by the Sufi orders. In the case of Jamil Shah Datar, Naimi states that he was first a Chishti, before turning to Naqshbandiyya (Naimi, 1997, 125). In his work on the literature and culture of deltaic Sindh, Khwaja Ghulam Ali Allana adds that Shah Jamil was a scion of Musa Kazim's family (Allana, 1977, 335). According to Allana, Jamil Shah Girnari was probably Pir Patho's *sajjada nashin* and he was the spiritual head of the Memons, maybe after converting them from Hinduism to Islam. The reverence they pay to him appears in their praise: 'Ya Shaykh Loqah din dunya ja dunka', meaning 'O Shaykh Loqah, you control the mundane world as well as the spiritual world'.[12] Jamil Shah Girnari is supposed to have died in AD 1244.

The Devi and the Sufis in Thatta

Thatta/Makli is another place where Shivaite cults are well attested, until the present day. Different sources state that there are two Shivaite temples devoted to the Devi: the first would be in Thatta proper (Briggs, 1938, 104), and the second is in Makli (Kervran, 1989 and 1994, 53). In Thatta, the temple is called Ashapuri Devi by Briggs. Some indications in his description lead one to think that what he called Thatta is, in fact, Makli. This place was a stop when the pilgrims were on their return journey from Hinglaj.

Asa or Asha is the goddess of Hope mentioned in the *Harivansha*, a lengthy appendix to the *Mahabharata* (ca.130). It is to be noted that Ashapuri Devi is a very important goddess in Kutch. She was for centuries the 'family deity' of the Jadeja Rajputs and her cult became a 'state religion' when King Hamir ascended the throne in 1472. In Kutch, her main temple is located at Mata-no-madh ('the abode of the Devi'), around 40 km to the south of the Rann of Kutch, and it is run by the Kapadis, a group of monks who seem to be local but close to the Kanphatas (Rushbrook-Williams, 1958, 105-6). This sect is probably an offshoot of the Kanphatas who became independent at an unknown time. The Sindhi poet Shah Abdul Latif (d. 1753) mentions several times in his long poem the word Kapari as another name for the Kanphatas.[13]

On the other side, the temple in Makli is named Mata Bhawani or Singh Bhawani, and it is around a century old. It is said there is a subterranean passage between the sanctuary and Hinglaj. Both the temples are related to the pilgrimage at Hinglaj and there could hardly be two temples devoted to the Devi in the same place. The Ashapuri Devi and the Singh Bhawani temples are, therefore, one and the same temple: it is called Singh Bhawani by the Sindhis, and Ashapuri Devi by the Kutchis. Singh Bhawani, another name for Durga, the goddess seated on a lion, was the most important cult of the Devi in pre-partition Sindh. A temple was built for her in every town or important village. The cult was controlled by the *gurus*, who performed rituals of the Shaktas (Thakur, 1959, 116). Barley was sown in honour of Bhawani.

Among the sacred places of the Kanphatas, Briggs gives the name of Thatta or Nagar Thatta. He writes: 'The importance of the place for the Gorakhnathis is that beads which they greatly prize are obtained there' (Briggs, 1938, 103). The plateau around Thatta, namely the Makli

Hills, is strewn with pebbles and nodular lumps of hard and yellow limestone. People collect and string them for sale to the pilgrims on their way to Hinglaj. There are two kinds of rosaries, according to the sizes of the stones. The rosary with smaller beads is called *thumra*, or *Hinglaj ka thumra*, while the one with larger beads is named *ashapuri*, after the Devi who is venerated there.

According to a legend, Shiva and Parvati stopped here on their way to Hinglaj. While she was cooking millet and rice for Shiva, Parvati killed a demon whose blood ran all over the place including the food. When he was back, Shiva decided to throw the food away: the grains turned into the 'stones' which are now found and collected for the rosaries (Briggs, 1938, 104-5). According to another legend, the Devi was in Thatta where some *faqir*s were persecuting the Hindus. The Devi appeared riding a lion and slew the *faqir*s. Then she proceeded to Hinglaj where she finally stayed. The Devi was obviously Singh Bhawani but what is interesting is the fight she had with the *faqir*s. Maybe this legend refers to the rivalry between Sufis and Shaktas, the followers of Devi's form known as Shakti. Being located in Thatta, one can argue this event occurred when the Sufis became prevalent under the Samma dynasty, at the turning point of the 14th and 15th centuries.

The Devi is also worshipped in Kalankot, a place which is a few kilometres south of Thatta, in the prolongation of the Makli Hills. She is worshipped under the form of Kali, and the temple is called *Wani ka mandir*—*wani* being maybe a diminutive of Bhawani. The local tradition is rather contradictory. The temple is said to have been built four or five centuries ago, that is, in the 14th or 15th century, but the tradition states that the king of Kalankot, a Muslim of the Kalhora tribe, allowed a *guru* to build a *mandir* at this place. The fair occurred in October and goats are slaughtered (Kervran, 1989 and 1994, 53). Nowadays, the small temple built close to a pond is in very bad shape and it is very unlikely that it is still in use as the walls are falling down.

It is usually said that Makli was built to replace Pir Patho as a necropolis for the people of Thatta. In his *Tuhfat al-kiram*, Ali Sher Qani states that Makli is the burial ground for 175,000 tombs of saints (quoted in Lari & Lari, 1997, 20). A number of monuments like *maqbara* and *khanaqah* show that Sufism played an important and official role during the Samma dynasty. The Samma cluster at Makli gives very precious details. The *maqbara* and *khanaqah* of Shaykh Hammad Jamali were built during the reign of Jam Tamachi (1389–1392). The *maqbara* and *khanaqah* of Shaykh Isa Langoti were built a few years later, during the reign of Jam Fateh Khan (1412–1418) (Lari & Lari, 1997, 37). Surprisingly, the *maqbara* of Shaykh Hammad Jamali is in a bad state while Shaikh Isa Langoti's is in a good state of preservation, due to the devotion of the followers who continue to flock there and take care of the venerable saint's resting place (Lari & Lari, 1997, 62). Shaykh Isa Langoti is said to have come from Burhanpur, in present day Madhya Pradesh, India. Shaykh Hammad Jamali was protected by his patron Jam Tamachi while Shaykh Isa Langoti was not.

Finally, one can note that in Thatta/Makli area, there are remains of Sufi centres, while one or maybe two shrines devoted to the Devi under different forms are also attested. It is true that Shiva does not appear in the shape of a god, but many of his symbols, like the famous trident, can be seen in Devi's temples. Due to the lack of sources, it is not possible to go further in the study of a hypothetical relation between Devi temples and Sufi centres because it is not known when this Shivaite cult begun. In any case, before Thatta was chosen as a new capital by the Samma king, Pir Patho, a place located in the south, was obviously the most important Sufi centre of the area. It is probable that for political reasons, Jam Nizam al-Din, the Samma ruler, tried to create a huge new Sufi centre under his own control at Makli, close to the new capital of Thatta he had just built. In any case, it is quite interesting to highlight the fact that the previous sacred complex of Pir Patho had appeared in the time of the Somras, the predecessors and in some ways rivals of the Sammas. The first is rather linked with Nathpanthi narratives, while the other is linked with Shakti narratives.

Lal Shahbaz Qalandar Alias Raja Bhartrhari and the Region of Sehwan

Lal Shahbaz Qalandar

The Sehwan area is another place where strong connections between Shivaism and Sufism appear. They converge through charismatic figures who merge into the complex cult of Lal Shahbaz Qalandar. There are consequently several voices for the tradition of Lal Shahbaz Qalandar. One of them argues that the Persian Sufi settled in a place where a Shivaite temple stands although the French Archaeological Mission never discovered any remains relating to Shiva (see Collinet's chapter). In ancient times, Sehwan was called Siwistan and it is said that the name derives from Shiva. Thanks to the Chinese traveller Huien Tsang, it is well known that Sehwan was a stronghold of the Shivaite sect of the Pashupatas shortly before the Arab conquerors arrived in Sindh at the beginning of the 8th century. The tradition of Lal Shahbaz states that his real name was Usman Marwandi, born in Iran. He went to several sacred places in the Middle East before coming to South Asia, probably following the order of his sufi master he met in Iraq. In the valley of the Indus, Lal Shahbaz first stayed in Multan, then reached Sehwan, a place under the control of a king who was either a Hindu, or a Muslim heretic. His charisma, as well as his asceticism and the many miracles he performed, attracted many people.[14]

The most famous *laqab* of the Sufi is *qalandar*. Nowadays, all the given explanations intend to introduce him as a regular Muslim following *Sharia*. It is nevertheless well known that the name of *qalandar* was given to *be-shar* Sufis: they did not pay respect to the *Sharia* and they were probably linked to the Sufis of the Malamatiyya, those who were searching for blame from society as a proof of sanctity. Another striking point is that the Hindus venerate the saint under the name of Raja Bhartrhari. Once more, it is futile to try to find a historical connection between the two figures, or even to find the oldest sources that mention these connections. In these conditions, it is better to focus on the Shivaite figure of Bhartrhari. Maybe one can consider that the first mention of him is in the *Chach Nama*, where one of the branches of the Indus River is named 'Bartari', which could come from Bhartrhari. According to the legend, Raja Bhartrhari spent some time in a cave near Sehwan: was it in Laki?

Bhartrhari is usually seen as the archetype of Shivaite asceticism and many legends are attached to his name (Grodzins Gold, 1992). They all make him a prince of Ujjain who renounced the kingdom in favour of his brother Vikramaditya. Their sister Manavati (or Maynamati) was Gopichand's mother (Briggs, 1938, 244). He was apparently one of Gorakhnath's heirs and it is said that his *samadh* is in Tilla, in Pakistani Punjab (Briggs, 1938, 102).[15] The fourth original *panth* of Gorakhnath was known as Bhartrhari or Bairag, and he was the alleged founder. Bairag or Bhairava in Sindh is usually a name for the terrible form of Shiva, while the Devi's one is called Bhairavi. Bhairava is especially worshipped by the Kanphatas and by older Shivaite sects before them (Briggs, 1938, 159).

Turning back to the Pashupatas, Lorenzen stresses a very relevant point: 'It is possible that the ultimate source of some of his practises may be found in shamanism, but their psychological basis has changed completely' (Lorenzen, 1972, 188). This is a very important point because my own study of Lal Shahbaz's cult leads me to a similar hypothesis, according to which Lal Shahbaz could be seen to some extent as an heir of the Pashupatas. It is true especially for the ritual of dance. Needless to say that Shiva was the 'king of dance'. Dance was also a very important ritual among the Pashupatas. It was the most common way to reach union with the god. Shiva's furious dance called *tandava* was performed with the play of a drum called *damaru*, a word still used in Sindhi for a drum or tambourine. Nowadays, the most important ritual in Lal Shahbaz's cult is the dance known as *dhammal*. How the players use their drums, also called *dhammal*, how the followers dance to reach ecstasy, which is understood as the divine union, or at least the meeting with the *qalandar's* soul, all these could really be reminiscent of shamanistic rituals.[16]

A last point is to be noted. It is a custom related by Richard Burton who wrote in 1851: 'Every year, a girl of the Khonbati (specialized in using saffron flower) caste is married to the tomb, with music, and all the solemnities which are due to her' (Burton, 1851, 211). Oral tradition is not clear in this matter. Some people spoke about one Hindu girl who gave the keys of the *dargah* to the Sayyids at the beginning of the 20th century, others mention that a Hindu girl stayed in the *dargah* up to the time of Partition. The Khonbatis mentioned by Burton were a Hindu caste who specialized in dyeing clothes with the safflower (in Sindhi *khuhnbo* means saffron). In South Asia, the dyers are usually a low caste. Here, it seems that the Khonbati played a priestly role by marrying one of their girls to the dead *qalandar*. This special position was certainly due to the fact they dealt with saffron, which is the sacred colour of both Udero Lal and Lal Shahbaz Qalandar. Even if Burton mentioned that the symbolism of saffron existed in the wedding ceremony among the Muslims (Burton, 1851, 270), there was one ceremony of *khuhnbo* among the Daryapanthis. A few days before the wedding, some caste fellows and seven happily married women prepared the saffron colour to dye the ceremonial dress of the bride and bridegroom (Thakur, 1959, 176).

Laki Tirtha

Laki[17] is a very important place because it controls the passage from northern to southern Sindh. Under the Sammas and the Arghuns, it was the capital of the administrative division between north and south. It is located very close to Sehwan, about two miles south of the town. It is also one of the most important places of Shivaite cult in Sindh. Laki is named as a *tirtha* (or *tirath*), a pilgrimage centre. It was a compulsory visit for the pilgrim on his way to Hinglaj. The place is devoted to Kali or Shiva, according to different sources. There is a sacred bath where the devout has to give up all impurities before performing his duties in the temple. According to others, Laki was the place where the funeral rituals were to be observed instead of going to Hardwar (Thakur, 1959, 153).

Richard Burton, who called the place 'Dharma tirtha', draws a comparison with Neuron's bath in Fontaine-de-Vaucluse (France). According to him, a special custom was performed there when Brahmanism dominated the province. Renunciants, who were supposed to have reached a very high spiritual state, went there to commit ritual suicide (Burton, 1877, vol. II, 174-5). Today, the place is still visited by Hindus, especially for Havarti and Valsakhi. The author saw some Balochis having a bath there when he visited the place in March 2002. The spring is reputed to cure skin diseases.

Interestingly, Laki, bearing today the official name of Laki Shah Sadr, was a place where Shah Sadr, an important Sufi used to stay. The tradition relates that: (1) he was controlling the area when Lal Shahbaz arrived in Sehwan, and (2) he gave birth to a very important lineage of Sayyids in Sindh, the so-called Lakyari. In 1996, when Sayyid Abd Allah Shah Lakyari was chief minister in Sindh and Benazir Bhutto was Prime Minister of Pakistan, a new *dargah* was built. It is a huge building, not yet completed, in the traditional style inspired by Central Asian monuments. If one agrees that Sufi traditions refer to a symbolic discourse, it is possible to conclude that the visit Lal Shahbaz made to Laki, and the homage he paid to Shah Sadr, can be understood as a recognition and an acceptance of the Shivaite legacy.

Sehwan Sharif, which is the centre of Lal Shahbaz Qalandar's cult, seems to be the most significant place for the observation of the medieval religious legacy in Sindh (Boivin, 2005b). Sehwan looks like an archetype. As a matter of fact, it is in Sehwan that a real continuity can best be observed from the Shivaite school of the Pashupatas to the *faqirs* of Lal Shahbaz Qalandar. It is sufficient to mention here the most prevalent features like renunciation, heterodoxy, and ecstatic rituals for reaching divine union. There seems to be a real continuity from the Shiva Pashupati to the Sufi Usman Marwandi, including, by the way, other regional figures like Udero Lal. Finally, the figure known as Lal Shahbaz Qalandar could be understood in some ways as a synthesis of all of them. The charismatic figure was a reconstruction which was oriented by the Sufi values.

Jogis and Sufis in the Hyderabad Region

Gunjo Area and the Golden Triangle
A third place where connections between Shivaite cults and Sufi centres can be observed is the region of Hyderabad. Hyderabad itself is not really concerned, although the author visited a temple devoted to the Devi in the city, just close to the fort. Hyderabad is nevertheless like a centre from which important sites emerged to the south and to the north. About forty kilometres south of Hyderabad is Jhimpir. It is a place where a Muslim saint is venerated, and also where a temple is devoted to Shiva. At about forty kilometres north of Hyderabad is the Gunjo (or Ganjo) area. This place, where the Devi has a temple, is very close to Bhit Shah and Udero Lal. Not far from these places is the ancient city of Brahmanabad. This is the place in Sindh where a small remain of Shiva was found by archaeologists. It is a terracotta piece where Shiva stands with a trident and in company of Parvati and Ganesh (Cousens, 1929, 51).

Gunjo Takkar is a hilly area between Hyderabad and Hala, along the Indus river. This place is famous in Sindh because the poet Shah Abdul Latif refers to it in his poem *Shah-jo-Risalo*. Tradition states that he spent much time with the *jogi*s in Gunjo Takkar. There is now a temple devoted to the Devi, but it is not known if there was one in the times of the poet. The most striking thing is that Gunjo stands in the midst of three very important religious places: Tando Allahyar, Udero Lal, and Bhit Shah. The first town is the place of the biggest temple devoted to Ramdeo Pir in Sindh. The second is the main sanctuary of the river god, Udero Lal. The third is the sanctuary of the greatest poet of Sindh, himself a very important Sufi, Shah Abdul Latif (d. 1753).

Shiva and Amir Pir in Jhimpir
Near the Kinjhar Lake is a village called Jhimpir. It is located about forty or fifty kilometres south of Hyderabad. This place is very interesting because it is well documented. Through the different sources, it is possible to draw the recent evolution of the cults performed in Jhimpir. In the middle of the 19th century, the *Gazetteer of Sindh* reports a Muslim saint named Shaykh Amin, venerated by both Hindus and Muslims (Hughes, 1876, 321). Another *Gazetteer* published at the beginning of the 20th century states there is in Jhimpir a Muslim mausoleum and a Hindu temple (Aitken, 1907, 505).

The place was visited by a British traveller in 1883. David Ross reports that hundreds of devotees, Hindus and Muslims, visited the sanctuary. This is the place of a son of Ali, the first imam of the Shiites. It is one of the most important *tirath* of the Hindus for the expiation of minor sins. For major sins, the Hindus have to go to Narayansar, in Kutch. Ross speaks of a temple devoted to Mahadev near the mausoleum of Shaykh Amin. Thousands of people come for the annual fair performed in February. According to the legend, the place was previously called Hem Kot. Hem was a raja whose daughter, Parvati, had married Mahadev. During the wedding, water became scarce and Mahadev made a spring emerge. For generations, the temple was managed by a Brahman family called Mengraj (Ross, 1883, 26). Carter states that Amir Pir is a place where the crocodile (*wagho*) is worshipped. The location he gives indicates it is the same place, but he does not give more information on this cult (Carter, 1917, 206).

The sanctuary of Jhimpir is today managed by the Ismaili Khojas, the Aga Khan's followers. The sanctuary is said to be Muhammad al-Hanifiyya's. Non-Ismailis are not allowed to visit the place. The official doctrine is that Shaykh Amin was Ali's son through a woman who was not Fatima. The Shiva temple is still standing there but it is usually closed, although some Hindu families visit the place. It is only open for important fairs related to Shiva, as, for instance, Shivratri.

Hyderabad is a different case in comparison with Thatta and Sehwan. The area shows marks of later religious legacies. Although there is still a temple devoted to the Devi near the fort, the city was not a religious place by itself. It is located nevertheless at the centre of a religious complex: Gunjo in the north and Jhimpir in the south were two important places of Shivaite and Sufi pilgrimages. Moreover, the most problematic point is the location of at least three Hindu–Muslim places: Udero Lal, Bhit Shah and Tando Allahyar. Here again, these more recent religious places are connected with a Shivaite legacy, most of the time under the form of the Nathpanthi school.[18]

Conclusion

In surveying the Shivaite cults and the Sufi centres, the main goal was to determine whether a correlation could be found between Sufi centres and important Hindu sanctuaries, and what was its nature and meaning. Although many questions are still unsolved, a few points can be made in conclusion. First, it is important to state that all the Sufi centres were not related to Shivaite cults. There are several main Sufi centres that appear to have been created quite independently of the worship of Shiva, mainly located in northern Sindh. Even if it is said that Hinduism was more important in northern than in southern medieval Sindh, only a few places were connected to Shiva. In fact, it appears that only one main sanctuary is in this category: the famous shrine of Khwaja Khizr, worshipped as the Indus river by the Hindus, located in an island near Bhakkar. The connection is not really attested, knowing that it lies on the affiliation of Udero Lal to a Shivaite sect. Briggs is the main exponent of the theory of Udero Lal as Daryanath, a Gorakhnathi follower, although he has probably used Carter's articles on religion in Sindh.

Nevertheless, the majority of the Sufi centres were established in places that were important Shivaite Hindu centres. It is also important to note the places devoted to the Devi. The most interesting area is undoubtedly the Delta of the Indus river. Several sites allow us the opportunity to propose the hypothesis of continuity from Shivaite ascetics to Sufi ascetics, but a careful study of the devotional poetry, the rituals and also some artistic features like iconography and architecture could surely bring more elements to reinforce this theory.

Nevertheless, this composite culture was very common in the Indian subcontinent, as well as in other parts of the world. What is to be pointed out here is that from the Pashupatas to the *qalandars*, heterodoxy and heteropraxy were important parts of the medieval religious

The dargâh of Jamîl Shâh Dâtâr: Main Entrance, December 2005. © Michel Boivin

The shrine of Hâjjî Turâbî, December 2005. © Michel Boivin

Wani ka mandir at Kalankot, December 2005. © Michel Boivin

Shivaite symbols in Udero Lâl's temple, December 2005.

Temple of Singh Bhawânî/Asnâpûrî at Makli, December 2005.

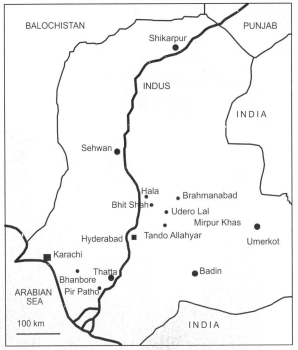

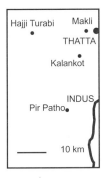

Shivaite and Sufi Centres in Sindh

legacy in Sindh. The spread of Ismailism can be understood in a similar way. The Ismaili community is still settled in Sindh and Karachi where the Khojas are a prosperous community. The followers of the Mahdi movement are also in present-day Sindh, especially in the Thatta area. The place where the entanglements of the different religious heritages are more visible is Sehwan Sharif. The town includes the different aspects which point to the religious specificity of Sindh. Here heterodoxy is based on the rejection of social conformism. This behaviour was basic among the Pashupatas as well as among the *qalandars*. Religious practice was also based on rituals like dance, which was thought to be a path to reach union with the divine, as also was renunciation.

It is obvious that the little available data do not allow for definitive conclusions. It is better to speak of the ambiguity of the relations between Shivaism and Sufism. The legends and traditions related to the Sindhi saints are structured like metaphorical discourses produced by different communities. Through this plurivocal discourse, the dominant feature is that of confrontation, either rivalry or competition. Although the data gives but few narratives of confrontation between Sufis and *jogi*s, it gives many narratives of confrontation between Hindus and Muslims, and it is not uncommon that Sufis are described as warriors: Lal Shahbaz Qalandar is also called Ghazi and he is said to have put Sehwan under his control at the head of an army of *faqirs*, while Pithoro Pir and his followers defeated a Hindu king. While turning to the symbolic discourse embedded in the rituals, the other side is featured by the transmission and the continuity, as can be seen by the common, or slightly modified, rituals both Shivaites and Sufis share.

3

URBAN SOCIETY IN COLONIAL SINDH
(1843–1947)

Claude Markovits

Abstract

This chapter looks at the economic, social and political configuration of urban areas in Sindh during the colonial era (1843–1947). First, some data on the urbanization of colonial Sindh are presented: the relatively high degree of urbanization of that province in relation to other areas of India is underlined, as well as the presence of a majority of Hindus in the urban areas. It is then argued that the rural-urban nexus of dominant groups in Sindh society straddled the communal divide: urban-based Hindu *banias* colluded with Muslim landlords, the *waderos*, to dominate and exploit the landless agricultural labourers, the *haris*. In the urban areas, however, growing tensions developed between a dominant Hindu administrative and economic elite of *Amils* and *Bhaibands,* and a tiny emerging Muslim middle-class. Faced with the hostility of its Hindu co-urbanites, that small urban Muslim middle-class had no choice but to ally with the *waderos* to fight for Sindh's separation from the Bombay Presidency in 1935 and eventual re-attachment to Pakistan in 1947. But the influx of *mohajirs* from India prevented it from enjoying the spoils of victory as it faced increasing marginalization in its own homeland at the hands of these more qualified immigrants who cornered most of the administrative and clerical jobs made vacant by the flight of the Hindus.

* * * *

If Sindh in general has attracted little attention from historians, urban Sindh has been even more neglected. A recent standard history of the province (Lari, 1994) lays scant emphasis on the urban areas and their overall role. There is a widespread perception that urbanization in Sindh is a recent phenomenon, linked to the post-Partition influx of *mohajirs* from India, and the conflict between *mohajirs* and Sindhis is often interpreted in terms of an urban-rural conflict. What is overlooked is the fact that, without even going back to Mohen-jo Daro, urbanization has deep historical roots in Sindh. During the colonial period in particular, the province underwent a process of urbanization which was of some depth. This process, however, did not affect the two major communities of the province in the same way. While the Hindu population became urbanized to a significant extent, the same was not true of the Muslim population, which remained overwhelmingly rural. It would nevertheless be misleading to put too much emphasis on this contrast. This study will argue that, throughout the colonial period, there was an urban-rural nexus in Sindh which operated across the communal divide. The erosion of this nexus in the post-1947 phase is an important factor in the new alignment of forces. After a presentation of some basic data on urbanization, the study will focus on the urban-rural nexus, and then discuss the city as an arena of inter-elite conflict.

Some Data on Urbanization in Colonial Sindh

In pre-colonial times, Sindh was already characterized by a relatively high rate of urbanization, which was linked to the privileged position of the province at the crossroads of major maritime and land trade routes (Mariwalla, 1981). The urban system, however, was characterized by chronic instability as old centres died and new cities rose, depending on the vagaries of the Indus and the ebb and flow of political change. The 18th century in particular saw a complete reshaping of the urban network, linked to the tumultuous political developments which took place during that period. In the 17th century, one city, Thatta, towered over all the other urban centres: it was a major seaport (the English East India Company briefly had a factory there in the 1640s), an important centre of textile production, particularly of chintzes and muslins, which were exported in great quantities, and the seat of the Mughal governor of the province during the period of Mughal rule (1612–1737). It had a large population, estimated to have been *circa* 225,000 in 1631–35 (Habib, 1982, 171), which made it one of the significant urban centres in the subcontinent, surpassed only by the three imperial capitals of Agra, Delhi, and Lahore. During the first decades of the 18th century, however, it lost most of its economic and political importance, as its port suffered from the silting of the river and as the new Kalhora rulers, who took over from the Mughals in 1737, transferred their capital to Khudabad. While Thatta entered into a decline from which it never recovered, new urban centres rose.

By the late 18th century, three towns had emerged as the main foci of trade and political power in Sindh. The largest and most prosperous was Shikarpur in Upper Sindh, which was under the direct control of the Afghans between 1747 and 1824. It had been founded in 1617 by the local Daudputra dynasty (who at a later stage became rulers of Bahawalpur) as a hunting (*shikar*) pavilion, and emerged during the second half of the 18th century, under the rule of the Afghan king Ahmad Shah 'Abdali' and of his successor Timur Shah, as the major financial centre of the entire Durrani 'Empire' (Gankovsky, 1981; Gommans, 1995). Its Hindu–Sikh (Nanakpanthi) bankers are said to have largely financed Ahmad Shah's mid-eighteenth century expeditions into the Punjab and northern India (Masson, 1842) and, in the first decades of the 19th century, they controlled financial transactions over a wide area extending from Calcutta to Nijni-Novgorod in Russia. With the decline of the Durranis, Shikarpur, which fell to the Amirs of Sindh in 1824, lost some of its importance, but remained the centre of an active commercial diaspora which played an important role in the economic life of Central Asia (Levi, 2002). Next in importance to Shikarpur came Hyderabad, founded in 1768 by the Kalhora rulers on the site of the village of Nerunkot, and made their capital by the Balochi Talpur Amirs of Sindh in 1783, after they had defeated the Kalhoras and burned their capital of Khudabad (Advani, 1940). Apart from its political functions as the capital of Sindh during the Talpur era (1783-1843), it was also an active mart, situated in a fertile region irrigated by the Indus and the Fuleli canal, and a sizeable centre of craft production, particularly embroidery (*zardozi*) (Askari and Crill, 1997), lacquer ware, and weapons. Of growing commercial importance was the port-town of Karachi, founded in 1729 by Hindu *banias,* relinquished by the Kalhoras to the khans of Kelat, and annexed by the Talpurs at the end of the 18th century. After 1750 it became the major port of Sindh and the seat of powerful merchant houses such as those of Naomul Hotchand and Wissundas Khemchand (Haider, 1974).

These three major towns were home to a large population of Hindu *banias*, who controlled the bulk of commercial and financial transactions within the province as well as its economic relations with neighbouring areas. In Hyderabad, another important group emerged amongst the Hindu population, that of the *Amils*, who occupied the top administrative positions in the fledgling Talpur state, and in particular managed the revenue system. The role of the *Amils*, a sub-caste of the *Lohanas*, the major Hindu caste in Sindh, was largely similar to that of the *Kayasths* in Mughal and post-Mughal northern India: they were scribes, whose literary skills and good knowledge of Persian made them indispensable to the functioning of the state. But they had close links to the Hindu bankers, also belonging to the *Lohana* caste, who were the financiers of the state. It is important to note that the economic dominance of Hindu groups was a feature of pre-colonial society, and not an outcome of the establishment of British rule. As to the Muslim population in the three major towns, it consisted on the one hand of a mixed Balochi–Sindhi military and political elite, and on the other of various groups of merchants, artisans, and day labourers, who were ethnically Sindhi in their great majority.

Of lesser towns, some, like Hala, Nasarpur and Gaubat, deserve mention as centres of various craft productions (embroidery, lacquer work, cotton cloth) that had a particularly large population of Muslim artisans. Other towns were either administrative centres, such as Khairpur and Mirpur, which were the seats of junior branches of the ruling Talpur family, or marts of only local importance, whose population included an important Hindu component.

While the province had an urban grid of some density, its urban centres did not constitute an integrated and hierarchically ranked network. There was one major north-south alignment of towns along the Indus Valley linked with the Punjab, which connected with two subsidiary east-west axes: one, of which Shikarpur was the pivot, led westward to Kandahar via the Bolan Pass and Quetta, and eastward to Jaisalmer and Bikaner across the Thar desert in the 19th century; this became one of the major routes linking northern India with Central Asia. Another route branched from Hyderabad towards the Marwar region of Rajasthan via Umarkot (famous as Akbar's birthplace). The towns of Sindh were thus integrated within regional and even interregional urban systems extending much beyond the boundaries of the province.

Although urbanization had its roots in the pre-colonial era, the overall expansion in the urban system during the colonial period was undoubtedly impressive. While no detailed statistical data are available, a generally accepted figure is that, at the time of the British annexation in 1843, the urban population represented less than 10 per cent of a total population estimated to have been a little over 1 million (Burton, 1851, 375). In 1941, at the time of the last colonial census, the urban population had reached some 900,000 out of a total population of 4.5 million (*Census of India 1941*).

While no complete series is available permitting us to derive the rate of growth in the urban population of Sindh during the entire colonial period, the existing partial data show that it accelerated considerably after 1921, in relation to the rapid development of irrigated agriculture. In 1891, there was already a differential between the rate of urbanization in Sindh, 12.6 per cent, and the rate of urbanization in India, 9.4 per cent (*Census of India 1891*), which was largely due to the impressive growth recorded in the 1880s by Karachi, the main urban centre of the province. This differential increased significantly between 1891 and 1921, and stood at 6-7 per cent between 1921 and 1941. In 1941, the rate of urbanization in Sindh was 19.6 per cent as against 12.8 per cent in India altogether. Table I presents the main data on the urban population of Sindh in 1941.

Table I: The Urban Population of Sindh in 1941

	Population of Sindh	Hindu population of Sindh
Total urban and rural population	4,535,008	1,229,926
Urban population	891,703	527,799
Rate of urbanization	19.6%	42.8%

Source: computed from *Census of India 1941, vol. XII, Sind*, by H.T. Lambrick, Karachi, 1941, Table V, pp. 22-23.

The Table fails, however, to show that this high rate of urbanization was largely due to the demographic weight of the only two Class I cities in the province, Karachi and Hyderabad, which together accounted for more than 55 per cent of the total urban population. On the other hand, the Table indicates clearly that Muslims, who accounted for over 70 per cent of the population of the province, were in a minority in the urban areas, where Hindus accounted for 59.2 per cent of the total. While the Census figures show that there were still more Hindus in the rural than in the urban areas, they are slightly misleading: if one takes into account only 'Caste Hindus', leaving out the 'tribal' Bhils and Kolis who accounted for the majority of the Hindu population of the largely rural Thar and Parkar district, they can be shown to have been equally spread between rural and urban areas. This made the 'Caste Hindus' of Sindh the most highly urbanized group in India after the Parsis. Since in Karachi itself, Muslims accounted for approximately half of the population, Hindu predominance in the other urban areas was fairly massive (64 per cent).

In absolute terms, over a period of less than one century (1851–1941), there was an almost tenfold expansion in the urban population, from less than 100,000 to almost 900,000, an impressive figure indeed. Karachi's growth was particularly spectacular: from a small town of 15,000 at the time of the British annexation, it grew into a city with a population of 387,000 in 1941. But several other medium-sized and small towns also grew at a very high rate.

What were the economic foundations of this rapid urban growth in colonial Sindh? At the time of the British conquest, towns were mainly administrative headquarters and centres for the collection of rural surplus. They also had a sector of craft production. Given that the latter went into decline, and that modern industry remained very little developed in Sindh before the 1950s,[1] most towns and cities tended to become even more dependent upon their links to the countryside. Only the three major cities of the province, Karachi, Hyderabad, and Shikarpur, had more diversified economies. Karachi, in particular, underwent a spectacular transformation from a small port-town with a purely regional function into one of the four major port-cities in India, largely thanks to it becoming the outlet of the rich agricultural province of the Punjab. This was made possible through the construction of a modern harbour at the end of the 19th century, and the building of a railway line along the Indus valley (Banga, 1992). Although Karachi benefited also by the development of irrigated agriculture in Sindh itself (with the completion, in 1932, of the Sukkur dam which increased considerably the irrigated area in the province), its link to the Punjab was the major reason for its rapid growth. Shikarpur and Hyderabad, for their part, although situated in fertile agricultural tracts, had economies which were partly dependent on the remittances sent by their widely-dispersed merchant colonies (Markovits, 2000). Shikarpuri *shroffs* were ubiquitous in Central Asia, Afghanistan, Iran, and Xinjiang till the time of the Russian Revolution and sent each year considerable remittances to their home town. After 1917, they redeployed largely in India, where, under the misleading appellation of 'Multanis' they emerged as one of the foremost communities of 'indigenous' bankers, allowing the flow of remittances to continue more or less unimpeded till the time of Partition. As to the 'Sindworkies' of Hyderabad, they developed, from the 1860s onwards, a widespread network of trade in silk and 'curios' which, by the time of the First World War, covered most of the globe, from Kobe in Japan to Panama in Central America. They also remitted money on a large scale. However, in contrast to Shikarpur, Hyderabad also remained an important regional trading centre, as it was well placed in relation to some of the best agricultural land in the province, and was an active cotton and grain mart.

Other urban centres in Sindh were closely dependent on a rural hinterland, some of them developing administrative functions when new districts were carved out of the three original collectorates of Karachi, Hyderabad, and Shikarpur: Larkana and Nawabshah were two examples of new district towns. Sukkur, which supplanted Shikarpur as the district headquarters in 1881, went through a process of rapid growth in the 1920s and 1930s, directly linked to the spread of irrigation made possible by the building of the Indus dam.

In spite of the existence of a growing trend towards regional integration in the inter-war period, it would probably be a mistake to view the urban network of pre-Partition Sindh in isolation. It would make more sense to see it as part of a wider network encompassing also the towns and cities of Balochistan, the Punjab and the North-West Frontier Province, the areas which form present-day Pakistan. Commercial flows between the Punjab and Karachi in particular were probably larger than intra-provincial flows in Sindh.

If one looks closely at the composition of the urban population in terms of occupations and religious communities, one is struck by a certain degree of correlation between the two: while traders, government employees and professionals were mostly Hindus, craftsmen and day labourers were overwhelmingly Muslims. Given the fact that the respective shares of Hindus and Muslims in the total urban population did not change noticeably between the 1891 and 1941 Censuses, while most of the increase in population was due to migration, one can safely conclude that migrants to the cities were drawn more or less equally from the two communities.

In terms of their geographical origins, these migrants, whether Muslim or Hindu, seem to have been drawn equally from the Sindh countryside and from areas outside the province, including from Balochistan, which always had very close links to Sindh. In Karachi, migration from outside the province was the major factor of growth, as the developing port-city attracted merchants in great numbers from Bombay (in particular Parsis who came to play a major role in trade), Kutch (both Kutchi Memons who were Sunni Muslims and Kutchi Bhatias who were Hindus), Kathiawar and Gujarat proper, and workers and different classes of menials, mostly from the Makran area of Balochistan, but also from northern India and the Punjab. Migrant merchants from Sindh were mostly Shikarpuris, who played an important role in the cotton trade (Banga, 1992). There was also a stream of poor migrants, *haris* (cultivators), from the Sindh countryside. In the other urban areas, the majority of migrants appear to have been Sindhis, both small Hindu *banias* from the villages as well as Muslim *haris*, who hired themselves as casual labour. There were also, however, migrants from other areas in India, mostly Punjabis, who were often skilled workers, and Rajasthanis and others who took menial jobs.

By the 1940s, the urban areas of Sindh, especially Karachi, and to a lesser extent, Hyderabad and Sukkur, were a patchwork of communities of various origins, some from the province, some from neighbouring areas in India (leaving aside the European community, strongly represented in Karachi, but almost non-existent elsewhere). The urban elites were also a fairly heterogeneous lot. In this respect, there was a clear contrast between Karachi and the other urban areas. In Karachi, a commercial city, the dominant elite was composed of British and Parsi businessmen, who operated in close conjunction with each other. Other influential communities were mostly Gujarati Muslim groups (particularly the Kutchi Memons and the Bohras), as well as some Hindu communities from Kutch and Kathiawar. Shikarpuris represented the dominant Sindhi *bania* element, but in the 1930s their role tended to diminish. Non-commercial elites were mostly represented by Sindhi Hindus, particularly *Amils* who had come from Hyderabad and Thatta. In other towns and cities, the local elites were mostly made of Sindhi Hindus, the traditional dominance of the *Amils* (except in Shikarpur) being increasingly challenged by the rise of the *banias*, who were generally known as *Bhaibands*. A Sindhi Muslim elite, albeit tiny, was in the process of emerging, and more will be said about it later.

There was no apparent tension between Sindhis and 'outsiders', even in Karachi where Sindhis were probably only in a very slight majority before 1947. Sindhi appears to have been the general *lingua franca* in the towns, used by non-Sindhis as well, although the Censuses reveal the presence of pockets of Gujarati, Punjabi, and Hindi-Rajasthani speakers. Interestingly, Urdu does not appear to have been much in use in the urban areas of Sindh before Partition.

The tensions which were perceptible in urban Sindh in the 1930s and 1940s were mostly of a communal nature and were both a cause and an effect of the politics of the province becoming increasingly polarised along a Hindu–Muslim divide. However, taking a longer-term view, it is easy to exaggerate the importance of the communal divide. The following section examines this question in some detail.

The Rural–Urban Nexus and the Communal Divide

It is tempting to dwell upon the contrast between an urban society which was mostly Hindu . and a countryside which was overwhelmingly Muslim, but sight might then be lost of the existence of a rural–urban nexus which cut across the communal fault line.

I shall argue that pre-colonial society in Sindh was dominated by a nexus which I call the *wadero-Amil-bania* nexus, which cut across both the urban–rural and the Hindu–Muslim divides. This fact is easily obscured by some of the literature produced by the British in the immediate wake of the conquest, particularly by Sir Richard Burton's fascinating but in some ways misleading account published in 1851 (Burton, 1851). These writings tend to present the Hindus as a politically and religiously oppressed group, while at the same time emphasizing the control they had over economic life. As this chapter has already argued, the Balochi rulers of Sindh and their landowning followers, both Sindhi and Balochi, those known in Sindh as the *waderos*, were very much dependent on the literary and financial skills of the local Hindus. The symbiotic relationship which existed between the Muslim ruling group and its Hindu auxiliaries was not devoid of tension and could even at times evolve into open conflict. The *Memoirs* of Seth Naomul Hotchand, the greatest Hindu merchant-banker of Sindh at the time of the conquest, offer fascinating insights into this highly ambiguous relationship. They tell in particular of the role played by Seth Naomul's father, Hotchand, during an episode of open Hindu–Muslim conflict in Sindh in 1831–32, when he was captured by a Muslim crowd bent on converting him to Islam and was rescued only by the intervention of the ruler of Hyderabad, Mir Muradali (*Memoirs of Seth Naomul Hotchand*, 1982, 68). The episode reveals both the clout of the Hindu bankers, who had close links to the ruling dynasty, and their vulnerability.

With the advent of colonial rule, the nexus was somehow weakened but not altogether broken. The *Amils* quickly took to English education and massively entered the subordinate civil service in the province, providing the British with crucial support in the running of the newly conquered territory. On the other hand, the British, who came to Sindh with an already well-established Treasury system, did not need the services of the local bankers. But the link between the *waderos* and the *banias*, far from loosening, became on the contrary closer as, in the more commercialised agricultural set-up which developed under British rule, the former became increasingly indebted to the latter (Khuhro, 1978). This caused widespread fears amongst British administrators that the *waderos* would in time have to relinquish part or even the whole of their estates to the *banias*. Although these fears proved to be largely exaggerated, they inspired the British to pass a series of Acts called the Sindh Encumbered Estates Acts (the first one was passed in 1876), which made it difficult for creditors to foreclose in case of unpaid mortgage repayments. Whether or not due to the adoption of such legislation, transfer of land to moneylenders, although it happened, did not occur on the scale predicted, as *banias* in any case resorted to foreclosures only as a last resort and preferred to deal with the actual cultivators, the *haris*, through the mediation of the *waderos,* rather than directly. Those *banias* who lent money to the *waderos* generally resided in the towns, but they also supplied with funds the smaller village *banias* who lent directly to the *haris*. Recent research, in particular David Cheesman's work, has shown that in Sindh the *banias* were basically traders who used peasant indebtedness as a mechanism to procure at low prices agricultural products which they sold at higher prices across the province (Cheesman, 1997). They made their profits in trading more than in money lending, since the *haris* were generally too poor to reimburse their debts, while the *waderos* were too profligate. Basically, it was the advances of the *banias* which permitted the financing of agricultural production as well as the payment of rents to the *waderos*. Thus, a major *de facto* alignment in Sindh society was the one between the *waderos* and the *banias* on the one hand and the *haris* on the other. It straddled both the communal and the urban–rural divide.

In the increasingly communalised atmosphere of the interwar period, both sides were understandably loath to acknowledge this unholy alliance. This comes out for instance in the report of the Indian Statutory Commission of 1928 (*Indian Statutory Commission, vol. XVI,* 1930, 239), from which I extract this significant dialogue between Professor H.L. Chablani, a prominent Hyderabadi *Amil* and spokesman for Sindhi Hindu interests, and Major Attlee (the future British Prime Minister), one of the members of the Commission:

Attlee: 'It has been stated to us that the poorer classes of the population are at present in the hands of the moneylenders; is that true?'
Chablani: 'I think both the moneylenders and the poorer classes are at the mercy of the zamindar in Sind'
Attlee: 'How is the moneylender in the hands of the zamindar?'
Chablani: 'The moneylender lives in isolated villages and he wants the protection of the zamindar. He cannot carry on his business without the protection of the zamindar'.
Attlee: 'Then the zamindar and the moneylender are in alliance?'
Chablani: 'Yes. It is an alliance of a slave to his master.'
Attlee: 'But the poor agriculturist is at the mercy of both'.
Chablani: 'Certainly'.

In Sindh, therefore, urban society cannot be analysed in isolation: many urban Hindus derived, directly or indirectly, their livelihood from the control exercised by the *waderos* over the land and labour of the *haris*. It is true that some of them also owned land, especially in the vicinity of the towns, but it was rarely the major basis of their wealth.

In spite of its tight hold over trade, finance and the professions, and of its fairly large landholdings, the Sindhi Hindu urban elite of the interior towns did not occupy a socially and politically dominant position. Its lack of social prestige, in contrast to the *waderos*, and its absence of spiritual clout, in contrast to the *pirs* and *syeds*, were decisive factors. Actually, most of the prominent *Amils* and *banias*, in spite of being Hindus (or rather Nanakpanthis, i.e. non-Khalsa or Sahajdhari Sikhs) were themselves *murids* of Sufi *pirs*, which meant that they recognized the spiritual leadership of these Muslim holy men (although they also revered Hindu holy men). The social and political limitations of this Hindu urban elite were reinforced by its fractured character, with competition growing between *Amils* and *banias*. As some sectors of the *bania* community, particularly the Sindworkies of Hyderabad, accumulated wealth on a big scale, they found it increasingly difficult to accept the traditional leadership of the *Amils* over Hindu society. *Banias* also tended to be socially more conservative than the *Amils*, especially in relation to female education. Apart from the growing rivalry between *Amils* and *Bhaibands*, there were also regional rivalries between Upper and Lower Sindh, and factionalism was ripe. In spite of its growing perception of itself as an endangered minority, the Hindu community was far from displaying unity in the political field. In the complicated politics of Sindh in the 1920s and 1930s, Hindus played mostly the role of 'spoilers', for, in spite of their domination of the provincial press, they did not achieve decisive influence on the course of provincial politics. However, they contributed significantly to the general political instability of the province (especially after the separation from Bombay in 1936), and earned a lot of bad will from members of the tiny emerging Muslim middle class, while they remained generally despised by the traditional Muslim elite.

Therefore, the urban–rural nexus which existed at the economic level did not translate itself into a political nexus. On the contrary, the increasing polarization of political life across communal lines strengthened the position of the *waderos* and *pirs* as the only foci of loyalty for the Muslim rural masses. It should be added that the policies followed by the British favoured the maintenance of political control by rural-based elements. In the Sindh Provincial Assembly which was elected in 1937 under the new 1935 Constitution, out of a total of sixty seats, only seven were urban, which meant that towns and cities were under-represented.

In spite of their relatively marginal position in the political system, from the 1920s onwards, it was precisely the towns and cities of Sindh which became the sites of increasing communal conflict, which contributed a lot to nurturing Muslim separatism in the province. This conflict has been recounted in some detail by various authors (Hasan, 1992; Talbot, 1988), but in the following section, emphasis will be on a particular aspect.

Inter-Elite Conflict in the Urban Areas

The most far-reaching change in the structure of Sindhi urban society during the colonial period was undoubtedly the emergence, starting in the second half of the 19th century, albeit gradually and slowly, of a Sindhi Muslim middle class. Not much is known about its beginnings, but it is depicted in such literary works as Mirza Qalich Beg's *Zinat,* written in 1890, considered to be the first Sindhi novel (Schimmel, 1974). Far from being a homogeneous social group, it consisted of three different segments: one, merchants and some master craftsmen who had risen through their skills, two, school teachers, clerical workers and others employed by the administration, and three, a tiny elite of journalists, professionals and *mullahs*. This elite was in the vanguard of the development of associations and political bodies, such as the Sindh Madrassa.

While rivalry for scarce government jobs developed over time between this tiny but growing Sindhi Muslim elite and the well-entrenched Hindu administrative and professional elite,[2] Sindhi Muslim merchants were not directly in conflict with the powerful Hindu merchant community. They were mostly niche traders, operating in some sectors which were neglected by the Hindus, like the leather trade, and they were highly dependent financially on Hindu bankers and moneylenders. Muslim merchants who were in a more conflictual relationship with Hindu businessmen tended to be mostly Gujarati Muslims, Bohras, Khojas, and Memons, based in Karachi. Amongst Sindhi Muslims, it was mostly those who aspired to government jobs who resented the dogged resistance on the part of provincial Hindu politicians to any suggestion of a system of quotas and job reservations for Muslims.

The *Amils* themselves, who represented but a tiny fraction of the Hindu population of Sindh, were not a homogeneous group. There was a divide between Hyderabadi *Amils*, the dominant section and non-Hyderabadi *Amils* (Larkana *Amils*, Thatta *Amils*). Within the Hyderabadi *Amils* themselves, there was a further distinction between Khudabadi *Amils* (who were supposed to hail from the former Kalhora capital), deemed to be the crème de la crème, and other *Amils* (Narsain, 1932). The Khudabadi *Amils* of Hyderabad were probably the most highly educated non-Brahmin group in the whole subcontinent. Already by the 1880s, the male literacy rate in the group was close to 100 per cent and the female literacy rate quite high also; the rate of English literacy was also exceptionally high. This group had horizons which went well beyond Hyderabad and Sindh. Already by the late 19th century, it was fairly common for Khudabadi *Amil* families to send their sons to the United States to acquire a higher education. Many Hyderabadi *Amils* pursued distinguished careers in the professions or the civil service (Kirpalani, 1993), in different provinces of India or even abroad. It is obvious that these people, who benefited in the last two decades of the Raj by the policy of Indianisation of the Indian Civil Service, were not the ones at risk from the introduction of quotas in favour of Muslims in the subordinate provincial civil service. However, *Amils* belonging to less privileged sections of the community felt threatened, and because of kinship and marriage networks linking the various segments of the Hindu community, it became a *mantra* for Hindu politicians in Sindh to fight against quotas of employment, which precluded any possibility of an urban-based alliance between Hindus and the emerging Muslim middle class. Thus, on the question of the separation of Sindh from the Bombay Presidency, which was discussed from 1928 onwards and eventually granted in the 1935 Constitution to become a reality in 1936, some Hindus were the first to moot the idea. However, when they realized that it could favour the rise of local Muslim politicians, they changed their position to one of fierce opposition, which made them very unpopular with provincial Muslim opinion, which overwhelmingly favoured the separation (Khuhro, 1982).

Thus faced with open hostility on the part of the Hindu elite to its political and social aspirations, the Muslim middle class increasingly tended to align itself with the *waderos* and *pirs* of the countryside, whose leadership it was too weak to confront by itself. The Sind Azad Conference created in 1932 brought together the landed aristocracy and the emergent Muslim middle class on a common platform of opposition to 'the threat of Hindu domination' (Ansari, 1992), but it was clear who actually called the shots.

As a result of the increasingly strained relationship between members of the Hindu and Muslim lower-middle classes, the towns and cities became the flashpoint of communal tensions in Sindh, starting with the Larkana riots of 1927, and culminating in the Manzilgah agitation in Sukkur in 1939 and the violence on an unprecedented scale which accompanied it (Khuhro, 1998).

Contrary to a widespread idea, the Hindu–Muslim conflict in Sindh was not primarily a class struggle between a Muslim peasantry and a class of Hindu moneylenders. While there were many instances of murders of *banias* by *haris* indebted to them, they were just ordinary events in the rural life of the subcontinent. Although the *waderos* were often implicated in these attacks (Cheesman, 1997), they were themselves too closely linked with the *banias* to allow a full-scale assault against Hindu moneylenders, at least not before Partition.

Communal conflict in Sindh largely took the form of a conflict over government jobs between a tiny but growing Muslim middle class and an entrenched and much larger Hindu middle class belonging mostly to the *Amil* community. After Sindh was made a separate province in 1936, the Muslim middle class benefited from increased state patronage but even then it could not completely break the stranglehold of the *Amils* on the provincial civil service.

It is only the massive exodus of *Amils* and other Hindus, after Partition, that seemed to open widely the field of government service to the Sindhi Muslim middle class. Its members had, however, counted without the arrival of the highly educated Urdu-speaking Mohajirs from India, who proved ideally fit to replace the *Amils* in the administrative and clerical posts. Partition, therefore, did not solve the basic problem of the Sindhi Muslim middle class of gaining access to government service, and it is not surprising that a conflict quickly arose between this group and the Mohajirs (Ansari, 1998).

Conclusion

The history of Sindh since the late 19th century is partly the history of a society which underwent a process of relatively fast urbanization (at least as measured in an Indian context), while land remained the only basis of social prestige and political power. There are some basic economic reasons for this discrepancy, above all the fact that the economy remained overwhelmingly agrarian, and that there was practically no industrial development before 1947. But other factors were also at work: the specific social morphology of Sindh towns and cities made them an arena for such fierce competition for scarce jobs between middle class groups that it prevented the emergence of an urban elite capable of challenging the domination of the traditional agrarian elites of the province. In pre-Partition days, the Sindhi urban middle class, although small, was sharply divided between an entrenched Hindu majority and an aspiring Muslim minority. The latter found that, in order to break the monopoly of the Hindus over government jobs, it had no other choice than to form an alliance with the dominant Muslim agrarian elites, the *waderos*, in which it could play only the role of a junior partner. After 1947, the Sindhi Muslim middle class thought that the time had come at last for its aspirations to be fulfilled, but it found itself again frustrated by the mass entry into Sindh of the Mohajirs from Northern India, whose literary and administrative skills were much greater than its own. While the *waderos* were left in undisputed control of their vast landholdings in post-colonial Pakistan, the urban middle class Sindhis were quickly reduced to the status of a minority in the two major cities of the province, Karachi and Hyderabad. The frustration of the aspirations of this group has thus been one of the major factors of political instability in post-1947 Sindh. It would appear that the legacy of the communal conflict of the 1920s and 1930s has stayed to haunt the winners.

4

A HISTORY OF VIOLENCE: ETHNIC AND SECTARIAN CONFLICTS IN KARACHI (1985–2005)

Laurent Gayer

Abstract

Karachi is a city of migrants and an important commercial hub which provides Pakistan with a window on the world. But Karachi is also a deeply fragmented city, plagued by an acute urban crisis that takes root in the failure of the development plans that successive Pakistani governments have delegated to foreign experts. The transnationalisation of the Afghan jihad in the 1980s also fuelled social and ethnic antagonisms in the city and contributed to the proliferation of violent entrepreneurs and ethnic parties. Both criminal elements and ethnic activists contributed to the ever-increasing fragmentation of urban space in the city, and to the multiplication of ethnic enclaves controlled by private militias. This extreme fragmentation of the city has benefited local jihadis and foreign terrorists who have taken shelter here since the fall of the Taliban regime in Afghanistan. However, Karachi will never be a 'sanctuary' for jihadi militants due to the hostility of local ethnic parties whose activists see themselves as enlightened secularists at war with the most retrograde elements of their society and their foreign allies.

* * * *

Karachi is not only volume. It now has the most hard-edged reputation of any South Asian city. It was born out of conflict, the child of Partition, and conflict has been its leitmotif (…).

– Rahul Bhattacharya.[1]

Currently one of the ten most populous cities on the planet, Karachi remained a small fishing hamlet until it received the favours of the Raj in the mid-1800s.[2] The 'young Alexandria of our young Egypt', as Richard Burton called it, had a strategic location, providing access to Central Asia and control over the Indus River. Moreover, if Karachi's port had no modern infrastructures, it was an important knot in the regional 'proto-globalized' economy[3] since the 18th century. The British believed that 'Kurrachee can hardly be said to possess a history'.[4] Yet, it had been linking Sindh and Punjab with the Persian Gulf, and further, with China and Africa for over a century.[5] The colonisation of Karachi, after its occupation by British troops in 1839,[6] connected it even more closely to the world economy. The British started modernising Karachi's port from 1854 onwards. The bay was dredged in order to make it fit for high tonnage ships, and modern docks were built.[7] In the 1860s, Karachi's economy benefited from the American cotton crisis[8] and with the opening of the Suez Canal, 'Kurrachee' became India's closest port to Europe, 5918 sea miles away from Southampton.[9] In the 1870s, McLeod Road became the hub of Karachi's commercial and financial activities, being home to an ever-increasing number of European firms and banks. In 1885–86, eight more European firms opened a branch in Karachi and the connection of Sindh with the Punjab through railway links made the transportation of wheat and cotton to its port far easier, so that in 1899 'it outstrip[ped] Bombay as wheat exporter—340,000 tons to 310,000 tons'.[10] In 1889, the construction of Empress Market provided Karachi with the second largest vegetable market in the world after Bombay and at the end of the 19th century, Karachi had become a serious rival to more ancient cities such as Bombay and Calcutta. The First World War turned it into 'the grocery of India'[11] and it played a key role in the logistic support to British and allied troops. During the Second World War, Karachi was yet again a major hub in the procurement of food and equipment to the allies' troops and it became a major 'ship hospital', where a thousand vessels undertook reparation between 1942 and 1945.[12]

Between 1947 and 1951, the massive influx of refugees from India, who came to be known as 'Mohajirs',[13] brought Karachi under intense demographic pressure but it also provided it with a highly competent workforce and an experienced bureaucracy, which ensured the economic and political success of the capital of Pakistan in the following years. Karachi's localisation had played in its favour when the Muslim League came to choose a capital. Lahore, the great rival of Karachi in West Pakistan, was considered too close to the border with India, and thus, strategically vulnerable, while Rawalpindi was a middle-range town which could not pretend to compete with its more illustrious rivals. Dhaka's case, for its part, 'had been doomed from the very start' due to the minor role played by Bengal in the Pakistan movement.[14] And whereas the Punjab and Bengal had collapsed amidst anarchy in the last months of the British Raj, Karachi had remained 'a relative haven of tranquillity.'[15] The city, whose municipality was the oldest of India[16] and which had become the capital of Sindh in 1937 after the province was separated from Bombay, 'could also boast of a nucleus of administrative buildings, which was what a central government suddenly faced with the problem of housing the offices of an entire state needed'.[17] Karachi was officially made the capital of Pakistan on 22 May 1948, when the Constituent Assembly decided that it would be separated from Sindh to become a federally-administered area. This decision fuelled the anger of Sindhi *ansars* (helpers) towards the *muhajirin* (refugees), whom they deemed to be arrogant city-dwellers full of contempt for the 'sons of the soil'.[18] The seeds of ethnic strife were thus planted in Sindh, which would soon become a battleground for aggrieved ethnic groups constructing their identities through their confrontation with the other(s).

Karachi's modern history is thus marked by an apparent economic success mitigated by violent ethnic, and more recently, sectarian conflicts. This history of violence has made Karachi (in)famous: as Indian cricket journalist Rahul Bhattacharya has suggested in his vivid account of a trip to Pakistan in 2004, 'Karachi's reputation precedes it, overwhelms it. Karachi of the mind's eye is drugs and madness and guns and bombs'. Yet, as Bhattacharya himself discovered, Karachi is also 'a mass of people who eat and drink and breathe and sleep and laugh and joke and work and play and get on with life'.[19] Moreover, the categorisation of Karachi's urban violence as 'ethnic' and 'sectarian' is deeply problematic. These conflicts initially had little to do with ethnicity and religiosity. In the 1980s, Karachi's urban crisis fuelled social antagonisms which turned into ethnic rivalries due to the particular social division of work in the city. The Afghan jihad also brought to Karachi a flow of arms and drugs which gave birth to a culture of ultra-violence amongst the city youth, for whom Russian TTpistols became the hottest commodity in town. Since the Afghan jihad has 'come home', in the 1990s and even more so after the fall of the Taliban,[20] Karachi's ethnic conflicts seem to have been supplanted by sectarian ones but this shift is open to question, as Karachi remains a largely secular city where jihadist and sectarian organisations have undoubtedly taken roots but where they remain marginal political actors.

The Ethnicisation of an Acute Urban Crisis

Since the colonial period, Karachi remains a 'dual city'.[21] If 'Kurrachee' was divided between the 'white' colonial town and 'black' indigenous neighbourhoods,[22] post-colonial Karachi developed around 'planned' and 'unplanned areas'. The former consists of residential and commercial areas developed by the Karachi Development Authority (KDA) or integrated into its development plans. The latter, which provide shelter to 50 per cent of the fifteen million inhabitants of the city, refer to squatter settlements developed through the illegal occupation or subdivision of public land, at the periphery of the city, along its natural drainage channels and railway lines and inside its river beds. Housing conditions and access to utilities, education, and health vary greatly between planned and unplanned areas. If the former can boast of modern educational, health, and recreational facilities, this is not the case in unplanned areas, where 'health, education and recreational facilities [...] are developed incrementally over time by the informal sector and remain inadequate and badly operated'.[23]

The origins of Karachi's squatter settlements, locally known as *bastis*,[24] can be traced back to Partition and to the subsequent formidable increase in the city's population. Between 1941 and 1961, Karachi's population grew by 432 per cent, a rate of growth 'no other city anywhere else in the world at any time in human history has ever experienced'.[25] All the *muhajirin* could not be properly accommodated in the city and a great number of them had to make do with *katcha* housing[26] for a while. In 1953, 250,000 of them were to be 'resettled', i.e. provided with decent accommodation, and in 1958, 100,000 refugees were still in this situation.[27] In the following decades, Karachi *bastis* grew in size and in number with the arrival of in-migrants from Punjab, Balochistan, and the Frontier Province.

Informal housing has taken two forms in Karachi: 'unorganised invasions' and 'illegal subdivisions'. The former started occurring after Partition, when squatters illegally occupied state land, whereas illegal subdivisions became more important in the 1960s, when peripheral land was developed and sold by 'independent' private persons who lack[ed] the property rights' over it.[28] These informal entrepreneurs, who came to be known as *dallals* (patrons), were in close contact with police officers, politicians and bureaucrats, these connections offering a certain degree of security against eviction to basti dwellers.

Until the beginning of the 1980s, most *dallals* were either Punjabi or Mohajir but this situation changed with the irruption of Pathan entrepreneurs in Karachi's informal housing market.[29] Many Pathan transporters, who often happened to be policemen,[30] started investing in real estate in the 1980s and so did several of the drug and arms barons who made their entry on to Karachi's political stage during the Afghan war. Within a few years, Punjabi and Mohajir dallals had lost control of Karachi's informal housing market to the Pathans, who imposed a new *modus vivendi* in squatter settlements: after land was seized by gunmen, plots were developed and rented to tenants who could be evicted at will. Coercion and violence were not new to Karachi's *bastis*, but they had never reached that level and the Pathans often met with resistance, particularly in Orangi, Karachi's largest squatter settlement, with an estimated population of about one million.[31]

Karachi's first major 'ethnic riot',[32] which took place in April 1985 and claimed at least a hundred lives, mobilised Mohajir, and more particularly Bihari *basti* dwellers versus Pathan gunmen who were trying to extend their influence to *mohallas* situated at the margins of their recently consolidated 'territories'. In Orangi, the main battlefield was situated between Banaras Chowk and the Metro Cinema, an area adjacent to new Pathan strongholds.[33] During the December 1986 riots, Pathan gunmen also attacked *mohallas* adjacent to their zones of influence, such as Aligarh and Qasba Colony. Most of the residents of these two bastis happened to be 'Biharis', i.e. 'stranded Pakistanis' freshly repatriated from Bangladesh. These newcomers were the most vulnerable inhabitants of the city, since they had not developed roots yet. However, they were often familiar with war and military organisation, as the founder of the first Canadian unit of the Mohajir Qaumi Movement (MQM) recalls:

> The Mohajirs who came from East Pakistan, they came from a war-ready people. They were the kids who had fought a war, so they made indigenous guns. I had reports that the steel poles for electricity, they're hollow, so they cut that down, make it the barrel of a big gun and train it towards the Pathans. They *make* it. So they say 'Ok, you come and try to kill us, but that gun is going to shoot on 20 miles, remember that…'.[34]

With each community boasting of its respective 'martial traditions' and stockpiling weapons to counter the enemy's threat, what were originally housing conflicts turned into ethnic rivalries. However, one should be aware that in their initial stage, the April 1985 'riots' did not oppose Pathan developers and Mohajir *basti* dwellers but transport-users, whether Punjabi or Mohajir, and transporters, who often happened to be Pathans. Akmal Hussain has identified Karachi's 'transport problems' as 'the immediate context' which made Pathan and Mohajir communities 'vulnerable to being emotionally manipulated into ethnic conflict.'[35] The owners of Karachi's minibuses, locally known as 'yellow devils', generally leased them out to individuals whose profit depended on the number of passengers they carried daily, thus encouraging them to drive recklessly. The absence of a bus terminal and of bus stations in Karachi led the 'yellow devils' to encroach on the pavement to drop and pick up passengers, thus threatening pedestrians. In 1984 and 1985, road accidents claimed two lives daily, in a city where the number of vehicles had more than tripled in ten years.[36] It was one of those accidents that prompted the April 1985 'riots'. On the morning of 15 April 1985, a Pathan mini-bus driver, eager to outrun a competitor, did not respect traffic lights and hit a vehicle before bumping into a group of students of Sir Syed College, in Liaquatabad, killing one of them, Bushra Zaidi. In the hours that followed the incident, angry young students organised a protest demonstration that was brutally repressed by the police. The attitude of the police, which was accused of molesting young female students after it entered Sir Syed College, fuelled the anger of Mohajirs and Punjabis alike and in the following days violence erupted all over the city, from Liaquatabad in the east to Orangi in the west. Far from being unorganised, these rioting incidents often involved young Mohajir and Punjabi activists from the Islami Jamiat-e Tuleba, the student wing of the Jama'at-e Islami. The young *jama'atis*, eager to provoke the police, set buses and minibuses on fire, which inevitably met with harsh responses. In the afternoon of 6 April, the army was deployed in Liaquatabad and Nazimabad, the Mohajir-dominated lower-middle class areas where violence had first erupted after Bushra Zaidi's death. But while the army was trying to defuse tensions in those two localities, a new incident set Orangi ablaze. A bus carrying Mohajir students to Bushra Zaidi's funeral was attacked by a band of armed Pathans in Banaras Chowk, a strategic location which plays the same role of 'interface' as Haider Chowk in Hyderabad.[37] In the words of Allen Feldman, the 'interface' is 'the topographic ideological boundary sector that physically and symbolically demarcates ethnic communities', where rioting functions as 'a traditional mechanism for setting and even extending territorial boundaries'.[38] In Orangi, Banaras Chowk was the main point of contact of Bihari and Pathan residents: it was an informal bus terminal linking Orangi to the rest of Karachi, and as such, it was 'a centre of all those activities involved with transport and its ancillary needs, ranging from repair shops to eating places'.[39] On 6 April 1985, it became a battlefield after Pathan gangs attacked Mohajir students, before invading the adjacent Abdullah Girls College, where they molested female students and damaged costly laboratory equipment.

The 1985 riot thus erupted in 'a context of general public grievances, which included the transport problem',[40] as well as the informal housing crisis. This urban crisis only took an 'ethnic' tone due to the communal division of work in the city and to the ethnic affiliations of the main protagonists in Karachi's new real estate politics. In other words, all inhabitants of Karachi came to see the Pathans as factors of nuisance and insecurity not because of their ethnic origins but because of their professions, and the clashes which occurred between Pathans and Biharis in April 1985 and December 1986 had less to do with ethnicity than with the new politics of real estate development in the city's squatter settlements. The new demography of the city also came to play a key role in Karachi's decline into violence in the mid-1980s.

A Playground for Aggrieved Youths

If Karachi's transport and housing problems are endemic, living conditions improved considerably in Sindh cities during the 1970s and 1980s. In 1987, the year the Mohajir Qaumi Movement (MQM) met with its first electoral victory, unemployment was actually much lower than in 1971–72, water was available in most parts of the city and transportation had become far easier than in the precedent decade. Thus, 'Sindh's urban crisis cannot be dismissed as simply a reaction to a lack of urban services and employment. Nor can the government's incapacity to address the situation be explained away completely by saying that the administration has been bought over by the mafia. There are bigger forces at work'. For architect Arif Hasan, these 'bigger forces' were 'colossal economic and demographic changes that have taken place in Pakistan in general, and Sindh in particular'.[41] In 1987, almost 36 per cent of Karachi's population was between the ages of 14 and 30 and 80 per cent of the individuals belonging to this age group were born in the city. Seventy-one per cent of them were literate, as compared to the overall Karachi literacy figure of 55 per cent and the overall Pakistan figure of 26.17 per cent. Almost 28 per cent of this age group had passed its 'matric' and 22.4 per cent of its members were graduates. The majority of them were white-collar workers or artisans, a large number of them being self-employed.[42]

Karachi and Hyderabad's slip into violence in the 1980s and 1990s was the outcome of these demographic and social changes, as they expressed the frustration and the aspiration of a more numerous and more educated youth, which fought among itself while rejecting the authority of traditional local leaders such as *muezzins*, *izzatdars* and *dallals*. For this restless youth, violence became a lifestyle, a 'daily routine' with its own norms, rituals and aesthetics. The stigma attached to violence, particularly among Mohajirs of the first generation, was reversed and young supporters of the MQM often claimed to be 'real terrorists' (*pakka dahshatgard*), 'commandos', 'great warriors' (*acche fighters*) or even 'butchers' (*qasai*).[43] This glamorisation of violence turned it into a social fact both preceding and extending the violent performances through which it was occasionally actuated. For these playful youths, violence was not only a part of life, it was life itself.

The rise and spread of these violent lifestyles was concomitant with a power shift on Sindh's campuses in the middle of the 1980s, which saw Mohajir students withdrawing their support from the Islami Jamiat-e-Tuleba (IJT) to join the Mohajir Qaumi Movement and its student wing, the APMSO. Until then, Mohajir students had been the backbone of the IJT in Karachi, their parents being ardent supporters of religious parties such as the Jama'at-e Islami and, in the case of Barelvis, the Jamiat-e-Ulema Pakistan (JUP). The Mohajirs' support to the religious parties was not a manifestation of their 'fundamentalism': for these refugees and their siblings, it was an attempt to join the Pakistani mainstream, as Muslims and not as 'refugees'. Since they could not rely on an ethnic identity of their own, as the Sindhis, Punjabis, Baloch, and the Pathans were able to, the Mohajirs could only rely on the larger Muslim *political* identity derived from Jinnah's two nation theory. Their support of political Islam was thus inspired by their specific identity politics rather than by their endorsement of the Islamist *weltanschauung*. On the contrary, the Mohajirs were urban dwellers prone to cultural liberalism and many of them were at odds with the religious parties' ideology. Most of the founders of the APMSO, including Altaf Hussain himself, came from the IJT, but their relations, with the religious parties has gone sour since they divorced them to organise on an ethnic basis.

Thus, the first half of the 1980s was a crucial period for Sindh, during which campus politics spilled over local and provincial politics, before affecting relations between the province and the centre. The large-scale influx of firearms into the province, courtesy of the Afghan jihad, turned its campuses into battlefields. In Karachi University, *kalachins* made their first appearance in August 1979, in the hands of Husain Haqqani's bodyguards.[44] In the following years, the IJT trained units of armed militants would take up positions at strategic points in the campus as soon as incidents broke out. Until the beginning of the 1980s, these militants' most bitter enemies were left-wing groups such as the Punjabi Students Federation. In 1982, a series of incidents between AMPSO and IJT activists started up a new confrontation in the city's campuses, which culminated in the clashes of September 1988, during which over 50 students were injured.[45] By that time, the APMSO had acquired a veritable arsenal, which was intended to counter the *jama'atis* in Karachi and Sindhi nationalist groups such as the Jiye Sindh Students Force (JSSF) in the rest of the province. After the riots of April 1985, MQM activists started distributing weapons to their supporters during public meetings, only asking for a 'donation to the party' in exchange; ammunition was five rupees a piece and the buyers were given an *ajrak* (Sindhi shawl) to conceal their purchase.[46]

The APMSO bought its first weapons from the IJT and the National Students Federation (NSF) while the MQM built a part of its armoury by trading cars for guns with the Pakistan People's Party (PPP).[47] Feuding organisations were thus freely trading arms with each other throughout the 1980s, forming what Elizabeth Picard has termed a 'militia system' (*système milicien*) in the cases of Lebanon and Northern Ireland.[48] However, at the end of the 1980s, the rules of gun-running changed in Karachi and Sindh at large. In 1989, a report of the magazine *Newsline* suggested that 'in the last one year, the business has been taken over by a new breed of independent underground entrepreneurs—students and political activists patronised by political parties who maintain what one student terms the 'minimum safety distance'. These boys have not only taken over the local distribution network, but also bring in their own supplies through regular visits to the tribal areas. They travel in small groups, always by train, and return to Karachi with their bags brimming with metal'.[49] The Mohajir students who resorted to that trade were initially apprehensive, thinking that the Pathan gunsmiths would refuse to sell them weapons because they would be turned against their brethren in Karachi. But ethnic prejudices were set aside by the Pathans when striking deals with Mohajirs. A Mohajir activist, describing his first experience with a Pathan gunsmith, thus recalls: 'I was apprehensive at first. I asked him what would happen if he went back on the deal saying that we were killing his Pathan brothers with his guns. And he said '*Tum kaisa Musalman ho? Hum ney Pathan ko khana hay? Hamain roti chahiey*' [What kind of a Muslim are you? I can't eat Pathans. I need my bread].[50]

Between 1986 and 1989, the prices of guns went down by 40 to 50 per cent in Karachi. The TT-pistol sold for Rs5500 in 1987. In 1989, it was priced at Rs3000.[51] In the Frontier, the price of an AK-47 went down from Rs40,000 in 1980 to Rs16,000 in 1989. During ethnic clashes in Karachi and urban Sindh, 'a rise in the prices of weapons was noticed because supplies were reportedly being rushed from the NWFP,'[52] but the large influx of arms in Karachi in the following years stabilised the prices of weapons and eventually led to their decrease. In this environment, a culture of ultra-violence developed among Karachi's and Hyderabad's youths[53] and firearms became a 'fetish' for a whole generation, i.e. objects which cease to be purely functional and take on 'an abstract power, an autonomous agency'.[54]

Violent Dreams of Extraversion

Until the military coup of 1999, most Karachi *mohallas* remained ethnic enclaves regulated by 'armed clientelism'.[55] Many streets had 'their own soldiers, an armoury, and a young general', who considered themselves 'members of a heroic vanguard.'[56] With these armed youths taking charge of *mohalla* affairs in the city, public spaces came under attack and most Karachiites retreated to the private sphere. Like in Beirut, this epidemic of violence led many of its residents to 'a search for security through segregation [which] led to the generalisation of segregation and insecurity.'[57] The destruction of Karachi's 'common world'[58] gave birth to a myriad of micro-territories which rapidly became hotbeds of separatism.

This ghettoisation process was not only nurtured by dynamics of ethnic polarisation and social introversion but also by projects of economic extraversion. Karachi remains the corporate capital of Pakistan; in the mid-1990s the liberalisation of Pakistan's economy and the resulting increase in foreign investments and in the capitalisation of the Karachi Stock Exchange (KSE) gave credence to those who prophesised a grand destiny for Karachi, on the Hong Kong or Singapore pattern. It is in this context that Mohajir activists started caressing the idea of independence for their city or even for their neighbourhood, in order to take part in globalisation on their own terms and for their own benefit.

In 1994, the rumour spread that Karachi would become the 'new Hong Kong' after the retrocession of the island to China. Rumours were also circulated that American companies were planning to buy huge terrains along the coast and that the Aga Khan had urged his followers to invest in real estate in Karachi. These rumours were probably circulated by real estate entrepreneurs to give the market a boost and it is attested that in 1994–95, real estate agents from the five city districts based their main argument for buying around 'the bizarre speculation that Karachi may well become a [new] Hong Kong.'[59] The rumours did succeed in boosting the real estate market, but they also had important political outcomes. Karachi has remained the financial capital of Pakistan since Partition[60] and these promises of prosperity have led many Mohajirs to fantasize about Karachi's independence, privately at least, since the MQM has always been careful not to alienate the 'establishment' it claims to oppose by endorsing separatist projects publicly.[61]

Although separatist ideas seem to be more prevalent among Mohajirs settled abroad than among those who remain based in Pakistan, it is primarily because their immediate environment is more favourable to free speech. When they were confident that neither Pakistan officials nor

MQM leaders would know about what they would tell me, several of my interlocutors in Karachi admitted that the separation of the city from Sindh and eventually from Pakistan was the only viable solution to the 'Mohajir problem'. Moreover, the first overseas members of MQM were more favourable to political compromises than their comrades in Pakistan and many of them, particularly in North America, were evicted from the party at the beginning of the 1990s due to this greater moderation. For many Mohajirs settled abroad, the experience of emigration or exile actually had a tempering effect; they endorsed the democratic values of their place of residence and often came to be at odds with the authoritarian political culture of the MQM.

When a new faction appeared inside the MQM (Altaf) in the summer of 1999, advocating the liberation of Karachi and Hyderabad through armed struggle, it was led by a Pakistan-born British citizen,[62] but it included several influential members of the MQM Coordination Committee based in Pakistan, such as Khalid Maqbool Siddiqi. The resignation of the seven dissidents was refused by Altaf Hussain and they were reintegrated inside the party after Imran Farooq, the suspected leader of the MQM 'militant wing' who had been 'underground' for the last seven years, mysteriously reappeared in London.[63] Farooq convinced the dissidents that the Mohajirs were not in a position to ask publicly for '*Urdu desh*'. Successive military operations had failed to eradicate the MQM, but they had proved that urban insurgency could not succeed in Karachi and Hyderabad. 1971 could not be repeated in urban Sindh and after the military coup of 1999, the only option left for the MQM was to make a compromise with the army and its intelligence agencies. Discussions between the 'Chief Executive' Pervez Musharraf and the MQM started shortly after the coup. In the words of Farooq Sattar, former mayor of Karachi and present parliamentary leader of the MQM in the National Assembly, '[General Musharraf's] coup was a bowl of fresh air for us (...). He saved us'. Although these discussions derailed shortly, they were promptly resumed by the MQM, whose leaders see Musharraf, a Mohajir himself, as their logical 'patron'. In the eyes of MQM leaders, Musharraf is a Mohajir before being a *fauji* (soldier): '[He] comes from an urban background. He is different from other military men. He does not come from a martial race but from a civilized race'.[64]

The deal between the army and the MQM was made public a few months before the general elections of October 2002[65] and it has ensured the party's political survival to date. But no one can predict how long the truce will last. The MQM has secured the post of governor in Sindh and it is presently using its alliance with the 'likeminded' PML (Q) in the province and at the Centre to strengthen its position in Karachi, primarily against the religious parties, which have become the MQM's *bête noire* in the last few years, since it defeated its Haqiqi rivals with the support of the army. However, the alliance between the MQM and the PML (Q) at the provincial and at the central level remains fragile. The MQM has been the nemesis of all coalition governments it has taken part in and its present alliance with the 'establishment' it has so vigorously combated in the past might well meet the same fate. 'Remember Moses, says Farooq Sattar, he lived with Pharaoh for many years, but he finally revolted himself...'.[66] Yet, for the time being, 'Moses' remains in exile in London.

Urban Governance and Spiritual Guidance from Afar

Karachi is the only megalopolis in the world which is, to a large extent, governed from afar. Altaf Hussain's exile to London in 1992, before Operation Clean-Up was launched by the army in Sindh, has contributed to the de-territorialisation of Karachi's urban politics. MQM representatives and ministers travel constantly between Karachi and London to take instructions from their leader and major political figures from other parties and nationalities have also paid visits to Altaf Hussain since the MQM has returned to power in Sindh and in Islamabad. In May 2005, for instance, the Chairman of Pakistan's Senate, Mohammad Mian Soomro, visited the MQM International Secretariat to meet Altaf Hussain. He was preceded by the Chief Minister of Sindh, Arbab Ghulam Rahim, who visited London a month earlier. In February 2005, a six member delegation of the Baloch Action Committee met with Altaf Hussain, whereas Nawab Bugti phoned Altaf in January of the same year to thank him for his stance on the Balochistan issue. In August 2004, it was the speaker of the National Assembly, Chaudhry Amir Hussain, who visited the MQM International Secretariat. A month earlier, Prime Minister Shaukat Aziz had phoned Altaf Hussain during his visit at 'Nine Zero', seizing this opportunity to invite the MQM's leader to return to Pakistan. Beyond these audiences, which reinterpret the Mughal tradition of *darbar*, Altaf Hussain makes his presence felt in Karachi through his frequent telephonic addresses to his supporters or to the press, which still receive large media coverage, both at the local and national level.

Despite his enduring exile, the leader of the MQM retains his authority over millions of Mohajirs, many of whom still see him as a *pir* (Sufi saint). Although Altaf tried to secularize this allegiance by asking his followers to refer to him as *bhai* (brother),[67] the devotion remains. This cult of the leader, which takes its main inspiration from the Leninist model rather than from Sufism, turned out to be the MQM's main asset in its globalisation. It ensured the ideological unity of the party and the centrality of its decisions, lying in the mind and the body of its charismatic leader, gifted with a foresight akin to magic. Interestingly, while talking with me, two young MQM activists exiled in Toronto had an argument about the localization of the strategic centre of the party. The first argued that its headquarters was 'Nine Zero', the former residence of Altaf Hussain in the middle-class area of Azizabad, in Northern Karachi. However, the second denied this by saying: 'No: Where Altaf *bhai* is, this is where the headquarters is. Altaf Hussain's personality is the headquarters'. To which the other added: 'Altaf Hussain is not a personality… He's a theory. Without him we would be lost. So we are not sad that he is not in Pakistan. If he's alive, one day we will achieve our goal'.[68]

The IT revolution offered an invaluable contribution to the MQM in its process of transnationalization.[69] Indeed, if Sufi masters always travelled and yet remained in touch with their followers, fax machines and modems now permit charismatic Muslim leaders to retain stronger ties with their audience, compensating their physical absence by electronic guidance.[70] Altaf Hussain could hence recently claim: 'Indeed, the telephone and the IT has [*sic*] never ever [been] used the way I have used them'.[71] Nasreen Jalil, a former MQM senator who lost her seat in 2002, even suggested that:

> [Since he is in exile in Britain] Altaf *bhai* is more available to the people over here, because he's constantly in touch with us, otherwise in Pakistan there were limitations. He himself remains in touch with everybody else. He can have conferences in several different countries at the same time… We are in Europe (Belgium, France, UK), America, Middle-East, South Africa, Japan, Philippines, Korea, and Australia… The Mohajirs there are working, and sometimes, Altaf Hussain addresses a dozen stations simultaneously through conference telephone calls and here in Pakistan he's been addressing rallies of hundreds of thousands of people on telephone. This shows the kind of attachment that people have for him and the party, that despite the fact that its head is in a remote place, people follow him….[72]

Altaf Hussain's charismatic authority has undoubtedly provided the MQM with a strategic tool in its transnationalisation process, protecting it from factionalism. Yet, this charismatic bond has also delayed the party's institutionalisation process. To prevent his lieutenants from contesting his authority, Altaf regularly sacks them or downgrades them. The MQM's 'politburo', the Coordination Committee, has not been immune to the *quaid*'s wrath and its turnover has increased in the last few years.

While the MQM struggles with itself to become a more banal political party, it has to counter a significant external threat: Islamists and jihadists, who have made Karachi their launch pad for waging jihad against Russian and later on American infidels. Since the fall of the Taliban, these sectarian and jihadist militants have come home and Karachi has become one of their sanctuaries.

Jihad Comes to Town

The outbreak of civil war in Afghanistan in the 1970s revived Karachi's primary function: providing support for military operations in Central Asia. In the context of Anglo–Afghan wars, this dusty port had appealed to the British because it was 'the most suitable for the disembarkation of troops, and for the collection of warlike stores'.[73] Almost 150 years later, Karachi had become the main port of entry for arms destined for the Afghan *mujahidin*, half of which never reached their destination. Karachi's banking institutions[74] have also appealed to jihadist groups from all over the Muslim world and at least 30 of its 165 registered *madrassas* are known to preach a rigorous and militant Islam.[75] The most famous of these religious schools is the Binori town *madrassa* (*Dar-ul Uloom Islamia Binori*),[76] which has become the hub of Deobandi Islam in Pakistan, alongside the Haqaniyah *madrassa* of Akhora Khattak, due to its role in the rise of the Taliban and later in the foundation of the Jaish-e Mohammed (JeM).[77]

Sectarian groups, such as the Sipah-e Sahaba Pakistan (SSP) made inroads into Karachi's mosques in the mid-1980s, but the city did not witness sectarian killings before the mid-1990s.[78] The first attack of that kind took place in July 1994, when a hand grenade was thrown at a bus transporting Shias from a religious gathering. The Shiite party Tehrik-e Nifaz-e Fiqh Jafria (TNFJ) claims to have lost 29 activists in the three months that followed this incident, whereas the SSP claims that 50 of its activists were gunned down during the same period.[79] Even if these claims are open to question, the number of victims of sectarian attacks did increase in the following months and years. Sectarian violence claimed 98 lives in 1995, 13 in 1996, 28 in 1997, 8 in 1998 and 58 in 2001. In 2001 and 2002, sectarian terrorists stopped targeting mosques and *imambargahs*, which had become heavily guarded, to focus on Shiite 'professionals' (doctors, lawyers, etc.). However, on 22 February 2003, two men riding a motorbike attacked an *imambargah* in Rafa-i Aam Society and killed nine people. On 7 May 2004, 23 people were killed and over 100 injured in a suicide attack on Hyderi mosque and on 31 May 2004, 23 people were killed in a bomb blast at Imambargah Ali Reza. A year later, on 28 May 2005, another suicide attack on a Shiite *imambargah* took place in the Gulshan-e Iqbal locality. The invasion of Iraq, in 2003, and the subsequent political rise of Shias in the country seems to have galvanised Sunni extremist outfits, who are presently trying to kill two birds (shias and supporters of American hegemony) with one stone.[80] Although Shiite sectarian groups are much weaker today than in the mid-1990s, they have not stayed idle and are suspected to be behind the murder of Maulana Haroon Qasmi, a local cadre of the SSP, which took place on 30 January 2005.

Since 1995, foreign interests have also come under attack in the city. In 1995, an agent of the CIA, Gary Durrell, and another of the NSA, Jacqueline Van Landingham, were gunned down in their van on Sharah-i Faisal, the city's main artery, which links the airport to the city centre. In November 1997, five employees of the Houston-based company Union Texas were killed in a similar manner and attacks on foreign targets have multiplied since the beginning of the American 'war on terror'. In January 2002, American journalist Daniel Pearl was kidnapped in Karachi and a videotape of his execution was received by Pakistani authorities a month later. On 8 May 2002, eleven French engineers died in a suicide-attack which was the first of its kind in Pakistan. On 14 June 2002, the American consulate was the target of another suicide-bombing, which resulted in the death of 15 Pakistanis. In December 2002, the Macedonian consulate was bombed and three Pakistanis with their throats slit were found in the rubble. On 26 May 2004, the American Cultural Centre was the target of another terrorist attack, causing one death, and on 15 November 2005, a blast occurred outside a KFC restaurant located in the city centre, killing three people.

If Karachi has become a breeding ground, a sanctuary and a battlefield for sectarian and jihadist militants in the last decade, their social base in the city remains circumscribed. Since it defeated the JI in the 1987 Karachi municipal elections, the MQM has remained unbeatable in urban Sindh and neither the Haqiqis nor the religious parties, MQM's arch rivals, have been able to cut deep into the MQM's vote-bank. The JI did sweep eleven of the eighteen city districts in the last municipal elections, which were held in 2000, but this success was primarily the outcome of the MQM's boycott of the elections. During the October 2002 general elections, the Haqiqis won one National Assembly (NA) seat[81] and the Jama'at four, but the MQM won 17 NA seats[82] and 42 Provincial Assembly (PA) seats. Until then, the MQM had never secured more than 15 NA seats and 31 PA seats, in 1990 and 1988 respectively. Such comparisons do not make much sense, though. The number of NA seats increased from thirteen to twenty in Karachi during the last general elections, and similar increases have taken place in other parts of the province. Moreover, substantiated allegations of poll-rigging make the results of these elections unreliable.

Clashes between MQM and Muttahida Majlis-e Amal (MMA) workers[83] have become more frequent in the city since the October 2002 elections. During the electoral campaign, MQM and MMA activists even exchanged gunfire in the Paposh Nagar locality.[84] Violence also erupted between MMA and MQM supporters during the by-elections of May 2004, leading to 15 deaths. In February 2005, clashes also erupted between APMSO and IJT supporters on Karachi's college campuses, leaving a dozen students injured.[85] MQM militants are also suspected to be behind the murder of Jamal Tahir, an activist of the JI who was gunned down in Karachi on 29 May 2005. During his funeral, a sympathiser of the JI was kidnapped and his bullet-ridden body was discovered a few days later. In June 2005, MQM activists also clashed with Barelvi activists of the Sunni Tehreek.

As we saw earlier, the conflict between the MQM and the religious parties, particularly the JI, is already decades old. This rivalry, which has its roots in Karachi's criminalized campus politics of the early 1980s, has been at the heart of Mohajir identity politics. 'Mullah-bashing' has served the party at the national and at the international level. In urban Sindh, it was used to cut into the religious parties' vote bank and to craft a Mohajir identity which links ethnicity with religiosity, equating 'Mohajir-ness' with 'secularism' and 'Punjabi-ness' or 'Pathan-ness' with 'fundamentalism'. The MQM has also used this tale of 'law-abiding secular Mohajirs *vs.* evil jihadis' to conquer hearts and minds abroad. The MQM started using this anti-jihadist rhetoric for international purposes before 9/11. Facing accusations of terrorism and criminalisation, the MQM did not receive the support it expected from the 'international community' in the 1990s, and it saw in 'mullah-bashing' an easy way to improve its image abroad. In the post-9/11 context, the MQM has reiterated its attacks against jihadis, surfing on the global 'green scare'. When the JI and other religious parties started demonstrating in Karachi against American military operations in Afghanistan, Altaf Hussain asked his followers to organise a massive 'anti-terrorist' rally in the city. MQM activists based in New York and New Jersey were also mobilised in this transnational public relations offensive. At Altaf Hussain's request, they set up relief committees providing help to the victims of the attacks.[86]

Although the MQM is using secular values to promote itself abroad and to counter its rivals in Pakistan, it has never been a truly secular party, at least in the Western sense of the term. In the past, Altaf Hussain's Islamic rhetoric has taken two forms: a reinterpretation of the Shiite tradition of self-sacrifice and a re-enunciation of the principles guiding the Sufi *pir-murid* relationship.[87] The MQM party workers murdered by the police or by the Haqiqis are qualified as *shahids* (martyrs) and their families are praised and taken care of. During Moharram, the MQM also provides medical help to those wounded in *ashura* processions and it uses the commemoration of Imam Hussain's martyrdom not only to keep alive the memory of its own martyrs, but also to sustain new vocations among its supporters. As I have already suggested, the relationship between *pir* Altaf and his *murids* is also infused with religious symbolism and it is reminiscent of the Naqshbandiyyas' *suhbat*, which reveals itself in *tawajjuh*, 'the concentration of the two partners upon each other that results in experiences of spiritual unity, faith healing, and many other phenomena'.[88] Before being admitted inside the MQM, candidates are given tapes of Altaf Hussain's speeches to meditate upon and the *pir* of Azizabad is often asked to embrace new born infants to make them benefit from his *barakat*. Thus, for the majority of Mohajirs, Altaf is not only a secular *pieta* embodying the sufferings of his people,[89] but also a spiritual leader who epitomises 'a human promise and ethical power beyond the ordinary'.[90] And like the Sufi saints he evokes in the minds of his devotees, Altaf Hussain is an ambivalent figure: he is an object of devotion and love but he is also seen as an unpredictable and potentially dangerous character.[91]

Conclusion

Karachi remains a violent and fragmented city, confronted by an endemic urban crisis and a turbulent regional environment. The city has never really recovered from the demographic upheaval that followed Partition and its transport, lodging, and water infrastructures have been deficient ever since. Although the level of violence has decreased in the city since the end of the 1990s (notwithstanding a rise in terrorist attacks against Shias and Westerners), local politics remain highly volatile. The MQM's alliance with the Punjabi establishment at the federal level is fragile and the stability of the provincial government is precarious. Moreover, the MQM is at daggers drawn with the Jama'at-e Islami and its success in the local elections organised in 2005 has infuriated the Jama'atis. By regaining authority over the local bodies, which they had lost in 2001 after they boycotted the elections, Mohajir nationalists might be tempted to settle old scores with their Islamist foes. Yet, if peace is not in sight, Karachi has learnt to deal with conflict, reversing the famous verses of the Urdu poet Ghalib: Inherent in its destruction, is the seed of its creation.

Part II

GLIMPSES OF LITERATURE AND SOCIETY

5

BARMATI PANTH: A MESSIANIC SECT ESTABLISHED IN SINDH, KUTCH, AND SAURASHTRA

Françoise Mallison

Abstract

The Barmati Panthi movement, also called Maheshvari, is prevalent among the Meghwal Untouchables of Kutch and Sindh. It shares many features with the so-called '*loka dharma*' of the southern and western parts of Gujarat, which respectively belong to Shaktism, Tantrism, Nathism, and Santism, especially in its rituals and hymnology. The strangest feature is certainly that these movements have in common a messianic element, a rare feature in Hinduism in spite of the presence of Kalki. We may be sure that in the case of the Barmati Panth, this feature is due to the influence of very specific Ismaili preaching whenever active.

* * * *

The province of Kutch has cultural links with Sindh thanks to its language (Kutchi) and religious traditions, but from feudal times onwards it was, politically speaking, always a part of Gujarat as an extension of the province of Saurashtra. If one follows the peregrinations of the Barmati Panthi founding gurus and saints, as described in their hagiographies, through these three regions: Saurashtra, Kutch, and Sindh, one notices the striking continuity of their religious culture. The wealth and originality of their religious traditions, often termed '*lok dharma*', is astonishing: the great number of popular shrines representing local deities and holy men and women, more or less deified, who in many cases initiated regional *sampraday*s; or the profusion of rites, cults, pilgrimages, and festivals freely shared by a population of low castes, craftsmen, peasants, shepherds, and outcastes.

Even more remarkable is the fluidity (or opacity) of features and definitions of the different religious communities concerned: be they followers of the *loka-devi,* adepts of the tantric Mahamarg, disciples of the Naths or the Sants, they all have in common certain elements of their rituals or sing together *bhajan*s drawn from the corpus they share and which is called *santa-vani*. The fascinating similarity of the *puja* called *pat-puja* (in which the offerings are placed—and the *yantra* drawn—on a four-legged little plank) in all these communities cannot but intrigue the observer and even more the fact that many of these movements share the messianic belief in a saviour who will return in order to put an end to the miseries of the *Kaliyug* and whose name, Nikalank, seems derived from that of Kalki.[1] In that context one needs to remember that the preaching of the Nizari Ismaili Shia Islam which especially concerns this part of India also includes several hymns (called Ginans) shared with the *santa-vani* corpus, together with an essential ritual called the *ghat-pat*, reminding one of the *pat-puja*; it announces the return of Ali, under the name of Naklanki-Niskalanki, riding on his white horse to preside over the day of final judgement.

There are studies concerning the Ismaili origin of Nakalanki in Rajasthan[2] or the priority of the Nizari Mission to so-called Hindu movements more or less belonging to popular Tantrism, established by holy men called *pirs*, and propagated among Untouchable castes. A case in point is that of the Barmati Panthi or Maheshvari in Kutch and Sindh.

The Barmati Panth

The name 'Barmati' is said to refer either to the foundation story according to which Shiva created twelve (*Bar*) men or spirits (*mati*) from the twelve drops of sweat that fell from his face while he performed ascetic austerities,[3] or to a funeral rite lasting twelve days.[4] Nowadays the Barmati Panthis prefer to call themselves 'Maheshwari Panthis' because of their devotion to Shiv-Mahesh. They belong to the Meghwal (*Meghavala*) Untouchable caste of Kutch and Lower Sindh.

According to their historian Mohan Devraj Thontya[5] the Barmati Panthis form one of the many branches of Nizari Ismailism, founded by a local *pir*, in this case Matang Dev, who separated from the Islamic sect in course of time in order to re-affiliate themselves with Hinduism. The Barmati Panthis worship their founding saint and his three descendants as incarnations of godhead. They are: Matangdev, Lurangdev (or Lunangdev), Mataidev, Mamandev, whose four *samadhis* called *cardhams* or *gaddis*, have become pilgrimage places (one meets with a similar development in parallel movements, for instance in the cult of Ramdev Pir). These four places are kept by the descendants of the four holy men who assume the functions of the *pujari*. They are located in Sindh: at Seni Thar near Ali Bandar (for Matang), at Tharai Dhandh (for Lurang), at Bhadra Dandh (for Matai) in the Division of Badin, Deltaic Indus, and the fourth one at Makli, a royal necropolis near Thatta (for Mamai). The first three are situated on the bank of the Fuleli, formerly the eastern branch of the Indus which emptied itself into the Rann of Kutch,—a very Ismaili area, historically speaking, with the sanctuary of Pir Taj-al-din, and where Pir Dadu and his two slaughtered brothers had been staying.[6]

At present, the holy places in Sindh are out of reach for the Barmati Panthis of Kutch; this is why they had to develop secondary places of worship in their place, such as the samadhi of Matiya, the son of Mamai, and of his friend Pir Tamaci, at Gudatar near Nalia; the Ganesh Mandir at Luni near Mundra (a *sthanak* of Lurangdev, himself an *avatar* of Ganesh); Mamaidev Bagathada at Anjar where the hairs and nails of Mamai are buried; and the cave in the Candruva hill near Bhuj where the founding saints and their disciples had practiced austerities.

The 1947 Partition has re-strengthened among the Maheshvaris a feeling of belonging to Hinduism and in a certain way has been instrumental in favouring a re-interpretation of their tradition such as we must consider it nowadays. They have formed associations based on mutual help in order to improve their lot, as did the high caste Sindhi Hindus who had fled to Gandhidham, a new township established for them in Kutch. Two recent books describing the Maheshvari movement and based on their traditionally transmitted texts called Ginans (the same name is used for the Khoja Nizari Ismaili hymns), namely the *Mamaideva Purana* (1974)[7] and the *Matanga Purana* (1992),[8] were, incidentally, published from Gandhidham.

The life story of the founding saint Matangdev, said to be based on historical facts, is a garland of hagiographical legends. The most reasonable period that might be assigned to his lifetime would be the 14th century.

Matang is said to have been born near the Hindu capital of Gujarat at Anahilavad Patana into a Brahmin family, and to be an incarnation of the divine light, *Nur,* come to save the world from the evil caste system, or more simply to put an end to the *Kaliyug.* It could be that his Brahmin father had married an Untouchable woman into whose house he had gone to hide, after fleeing from his brothers whose astrology manuscripts inherited from their father, a well-known *jyotisi,* he had stolen. Another story is quoted saying that he was Chanch or Chach, the disciple of Satgur Nur, the earliest of the Ismaili preacher *pirs.* Matang's vocation was neither learning nor farming but social service. After having spent some time with austerities on Mount Abu he returned in order to alleviate the lot of the Untouchables, especially of the Meghwals who distrusted him but whom he conquered through the imposition of moral and purificatory rules, the 36 *Dhroka*s.[9] It seems that he campaigned against the Tantric rites—although he was also considered to be the brother of Devayat Pandit, the great Tantric Mahamargi guru as well as a 'local' Ismaili *pir.* He married the daughter of a Meghwal chief who bore him a son, his successor Lurang. He also married the daughter of a Rajput chief, but their son Monand, refusing the social ideas of his father, perished in the Rann. After leaving Saurashtra, Matang entered into alliances with more or less Rajput tribes, i.e. the Sammas, Sumras, Sodhas, and Jadejas, from Sindh and Kutch, helping them with the re-conquest of their territories. So did his successors who often died a violent death, like Matang himself, on the battlefield. Until recently the throning ceremony of the ruler of Kutch included a legitimisation rite in which a Matangi Meghwal priest had to apply a *tika* on the future ruler's forehead. Why such an alliance? Was it that Matang had understood that in order to make society change, it was necessary to form alliances with the political elite of the time and the place. This is what the present-day historians of the community tell us. Anyway it is true that in Kutch a kind of clientelist relationship existed between the Rajput ruler and the Untouchables[10] which was wiped out by the rule of the English who had given their preference to the emerging Vaishya merchant castes rather than to the Rajputs.[11] Matang's social service activities were, according to these historians, at the root of his breach with the Nizari Ismaili Mission of which he is said to have been a member. Indeed, Matang is said to have decided by himself not to cooperate any longer with the Ismailis who, according to him, had reconciled themselves with caste hierarchy after having worked for the uplift of the low castes.[12]

According to the Ginan of Mamaidev, the relations between Matang and the Ismaili mission were very complex: Matang is considered to be the re-incarnation (*avatar*) of Ali himself: Ali having been born as the ruler of Alamut (the fortress from where, in Iran, the Nizari Ismailis spread their conquest and missionary activity), launches his appeal from Alamut, and Satgur Nur (who in the Ginan of Mamaidev is called Aspar Pandiya) answers his call and leaves for the 'East' (i.e. India). He is charged by Ali to deliver a ring and manuscripts in the village of Mandro in Saurashtra to his new incarnation, i.e., to Matang. A short while before the meeting of Satgur Nur and Matang at Mandro, Chach/Chanch who is the servant of Palande, Satgur Nur's wife, and also Satgur Nur's disciple, in the shape of a crow takes away his master's manuscripts and ring but is caught again by Satgur Nur in the shape of a parrot. Matang then takes in this cycle the place of the Imam Ali, the Qaim or Kayam who has come for the end of the world and the last judgement riding his white horse Duldul. He is no more the disciple of Satgur Nur under the name of Chach/Chanch as we have seen in another cycle of legends. So far the Ismaili context.[13]

Other Ginans introduce Matang as Naklanki who will achieve the *Kaliyug*. This constitutes another ambiguity, as Matang has already arrived and done his saviour's work. During a solemn rite on the Karumbho Rock in Saurashtra he has celebrated a miraculous human sacrifice: the victim, who is alive, distributes as *prasad* the flesh of his body, but only one out of three initiated participants accept, and are thus saved. Thus becomes necessary a fifth era, the '*Pancorath yug*' and the descent of an eleventh *avatar*,[14] Muro Raja, in order to finally save the world and abolish caste society.

In the Ismaili context, Naklanki represents Ali who is expected at the end of time, and Dominique-Sila Khan[15] has shown that the messianic cults in honour of Naklanki, although inspired by the tenth *avatar*-to-be of Vishnu, nevertheless owe everything to the Nizari Ismaili preachers who had preceded these cults (which later returned into the fold of Hinduism).

Finally, people also say that Matang is nothing but an avatar of Shiva-Mahesh (this explains the Maheshvari name), his son Lurang being the avatar of Ganesh. Shiva, in the Mahapanthi Tantric or Nath context, is the founder of both these communities.

The successors of Matang, also deified, do not assume the same messianic function: Lurang enters into an alliance with the Sumras, sorts out the succession crises of the Sammas, marries the daughter of one of the Sodha chiefs and leads Meghwal troops. From the city of Tharai Dhandh where he had established himself in Sindh, he retreats to Kutch because of defeats and persecution. He dies after requesting the earth to swallow him up. Matai, born in Kutch near Anjar, wields magic and tantric powers. He is said to have contributed to the installation of the Jadeja dynasty in Kutch; he dies serenely in Sindh. Mamai, the youngest and ablest of Matai's sons, is the actual founder and organizer of the movement to which he writes his texts, the Ginans; he assists, among others, the Jethwas at Gumli (near Porbandar) in Saurashtra, and moves back and forth between Sindh and Kutch. He dies in Sindh, beheaded at Thatta by King Bambhaniya, a Samma convert to Islam, not without having pre-programmed the decline of his sect by installing at its head the least suitable of his sons.[16]

This cursory view enables us to list three features which point to the Ismaili preaching underlying and shaping the Barmati movement:

1. The need to send out a Mission to convert and educate the people, this implying reforms for social uplift [for instance, one possible explanation for the presence of the mysterious seventy-two Jakhs in Kutch, seventy-two horsemen with a manuscript roll under their arm who reached there from nowhere to free people from ignorance and tyranny, could be that Matang or Devayat Pandit might have been their chief].[17]
2. The importance of astrology, of the preaching of things to come, of the efficiency of mantras and rites to foretell.
3. The expected arrival of a saviour who is to achieve the improvement of this world undertaken initially by the Mission.

The arrival of this saviour is announced through terrible forecasts, wars of destruction being the ultimate echoes of the persecutions endured by the not always so orthodox faithful. But this always happens in a familiar context. Thus in the Ginan of Mamaidev '*Ali bhada ji vagata*'[18] (The Narration of Ali the Brave) one may read:

Cetara mase gata samane se sambharo, aya kataka vembhara tana,
Bhare kataka piche kheda, Ali jo dhada avyo anata apara./5/

Luni: Ganesh Mandir (Lurangdev) — Wall-paintings of the 'Cár Dhárm' in Sindh. © F. Mallison

પૂ. શ્રી માતંહંદંશનું સ્વધામ - ભાદા (હાજીયાવણ)સિંધ

પૂજ્ય શ્રી લુણંગદેવનું સ્વધામ - ગામ ઠરઈ સિંધ (પાકીસ્તાન)

પૂ. શ્રી ધુણીમાતંગ દેવનું સ્વધામ - ગામ-સોડી (આદીહંદકણા) સિંધ પાકી

Sites of Deltaic Sindh

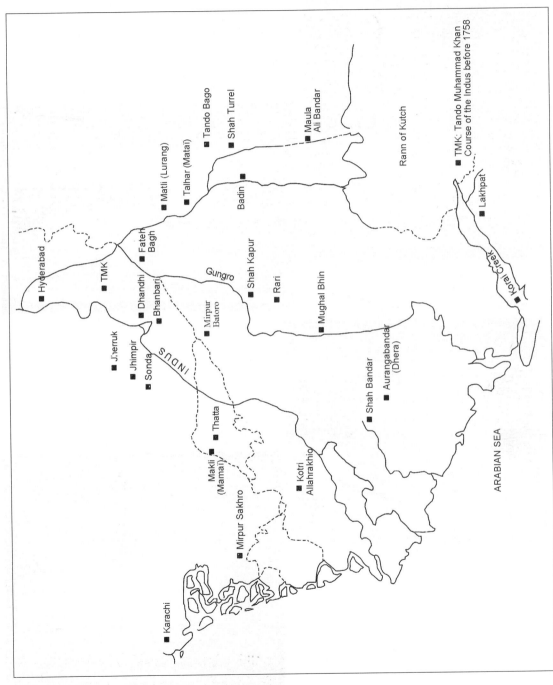

Map: Courtesy Michel Boivin

Listen, oh People, in the month of Caitra came an army full with destruction; the army hits and pushes from behind but the soldiers of Ali reach here, numberless./5/

Vaisakha mase Bhibhi Phatama penase, gambhira dhunaka hava dharase,
Rava divo ne cori Giranara, teni dhamara mangara dese Sagado somsara./6/

In the month of Vaishakha, Ali will marry Bibi Fatima, then will resound the roar of the drum. The sun will be his lamp, and Mount Girnar[19] will be his *Cori* (wedding canopy); as a gift, the entire world will sing the wedding songs./6/

The strange stories told by the Barmati Panthi hagiographic legends, in addition to their unusual messianic element, illuminate in their own way the religious history of Sindh. It is high time for the texts,[20] rites, and holy places of this community (and of quite a few related ones)[21] to be reckoned and recorded if one wishes to keep track of the ancient yet still alive popular cults, as they are more nuanced and abundantly detailed than the ideologies and classifications established during the 19th century.[22] They enrich the study of the religious history of this part of the Indian subcontinent.

6

JHULELAL AND THE IDENTITY OF INDIAN SINDHIS

Dominique-Sila Khan

Abstract

The Sindhis who have migrated to India after Partition generally term themselves as Hindus, although their cultural and religious heritage can be termed 'liminal'. While worshipping various Hindu deities, many of them revere the Guru Granth and perform their domestic rituals according to the Sikh tradition. Simultaneously, they continue to be disciples of various Sindhi Sufis, in particular, the famous Pir of Sehwan Lal Shahbaz Qalandar. During the last decades a strong feeling of otherness has prompted them to search for a distinct identity that would help them integrate into the Indian state while preserving their own cultural heritage. In this way the saint and deity Jhulelal, also known as Khwaja Khizr, has become a new marker of their identity. On the other hand, Hindu nationalist and reformist movements have had a deep impact on the community. As a consequence the syncretic nature of their traditions is often perceived as a contradiction that the exiled Sindhis find difficult to admit.

* * * *

In our century the reshaping of nations and states along cultural, religious, or linguistic criteria has contributed to solving a number of problems while generating new types of issues. Across the Pakistani border many Sindhis are now part of North Indian society. Although a few of them are Muslims, those who call themselves Hindus are, by and large, the more numerous. Most of them are concentrated in three states: Gujarat, Rajasthan, and Maharashtra. They have become a familiar sight in the urban landscape of these regions and despite the fact that they are a minority (less than one per cent of the total population of India) they are said to play a key role in various domains such as business, finance, religion, and politics. The average Indian tends to view them as a separate group which, curiously enough, he classifies along religious lines, listing the various communities of his country as 'Hindus, Muslims, Sikhs, Christians, Jains and Sindhis'.

This feeling of 'otherness' seems to be shared by the Sindhis too, and although the young generations tend to merge into the mainstream of Indian—mostly Hindu—society, constant efforts are made to preserve and revive their dying culture. In other words, exiled Sindhis are in search of their identity. This study seeks to investigate the various problems which they face while striving to solve an apparent contradiction: can one be a true Indian citizen and at the same time remain a Sindhi far from Sindh? This study is also an attempt at analysing the role played by religion, culture, and politics in this new quest of identity.

A Hidden Treasure: The Exodus

The popular iconography found in Indian Sindhi magazines and publications often shows a typical scene: two adults accompanied by children carrying on their head a suitcase and a few bundles, walking under a stormy sky. The caption says: 'a Sindhi family exiled from its motherland after Partition'. This is, of course, an allusion to the Sindhi Hindus who chose to cross the new Pakistani border in 1947 and settled in India. Interestingly enough, the commentary which invariably goes with this image has been drawn from the words of a Muslim Sindhi writer, Khwaja Ahmad Abbas:

> ...after the excavations done at Mohenjo Daro, we have learnt that the civilization of Sindh was several thousand years old and was superior to other civilizations. The Sindhis are the heirs of this ancient civilization. While our Sindhi brothers were leaving the province of Sindh to cross the Indian border, the customs officers who stood at the frontier searched them and took away all their belongings, but they forgot one detail: the Sindhis were carrying with them something which was more precious than these belongings: the culture, language and literature of Sindh.

Even if a feeling of 'otherness' had arisen in consequence of apparent religious differences with their Muslim brothers forming the majority of the population of Pakistani Sindh, the 'hidden treasure', that is to say their cultural heritage, forced them to maintain a permanent link with their motherland, regardless of these or other differences. In Pakistan, newcomers coming from Punjab or from India settled in Sindh, so there also the Sindhis were in danger of becoming a minority. Thus, across the border started a new dialogue which tended to blur religious differences in order to protect a threatened common heritage.[1]

Meanwhile, the majority of those who settled in India were under the impression that the historical process which brought them to a different country was an irreversible one. Many agreed to sell their land and property and the Indian government offered them new lands in reserved areas. For example, in Jaipur which has been the focus of my study, they had first been accommodated in refugee camps (the area near the central bus stand, known as 'Sindhi camp' still testifies to this fact) before being allotted particular *mohallas* in the city or in its suburbs. Soon the Sindhis managed to build houses and shops and in a comparatively short span of time those who had come with empty hands, nurturing in their soul the 'hidden treasure', became literally one of the wealthiest communities of North India. Their active participation in commercial, financial, social, and other enterprises enabled them to carve out for themselves an outstanding place in modern Indian society.

However, this very success started to be perceived as a threat: as the young generations began to feel at ease in the urban landscape of Rajasthan, Gujarat, or Maharashtra, fluently speaking Hindi and other local languages, sharing the customs and interests of their fellow countrymen, they gradually forgot their language and literature,[2] and consequently also the feeling of 'otherness' which was supposed to arise from their specificity as a distinct regional/social group. In other words, the material treasure which had been recently accumulated was endangering the secretly smuggled heritage.

The Religion of Indian Sindhis: A Many-Faceted Jewel

It is not uncommon to hear an Indian Sindhi asserting that the sole cause of the exodus was the feeling of religious difference and that his aim in leaving his native province which had become a part of Pakistan was to 'save the Hindu Dharm'—a recently coined term used to refer to a vast set of beliefs and practices which scholars, for the sake of convenience, generally designate as 'Hinduism'. If this were so one cannot help being surprised when considering a number of intriguing facts.

The Hindu Sindhi community is practically a casteless society: no Untouchables, few Shudras, among the famous Sunars (goldsmiths) and an overwhelming majority of people defining themselves as Kshatryas, known as Lohanas or Bhaibandhis. Describing this group in 1855, R.H. Thomas (reprint 1993, vol. II, pp. 651-4) had already distinguished two broad categories: the Amils and the others, including the 'Soucars'. One should also mention the priestly class of Thakurs, as far as they are associated with the cult of the Sindhi deity Jhulelal about whom more will be said later. Caste discriminations and barriers seem to be unknown in the traditional Sindhi world, to the extent that other Indians tend to view the whole Sindhi community as a Hindu caste with a specific religious and cultural heritage, more or less in the same way as they perceive the Jains.

On the other hand some Sindhis still remember the days when, freshly arrived, and hardly settled in their new country, they were not allowed to draw water at the common pump by most Hindu high-and middle-caste groups who treated them practically like Untouchables, although they posed as the defenders of Hindu Dharm and claimed to be Kshatryas. As one of my Sindhi informants confessed, 'people had all sorts of misgivings concerning our community: we were considered impure and somewhat in a limbo, between Islam and Hinduism'.

Actually, defining the community is in itself a tricky issue to which a Sindhi author, Sundarlal Rajpal, alludes in the title of one of his articles published in the magazine *Sindhu Dhara Times* (May–June 1996, pp. 11-12), 'k*ya sindhi samaj dharm, jati, panth ya sampraday hai?*' (is the Sindhi community a religion, a caste, a sect, or a religious order?). The question is left unanswered for one simple reason: much in the same way as the Sindhis cannot be identified with one caste (*jati* or *varna*), they are not the followers of one particular religious tradition, nor do they stick to a single set of beliefs or practices. Observing them in their everyday life one may notice an intriguing fact: the same person who will piously repeat the name of the Sindhi deity Jhulelal, worship various gods and goddesses of the Hindu pantheon, may also, incidentally—when surprised or shocked—invoke the name of Allah, and perform a number of domestic rituals, including marriages, with the *Guru Granth*, the holy scripture of the Sikhs.

It is the same Sindhi who, in the bridegroom's procession, stops with him, on the way to the bride's house, at some Hindu temple and listens to the praise of the Sufi Pir, Lal Shahbaz Qalandar invoked in a very popular song sung by the local band.[3] He has selected the date of the marriage according to the phase of the moon, and will have it celebrated according to both Hindu and Sikh rituals.

The simultaneous reverence for deities and saints belonging to various traditions is by no means an exclusive feature of the Hindu Sindhis, and the same phenomenon is frequently observed in many Hindu milieus. However, the highly 'syncretic' religion of the Sindhis displays some unusual traits and ought to be carefully analysed from an historical, as well as from a contemporary perspective, before one can fully grasp, in all its complexity, the issue of Sindhi identity and understand how a particular religious figure, Jhulelal, could be raised to the rank of a 'national deity'.

The Historical Perspective

The scarcity of documentary evidence has prevented scholars from elaborating a fully consistent picture of the history of religions in Sindh, as well as of the emergence of the Lohana community. Drawing from Carter's (1917), Maclean's (1989), and A.Z. Khan's (1975) studies as well as from some modern Sindhi sources (mainly articles from various magazines published by the community), one can, however, make an attempt at reconstructing its main phases.

The geographical and economical importance of the Indus makes it probable that, as oral tradition has it, the worship of this river has been one of the most ancient forms of religion in Sindh. It must have coexisted with the cult of various Vedic or local deities, including trees, snakes, and other animals. As Maclean has shown (1989: 6,42), roughly till the 8th century AD, Buddhism played a dominant role in this region of the subcontinent. After having examined the rich material found in the famous *Chach Nama*, the author concludes that two Lohana brothers, Mokah and Rasil, sons of Basayah, must have been Buddhist kings ruling over an extensive part of Sindh, including the region of Bet and the eastern portion of the delta, up to Kutch. According to him (Ibid.), this dynasty was strongly opposed to the Brahmanical family of Chach whose most famous descendant Daharsen, was defeated by the Arab conqueror Ibn Qasim. It seems that Buddhism was more prevalent in the north and spread mainly in the merchant classes, whereas the Brahmanical religion was more important in the south of the province among landowners.

Very little is known of the emergence of the Lohanas who may have evolved from various castes. Suffice it to say here that claiming a Kshatrya origin,[4] they became a major trading class. Their conversion to Buddhism and their opposition to the Brahmanical power must be considered an important element of their history. According to some modern Sindhi authors writing in various Sindhi publications in India, Buddhism may have played a major role in the shaping of a society in which caste barriers were absent or negligible.

Despite the lack of specific written sources it can be surmised that Jainism also had some impact on the religious history of Sindh.[5]

At a time when Buddhism seems to have disappeared from Sindh, as Buddhists converted to Islam or reverted to various forms of Hinduism, the oral tradition, filling the gap left by history, mentions the emergence of a new sect referred to as Darya Panth or Daryashahi Panth (A.Z. Khan, ibid.). As if to compensate for the lack of documentary evidence, numerous colourful legends propose different versions of a story in which the leading role is played by its founder variously known as Uderolal, Lal Sai, Jhulelal, Amarlal, Darya Nath, Darya Shah, Khwaja Khizr, Shaikh Tahir and Zinda Pir. The most striking feature here is the ambiguity of this sacred figure revered by both Hindus and Muslims.

Incidentally, the date of AD 952 given by modern Sindhi authors as the birth date of Jhulelal viewed as the 'spirit' of the Indus and an avatar of the Vedic god Varuna, coincides, as already noticed by Carter (1918: 206) and Maclean (1989: 112), with an inscription found on a Muslim grave located on an island near Rohri, said to be the tomb of Khwaja Khizr, the Muslim form of Jhulelal.

From a syncretic point of view, still defended by many Hindu Sindhi writers, the saint appears as a great reconciler of religious differences: in this light, even his legendary attack against the Sunni ruler of Thatta does not bear any anti-Muslim connotation, Jhulelal/Khwaja Khizr's message symbolizing rather the philosophical and tolerant spirit of Sufism versus a more legalistic and rigid form of Islam.

The striking episode of the dispute which ensued after his disappearance from earth[6] (and which strongly recalls similar legends associated with the Saints Kabir and Nanak) was, according to the tradition, solved in a way which could satisfy both communities. A celestial voice ordered the quarrelling disciples to build side by side a temple and a *dargah*: the saint declared that his shrine should be acceptable to both Hindus and Muslims, thus a part of it should be like a temple and the other like a mausoleum: he 'belonged to all of them'. However, he did not allow any image to be installed in the temple, his cult being performed only with light and water.

The hagiography of Jhulelal is too rich to be retold here in detail, for which we refer the reader to the articles listed in the bibliography. However, the following question can be raised: is it just a mere bunch of legends linked with the blurred memories of some ancient cult of the Indus tinged with Sufism, or has there been a real sectarian tradition referred to as Darya Panth? In their magazines published in India, some Sindhis have alluded to an intriguing fact: Jhulelal is often represented as an old man riding a fish, holding a book in his hand, but no scripture connected with the Darya Panth has subsisted to this day.

Nevertheless, a number of elements point to the existence of some ancient tradition which would have been buried gradually under a mass of legends. If we accept the tenth century as the time when its founder and exponent had flourished in Sindh and spread his teaching, it would be anachronistic to associate the syncretic Darya Panth with much later movements, like those started by Nur-ud-din Rishi, Kabir, Nanak, or Dadu. Even the Sufi orders were still to come to the subcontinent. One can postulate some connection with the Nath Sampraday, as far as Jhulelal/Darya Nath's sect is listed among one of the oldest orders of the Kanphata Jogis (Briggs Ibid.: 65) and sometimes said to have received initiation at the hand of Gorakhnath himself, one of the most famous exponents of this tradition. However, one must not forget the encompassing nature of the Nath movement which, much later, became connected with a single sect.

In the Nath tradition Darya Nath's dual personality is also noted, as he appears as Darya Shah or Khwaja Khizr. Islamic elements, however, seem to be prevalent in the tradition. Jhulelal's *samadhi* is, in fact, a Muslim tomb, and his so-called 'Hindu' shrine contains no image. The custom of *chaliha* (forty days' fast and austerities connected with the saint's tradition) is also strongly suggestive of the Sufi *chilla*. Finally, another popular representation of the saint as a bearded horse rider typically portrays him as a *pir*. There are even legends in which he is seen in the company of the famous 13th century Qalandar Lal Shahbaz. Yet, as has been said earlier, if we take for granted that the founder of the Daryashahi sect flourished in the tenth century, it would be difficult to trace any historical Sufi connection at such an early period.

A.Z. Khan (Ibid.: 212-213) seems to be the only author to have noticed a number of similarities between the Darya Panth and Fatimid Ismailism. During the 10th century this form of Shia Islam was prevalent in Sindh (Maclean, ibid.: 126-153), particularly in the region of Multan. Khan (Ibid.) suggests that the sect may have been connected with Ismailism or been influenced by it. But the subject has not been further investigated by him. He has not noticed, for instance, that the very period when Jhulelal/Khizr is said to have flourished is associated with an important event in the history of the Ismaili mission in Sindh. It coincides with the activities of an anonymous 'heretic' da'i (Maclean, ibid.: 132) whose heresy consisted not only in having allowed the indigenous converts to retain some of their earlier beliefs and customs, but also in claiming the legitimacy of a different succession of Imams and expecting the imminent advent of the Mahdi or Qaim, the messiah of the Shias. One could therefore contemplate the possibility of some forgotten link between the Daryashahi sect and this or another dissident movement of Ismailism. As I have pointed out elsewhere (D.S. Khan 1997: 227), the ambiguity and dual personality of a number of religious figures simultaneously viewed as Muslims and Hindus, fits very well into the framework of the Indian, acculturated form of Ismailism (Nanji 1978: 68), where it is said that many missionaries worked, according to the context, as Muslim dervishes or as Hindu jogis.

Be it as it may, without being able to come to any conclusion at this stage, we may at least surmise that the ambivalent/syncretistic nature of the Darya Panth and of its presumed founder Jhulelal/Khizr has left a deep imprint on Sindhi culture from the Medieval period to this day. According to a contemporary author writing in the Sindhi press published in India, the Darya Panth would have been the dominant religion of the Lohanas till the advent of the Qalandar Lal Shahbaz (13th century). This Muslim saint, later appropriated by the Sunni Suhrawardy order of Sufis, brought, to repeat the words of the same author, a message which was very much akin to the teaching of Jhulelal. It is even suggested elsewhere that Jhulelal 'paved the way for Sufism'. It may not be out of place here to point out that Lal Shahbaz is himself endowed with a multiple personality, in the same way as Jhulelal: he is simultaneously perceived as an incarnation of Vishnu, a Nath Jogi (Bhartrihari) and a Sufi Suharawady Pir (Ansari 1992: 19). Moreover, Ismaili tradition claims that he was in reality one of the early missionaries of the Nizari branch working in the area of Multan (Allana 1984: 35-36).

If it is a well-known fact that Hindu Sindhis had become *murids* of Lal Shahbaz, and at least till Partition, regularly visited his shrine at Sehwan, scholars do not seem to have noticed one more intriguing detail: in traditional hagiography Lal Shahbaz appears as a kind of alter ego to Jhulelal and is sometimes even totally identified with him, as one of his aspects. He is thus worshipped at Sehwan. According to Carter (1917: 205), Jhulelal in his Muslim aspect is also portrayed as *mast qalandar*. According to another version, both Jhulelal and Lal Shahbaz are listed among the twelve main qalandars of Sindh. The fact is that in the famous Qawwali song starting with the words '*Damadam mast Qalandar…*', supposed to be dedicated to Lal Shahbaz, the name Jhulelal also appears, and according to a Hindu Sindhi source, this is a song in praise of both 'Lals'.

Finally, although I found only one reference to Ismaili *pirs* in the Indian Sindhi press (Jotwani, 1995: 18), one must briefly mention that, among others, Pir Sadruddin (14th–15th century), is said to have converted many Lohanas to the Nizari branch of Ismailism (Shackle and Moir 1992: 7), whose descendants are mainly known as Khojas. However, curiously enough, these Lohanas are portrayed in Ismaili tradition as having been Shakti worshippers and no mention is made either of their affiliation to the Darya Panth or of their cult of Jhulelal/Khizr.

Following A.Z. Khan one must also refer to another major event which is said to have occurred at the beginning of the 16th century: coming under the influence of the founder of Sikhism and of the successive gurus, including the last one Gobind Singh, many Lohanas became Nanakpanthis, mainly, it seems, of the Udasi order. According to the same author this would have led to a noticeable decline of the Darya Panth. However, although these Sindhis adopted all the ten gurus and the Guru Granth as their holy scripture, they did not adhere to the Khalsa nor did they take part in the Singh Sabhas and other reformist Punjabi movements. Instead, they developed their own line of gurus and in Sindh started to build their own shrines, mainly known as darbars.[7] After Partition most of these shrines were transferred to India. Rajasthan has a few famous ones in Jaipur and Ajmer. Till 1984, when the then prime minister of India, Indira Gandhi was murdered by a Sikh bodyguard, it is said that Sindhis maintained certain links with the Punjabi Khalsa Sikhs and even contributed to the maintenance and repair of their gurdwaras.[8]

Further, modern Sindhi authors mention the leading role played by the great Sufi saints of the 17th and 18th centuries, in particular Sachal Sarmast and Shah Abdul Latif. At that time exchanges may have occurred between these Sufis and the Nanakpanthi Sindhi gurus, but more investigation would be required before determining the nature of this interaction.

It may be of some interest to conclude this brief survey with the words of a Hindu Sindhi author residing in India: 'The religion of the Sindhis whether of Muslims or of Hindus is not orthodox Islam or orthodox Hinduism, but a rather heterodox worship of saints and holy men' (Jotwani, ibid.: 18).

A temporary conclusion could be that defining the majority group of Sindhi refugees in India as 'Hindus' one resorts to a classification which is far from reflecting the complexity of the actual situation and must rather be viewed as the result of a historical process connected with the construction of new religious boundaries (Oberoi 1994, Mayaram 1997, D.S. Khan 1997).

The Emergence of Religious Boundaries

In the history of the subcontinent national, regional, or communal identity has often been sought by rallying people under the banner of a hero, a saint, or a god. Maharashtra nationalism has centred around the figure of Shivaji, while some leaders have extolled Maharana Pratap, a ruler of Udaipur, as the precursor of the modern Rajasthani State and Punjabi Sikhs have selected Guru Gobind Singh as the symbol of the Punjabi nation.

In Sindh there was no dearth of heroes or saints, but many of them were already associated with other social or religious groups. If Buddha had sunken into oblivion, Lal Shahbaz was now entirely appropriated by the Sunni Sufi orders: Nanak and Gobind Singh 'belonged' to the Punjabis, while Brahmanical gods and goddesses were shared by many communities. There remained the ancient cult of Jhulelal/Khizr. If the Darya Panth had lost its identity as a sect in the course of history, to the extent that nowadays some Sindhis deny that there has ever been such a Panth, the reverence for the Sindhi saint connected with the Indus had still been preserved. It is true that, far from Sindh, pilgrimages to Jhulelal shrines and regional festivals had practically ceased. Among the Lohanas the Thakurs—said to be the descendants of Jhulelal's disciple and cousin Pagar—were the only repositories of this half-forgotten tradition.

It was difficult to unite the exiled Sindhis around issues of language and culture, and this is why Ram Panjwani, a writer, a singer, and an actor, understood that people could more easily rally under the banner of a hero and saint. In 1959 he launched a movement which in Sindhi milieus was later compared to a 'cultural revolution': he resuscitated a dying god (the words often found in Sindhi articles are 'the recreation of a deity') and revived his cult. Thanks to his multiple personality, Jhulelal could simultaneously be their god, their hero, and their saint. Ram Panjwani proclaimed that Caiti Cand (the new moon of the Hindu month of Caitra) would be celebrated each year as the *Sindhyat diwas* or 'day of Sindhism'. This date which coincided with the annual flow of the Indus was, according to the legend, the day when Jhulelal was incarnated. In order to organize this event on a grand scale, various committees were created, and eventually in 1979 their activities encouraged the foundation of the Bharatya Sindh Sabha.

In the wake of this, different cultural events were organized to promote the language and culture of Sindh and Sindhi magazines and books, in English, Sindhi, and Hindi, were published, while temples to Jhulelal, a new feature in the urban landscape of India, started to be built. At this stage it may be of some interest to mention here that the celebration of the first Caiti Cand festival at Baroda (Gujarat) and a committee named 'Sri Lal Sahib Mandal' were instituted by Hindu Sindhis at the big shrine of the Sufi Sachal Sarmast—since no temple to Jhulelal had yet been built.

If one bears in mind the complex history of Sindhi Lohanas it will be clear that the tradition of Jhulelal, being highly syncretic by nature, could perfectly embody the main values and ideals of this community. As a Sindhi author has put it: 'The Sindhis on both sides of the Indo-Pakistani international border very often raise voices of dissent against fundamentalism, which goes against the very grain of syncretism, a great Indian subcontinental value deeply entrenched in their psyche' (Jotwani, ibid: 17).

Many authors stress the fact that Jhulelal appeared in two forms to explain to his devotees that there was only one God, whether one chooses to call him Allah or Iswar. The Sindhi god has emphasized the bond of brotherhood among all Sindhis, Hindus as well as Muslims. In this perspective the aim of Jhulelal was precisely to unite the two communities; that is why the shrines dedicated to his cult became the nucleus of a pilgrimage for both. This perspective which is sometimes defined as an example of 'secularism' before the term had been coined does, however, represent but one side of the picture.

One cannot ignore the fact that opposite trends have been at work approximately for one century (that is to say even before Hindu Sindhis crossed the new border), as a result of which Jhulelal, the new symbol of the exiled Hindu Sindhi community, can be perceived in a drastically different light. Let us be reminded briefly that the legendary dispute which ensued after Jhulelal's disappearance from earth had been solved by the saint's injunction: two shrines were to be erected side by side, for the worship of the two communities; but even in the temple there should be no image. In this way both sacred places became acceptable to all. It seems that for centuries the sacred space of Jhulelal/Khizr shrines has been shared peacefully by Hindus and Muslims. But as one Sindhi author recalls (Israney 1994: 34), a major event took place at the deity's shrine which was located on an island in the Indus, near Rohri:

> Towards the end of the last century, on the instigation of some fundamentalist, the Muslims service men of God drove away the pujaris from the island; That is why Hindus built a big, magnificent temple on the land opposite to the island (…) This is how Hindus left the Zindah Pir of water and established their own Zindah Pir on the dry land. By 1940 both places were in ruins.

Of course this event must be understood as a consequence of the emergence of clear-cut religious identities towards the end of the 19th century—a phenomenon which is said to be the result of the 'categorizing' activities of the British colonial census, as well as of the efforts of a number of revivalist and reformist bodies, both Islamic and Hindu. Newly cast definitions of what Hinduism and Islam 'should' be led to conflicting versions of the hagiography of the ubiquitous saint Jhulelal/Khizr whose aim had been, according to some traditional sources, to reconcile religious differences. As Maclean has it (Ibid.: 113), the saint 'was associated with miraculous powers which are employed for the benefit of the Muslim community against the non-Muslims of Sindh (…)'. Khwaja Khizr was said to have saved a Muslim woman performing the pilgrimage 'by diverting the entire Indus River away from the capital of the Hindu king, thus bringing both the king and his non-Muslim community to ruin' (ibid).

The author, however, does not seem to be aware of the fact that an opposite version of the saint's role has become popular with certain Hindus: for them Jhulelal has become the saviour of the Hindus persecuted by the Sunni ruler of Thatta, Mirakh Shah. Although historical records do not mention any ruler of this name (his Persian title 'Shah' sounds rather anachronistic for the 10th century), this version must be understood as an attempt at reconstructing history according to one's personal convictions. To understand how such a transformation could take place one must briefly mention the role played by the Arya Samaj among Sindhis, towards the end of the 19th and the beginning of the 20th century, proposing its own version of Hinduism and inventing a new ritual of purification (*suddhi*) to integrate half-Muslim or low-caste communities into their organization (Jaffrelot 1994: 78-89). The Arya Samaji activist Narayan Dev, sometimes referred to as '*Dayanand ka vir sipahi*' (the Arya Samaj founder's heroic soldier), is still extolled as a Sindhi martyr; after having made many conversions he died in a street fight in 1948.

Later on some Sindhis came under the influence of the Hindu Mahasabha, the Jan Sangh, the Rashtrya Swayamsevak Sangh, and the Bharatiya Janata Party. These new political orientations did not, of course, remain without effect on the perception of the 'recreated deity' Jhulelal, who, in this new light, became the symbol of the identity of non-Muslim Sindhis. As Sanskritization and re-Hinduization gradually transformed a number of religious beliefs and practices throughout India, Jhulelal, an old man riding a fish (his most popular iconography), was identified with an avatar of the Vedic Varuna and the mysterious book held in his hand was said to be the Bhagavad Gita. He was also proclaimed to be an incarnation of Krishna (his 25th avatar) and some Sindhi authors supported this view by quoting a famous fragment of the Bhagavad Gita where Krishna declares 'among the nagas I am Ananta, among aquatic creatures I am Varuna'.

The whole history of Sindh was reconstructed along these lines. The Brahmin ruler Dahrasen was extolled as a hero who fought against Ibn Qasim, while the Arab conquest was perceived as the 'first germ of partition'; Buddhism and its 'wrong conception of non-violence' was to blame for the weakening of Sindh: thus Sindhi Lohanas readily forgot that ancient Buddhist Lohana kings had been strongly opposed to the Brahmin dynasty of Chah and Daharsen. Brahmins acquired an unprecedented prestige in a community which had always denied them any kind of priority or superiority. Reproduced in a special issue of the RSS magazine *The Organizer* published for the Caiti Cand festival (April 1995), a fragment of Vir Sarvakar's speech echoes this reconstruction of history. The leader of the Hindu Mahasabha who has been the author of a famous pamphlet issued in 1923 'Hindutva: who is a Hindu?', sought to attract the Marathi Sindhis by giving them the rank of 'best patriots and highly orthodox Hindus' (ibid.: 6); he claimed that the Indus river (Sindhu) from which the word 'Hindu' derives is still more sacred than the Ganges because it is supposed to be the place where the ancient Rishis had the first vision of the Vedas.

The conclusion of Sarvarkar was that 'one cannot be Hindu without Sindhu' and that there should be a new political ideal attempting to reverse the course of history: in other words that Sindh should legitimately be a part of the dream of a 'great India'. Following this idiom, 'no Hindu without Sindhu', the concept of Sindhyat was still enlarged and transformed to equate that of Hindutva, and Sindhis were forcibly identified with 'Sanghis' (members of the RSS). This version was very far from the syncretistic, idealistic vision of Jhulelal/Khizr as a reconciler of religious differences endowed with a dual personality, seen as a Sufi saint, a Nath yogi, and a Hindu deity.

Conclusion

How far has this particular bias affected the real everyday life of non-Muslim Sindhis settled in India? If nobody knows what kind of sect the Darya Panth was in reality, some going as far as denying its historical existence, Jhulelal has subsisted, and even been revived, if not recreated, as the powerful symbol of a threatened identity. The deity seems, moreover, to continue his own existence regardless of all political or religious manipulations. If it has gained or regained a place in the heart of modern Sindhis who have chosen to settle in India, many of them still continue to be the *murids* of Sindhi Sufi *pirs*, who came to bless the inauguration of an ambitious financial undertaking, the creation of the Indus bank; at the same time Hindu gods, goddesses and saints continue to be present in their Nanakpanthi temples where the Guru Granth is enshrined. Despite all these efforts, Jhulelal's temples are less numerous than are his popular images at the entrance of shops or in advertisements found in various magazines and brochures published by the Sindhi community. Was he an incarnation of the Vedic Varuna, an avatar of Krishna, a yogi of the Nath sect, a manifestation of the Coranic Khwaja Khizr who had drunken the elixir of immortality, a Sufi saint, an Ismaili missionary under the guise of a Qalandar, a precursor of Kabir and Nanak's 'syncretic' message?

While his real historical personality must remain shrouded in mystery till further evidence is found, his successive or simultaneous avatars in the Sindhi psyche appear to mirror the multi-faceted soul of a community in search of its identity. However, the material success of those who came with empty hands but with a 'hidden treasure' in their heart may be the most conspicuous one, as a Sindhi author complained, accusing his brothers of 'destroying a deity'. Could one go so far as to conclude that nowadays, much more than a symbol of syncretism or of Hindutva, Jhulelal should be perceived as a modern avatar of Kubera, the god of wealth?

7

LOHANA AND SINDHI NETWORKS[1]

Pierre Lachaier

Abstract

In the 19th century Lohanas were known as one of the largest Hindu trading communities in Sindh, Kutch, Saurashtra and in the western parts of Punjab and Rajasthan. However, after the Partition in 1947, those Lohanas who mostly came from Kautch and Saurashtra have built up their own and exclusive network of *jati* associations, whereas the others Lohanas who left Pakistan are to be found in a large proportion in the network of institutions and associations built by the Sindhi refugees. The author tries to understand why and how Lohanas seem to have forgotten after hardly half a century that they used to belong to the same community.

* * * *

Introduction

In the 19th century Lohanas were known as one of the largest Hindu trading communities in Sindh, in Kutch, in Saurashtra and on the western parts of Punjab and Rajasthan. However, after the Partition in 1947, those Lohanas who mostly came from Kacch and Saurashtra have built up their own and exclusive network of *jati* associations, whereas the other Lohanas who left Pakistan are to be found in a large proportion in the network of institutions and associations built by the Sindhi refugees.

In this study, I am trying to understand why and how, after about half a century, Lohanas became divided into two separate communities in such a way as not being able any more to admit of their common past social origin. The relevant information I collected among the Lohanas during my fieldwork and the literature about them before the Partition being sparse, the scope of this study is limited to a comparative exploration of both sides of the divide of the Lohanas from socio-economic and religious points of view.

The few colonial sources which I could consult are mainly the usual caste dictionaries (Enthoven, 1975), and the earlier *Gazetteers* of Sindh and Kutch which often quote the classical old works of R.F. Burton[2] and James Tod.[3] For Kutch, apart from the book of Rushbrook (1958) and the last *District Gazetteer* of 1971, recent sociological works in English mentioning the Lohanas are also few. For Sindh, I used Thakur's[4] *Sindhi Culture* (1959) and Anand's *National Integration of Sindhis* (1996). Recent publications by the Sindhis (Bharadwaj, 1988, 1990) and by the Lohanas from Kutch–Saurashtra are many, but not readily available in the market. They contain useful information, but should be resorted to carefully.

The Mythico-Historical Origin of the Lohanas

Lohanas have recently written for themselves some accounts about who they are and where they come from.[5] These mythico-historical stories articulate a few important events and beliefs which were already mentioned by Lohanas during the colonial period:

a. Lohanas descend from Rama's[6] son Lav and were previously called 'Lavranas' or 'Lohavranas'.[7] Lavranas or Lohanas have founded Lahore, in Punjab.[8]
b. Lohanas came from Afghanistan,[9] and migrated southwards to Sindh, Kutch, and Saurashtra under the pressure of Muslim conquerors.[10]
c. Lohanas ruled ancient kingdoms.[11]
d. Lohanas' main divinity is Daryalal,[12] the god of the Indus who incarnated to protect Hindus against a Muslim prince who wanted to convert them. Actually, Daryalal, or Amarlal, Jhulelal, Udero Lal, as he is also called, is said to be born around AD 1000 in Nasarpur, on the Indus, and he has been widely worshipped in Sindh by Hindus and Muslims. His birthday festival (Cheti Cand) is attended with fervour by Kutchi Lohanas and Sindhi Lohanas today. One of his usual representations shows him as an old white-bearded man sitting on a fish (a '*palla*') and holding a holy book in his hands.
e. At a later period, Lohanas served as ministers[13] to local princes from whom they eventually had to suffer many hardships. As we will see later, the Sindhi Lohanas called *Amils* also served local rulers, the *Amirs*, as *Diwans*.

Apart from some variable details which have been omitted here, these stories of origin have remained constant since Burton's time, which is at least one century ago.

The Lohanas before Partition

The Lohanas in Sindh

Today's Kutchi Lohanas in India are aware that they came from Sindh a long time ago. According to Thakur (1969:25) 'The Lohanas who form the mass of the [Hindu] population constitute an all absorbing caste which has given shelter to various elements of the population from the adjoining provinces from time to time'[14] and 'Unless a person is a member of any of the non-Lohana castes, he must be assumed to be a Lohana, members of which caste form the general body of Sindh Hindus' (Thakur, 1959:68). There were, however, some fifty Lohana subdivisions in Sindh, says Thakur (1959:58), and let us note that, although 'Human relations which bind various elements of Sindhi society are based, as elsewhere in India, on the institution of caste' (Thakur, 1959:56), we know too little about these subdivisions to be absolutely sure that their members did consider themselves as belonging to one caste-community before the Partition.

Priestly castes enjoyed the highest status, as elsewhere in India (Thakur, 1959:69). Saraswat Brahmans were close to the Lohanas whose priests they were. Then came the mercantile castes such as the Lohanas, Bhatias, Khatris, Chahprus 'the first being the principal caste and forming the general body of Sindh Hindu', says Thakur (1959:35 and ff.).

In the 18–19th centuries, a social differentiation appeared among the Hindu merchant communities between the Amils, who were employed in the administration of the Amir rulers,[15] and the other merchants who were soon to be called Bhaibands. The Amils acquired a higher status than the Lohanas from where they were mostly issued, and quickly became a hereditary group (Anand, 1996:7) although they continued to also be recruited from the Lohanas and the Khatris.

Under the British, Hindus and mainly these Amils learned English and grabbed the high posts that the colonial administration could offer: 'Thus the community came to be recognized as Diwan-Hindu-Amil in contradistinction to traders and shopkeepers who bore the well-established label of Bania.' says Bharadwaj.

In the second half of the 19th century, merchants who were often from Hyderabad, were selling locally made handicraft goods, the so-called 'Sindh-Works'. These 'Sindh-Works' were very much in demand in Bombay and in other places where the British resided. Soon, these enterprising merchants, who were to be called Bhaibands, started to emigrate to distant countries to sell their 'Sindh-Works': such were the Pohumal and the Vasiamal in Hong Kong,[16] and others in Singapore, Malaysia, Indonesia, Egypt, and the Middle East. They made a humble beginning as hawkers, it is said. However, it did not take long for them to develop prosperous businesses and 'Whatever the part of the world may be, the Sindhi firms employed managers, partners, clerks and even ordinary servants from among Sindh Hindus who were recruited from the entire Sind' (Thakur, 1959:37).[17]

At the time of Independence, a large majority of the Hindu refugees from Sindh in India were traders and merchants.[18] The smallest of them were shopkeepers, then came grain, cotton and oilseeds merchants, and at the top the 'Lohana Bhaibands',[19] owners of big firms called 'Khotis'. These Khotis were established in larger agglomerations, mainly in Karachi. They had agents and branch offices in Bombay, Ahmedabad, Nagpur, and were often dealing in wholesale and import-export of grains and textiles. In Bairagarh (Madhya Pradesh), up to 92 per cent of the Sindhis who settled there after the Partition are reported to be Lohanas engaged in business (Thakur, 1959:42-3).

The Lohanas in Kutch and in Saurashtra

In Kutch, whereas almost all Vania merchants and Brahmans have come from Marwar and Gujarat and talk Gujarati, the Lohana, Bhatia, and Bhanusali merchants have come from Sindh, sometimes from Multan in south Punjab, and talk Kutchi which is a Sindhi non-written[20] dialect.

According to the census of 1872, in Kutch, there were 369,184 Hindus and 118,063 Muslims. The most numerous Brahmans were the Saraswats (5,431 people) from Sindh; they were usually the family priests of the Lohanas, Khatris, and Bhanusalis.[21] The Lohanas worshiped Darya Pir, the Muslim name for Daryalal. Kutchi Hindu and Jain merchants and shopkeepers from Sindh and Gujarat together represented 31.93 per cent of the non-Muslim population, among which the 31,000 Lohanas represented 26 per cent of it.

In the 18th century Lohanas occupied high positions, such as ministers and bankers. However, in 1778, after their headman Devchand was put to death and a big amount of money was extorted from his relatives, '… a Lohana has never risen to the post of Minister, and few of them are now men of much wealth and position' (Campbell, 1880:55).

In 1880, there were around five hundred 'capitalists' in Kutch (Campbell, 1880:110). They were to be found mostly among the Brahmans, Banias, Bhatias, Lohanas, and Gosais, and among the Khojas, Memons. and Bohras. Some fifty firms were operating as banks, the largest of which had agents, branch offices, or their headquarters in Bombay and some of them in Zanzibar. Importers were usually Bhatias, Banias, Lohanas, or Khojas; they used to resell in towns and in villages upland, where shopkeepers and merchants were Lohanas and Banias. Kutchi merchants have a long experience of overseas trade, in East Africa, Arabia and in the Persian Gulf.[22]

However, during the colonial time, the ports of Kutch—Mandvi was the most important—were declining because they had silted up and could not accommodate the new vessels of higher tonnage. When the British people started to develop the port of Karachi after 1843, the coastal trade[23] had already some local importance in its surrounding area. According to the census of 1901, there were 446,513 inhabitants in the Karachi District and 'Among Hindus, the trading caste known as Lohana or Luvana is alone of numerical importance, with 35,000' (*Imperial Gazetteer*, 1908:5). In 1910 there were 50,000 Kutchi speakers in this district (Grierson, 1919: note 14). It is highly probable that Lohana merchants from Kutch had already settled there before other Lohanas, either from Sindh or from Kutch came and joined them after the conquest of Sindh.

At the time of Partition, big businessmen and a number of smaller merchants and shopkeepers were operating in Karachi which was linked closely with Bombay. Those who could transfer their business to Bombay, did so; the others migrated to elsewhere in India and abroad where they eventually settled in harder conditions. Some poorer migrants of Kutchi origin went back to Kutch where they could still have some land, and from there, they migrated farther up to other parts of India.[24]

The Lohanas and Sindhis after Partition

In India, Sindhi refugees have created many educational institutions, hospitals, cultural associations, etc. which tend to concentrate in the Greater Bombay area: they are managing some twenty colleges of various specialities,[25] many of them were founded by big Sindhi businessmen. These institutions often describe themselves as 'Sindhi', but their designation rarely mentions a caste name (such as Loar Sindhi, Chahpru Sindhi), or a place of origin such as Sukkur, Shikarpuri, Larkana, Multan, Jacobabad, etc. Sindhis have also built all-India and some foreign associations. However, their community remains divided on certain questions, such as which script, Arabic or Devanagari, should become the official one for the Sindhi language.

According to the 'Sindhis' International Yearbook',[26] the Sindhi Diaspora comprises around 3.5 million people, out of which 2,375,000 are settled in India where they mostly concentrate in Gujarat, Maharashtra and the Bombay area, Rajasthan, and Madhya Pradesh. Abroad, Sindhis are dispersed in some 150 countries all around the world and have settled mostly in Indonesia, Netherlands, USA, UK, Hong Kong and the United Arab Emirates.

The Sindhis' economic achievements in India or abroad are emphasized by all authors, sometimes with some ostentation, especially in Bharadwaj's books (Bharadwaj, 1988:245-399, 1990:254-350). The largest Sindhi firm in the UK is the Hinduja group (one billion pounds of assets) which controls the Indian company Ashok Leyland. Then come the Laxmi Shivdasani group (hundred million pounds sterling in assets), the Damodar Chainrai group (sixty million pounds sterling in assets), etc. (Bharadwaj, 1990:254-5).

In India, the Sindhi hit-parade is, however, more modest: there are many in the movie industry, in newspapers and reviews businesses, and some 1500 Sindhi industrialists produce all sorts of goods many of which are exported.[27] In the Bombay area, as many as nine million families depend on salaries from Sindhi firms and industries[28] and Bharadwaj concludes his success-board saying with some satisfaction: '… I was surprised I am proud to say that our contribution in the field of industry, business as well as marketing is number three after Marwari and Gujratis'.[29] But there is also another side to this coin: according to a young Sindhi shopkeeper selling chappals and tennis shoes I met on the roadside in Sangli, South

Maharashtra, the 150 Sindhi families locally settled and rather poor do not fit into this success board.

Bharadwaj does not give any details about any other group of merchants or trading communities of Sindh,[30] and he says nothing about the Lohanas, although those Bhaibands who developed a large Sindhi Diaspora in the 19th century were Lohana traders,[31] and '… the difference in cultural status of the people has kept alive the caste consciousness specially among the Amil and Lohana Bhaibands; and there is no indication that the caste prejudices have disappeared as a result of migration from Sind… The tendency is to regroup themselves with a regional background, which they possessed in Sindh irrespective of caste' (Thakur, 1959:72).

In 1996 in Nasik, there were four territorial Sindhi Panchayats whose members belonged to several endogamous groups: Chahpru merchants from Karachi, Hyderabadi merchants in auto businesses, Uttaradi from the north of Sindh, Diwans who are educated civil servants (probably the Amils), Bhatia money-lenders, Bhaget Brahmans and Khatri hotel-and bar-keepers. Far from being subdivisions of the same caste, most of these groups are different *jati*s and their common Panchayat is but a multi-caste association. Nasik Sindhis have started a common cooperative bank called the 'Jhulelal Cooperative Society', and some of them are in the jute bag business in which they have to compete with the local Kutchi Lohanas who have their own local cooperative bank and caste *Mahajan*. Nasik Lohanas and Nasik Sindhis do not mix, even though some of these Lohanas have come from Sindh after Partition, and even though some of these Sindhis belong to *jati*s which are well known in Kutch.

Lohanas of Kutch-Saurashtra after Partition

After Partition, Lohanas started to develop new local caste associations called '*Mahajan*', in Bombay and in its suburb, in Gujarat, Maharashtra, and in some other places in India and abroad. These associations, after having federated at the regional level, became affiliated with an all-India and world-wide association called '*Lohana Mahaparishad*' settled in Bombay. This Lohana Mahaparishad is made up of elected members coming from the local Mahajans of the 'Regional subdivisions' of Bombay, Gujarat, Saurashtra, Kutch, north-eastern India, central India (Vidarbha), South India, Africa, USA, and the UK, but there is no subdivision for Pakistan.

These Lohanas belong to more or less endogamous '*jati*s',[32] which distinguish themselves depending on where their members come or originate from. Kutchis are from Kutch, Halais from the Halar area of the Jamnagar district of Saurashtra, Ghogharis from Ghogha Bandar, a port close to Bhavnagar in Saurashtra, and Nagar-Thatta come from Thatta, which is an old capital of Sindh. These last are but a few, but their presence among the Lohanas is significant as well as the fact that the few Kutchi Lohanas living in Pune and Nasik who had been living in Karachi Since before Independence tend to form locally a separate wealthier Lohana faction: in other words, they and the Nagar-Thatta still somehow recognize and admit that they are Sindhi Lohanas among the other Lohanas.

Many among the Mahajans' leaders are merchants belonging to the middle or upper categories, and some of them are important industrialists. However, most of the Kutchi Lohanas who came to India after Partition were poor and little educated. In Bombay-Mulund, Pune, and Nasik they started gunny bag businesses (Lachaier, 1993), which some of them had already practised in Karachi. It is only after fifty years, that some of them have been able to establish average sized firms, specialized in packing materials, or can diversify their business activities in more profitable ways, or become high level professionals. From the petty, second-hand gunny bag dealers to the big businessmen, the Lohanas have been living under wide-ranging socio-economic conditions.

In the buildings of the Kutchi Lohana Mahajans, there is usually a temple-room dedicated to their main god, Daryalal, whose birthday is a widely attended festival. The only temple to the deity the Kutchi Lohanas have built in India is in Bombay (there are other Daryalal temples in India built by Sindhis, but Lohanas do not mention them). Kutchi Lohanas who have settled in Bombay and Maharashtra have made their Kutchi Saraswat Brahman priests come to serve them.

The Kutchi language is less and less spoken, even at home. Until the mid-eighties, Kutchi children in Pune used to go to Gujarati-medium schools. Now they tend to be sent to English-medium schools.

Lohanas have been known as a trading community. Today, and in as much as the politico-economic situation has become more favourable for them, most of them tend to pursue their traditional calling. Their strategy of networking and coordinating local jati associations at different geographical levels has been rather usual in India since the beginning of the 20th century at least.[33] The resulting transnational Lohana network is centred on India, where the Lohana Mahaparishad, their apex Bombay association, tends to build a more or less unified identity. But Lohanas do not usually fraternize with the post-Partition Sindhi refugees, and do not mix with them even for the Daryalal festival.

Sindhi Identity and Nationalism

We may think of this divide among Lohanas from Kacch-Saurashtra and Sindh as mainly resulting from their distinct regional identities which were reinforced during the colonial period, for 'It is true that Kutch remained for centuries set apart from the rest of India—though by no means from the rest of the world. It is true that ... (the small self-contained polity of Kutch)... had developed a tradition of separatism...' (Rushbrook, 1958). It is a fact that before Partition, the Kingdom of Kutch, with its feudal socio-economic institutions, remained relatively isolated and rather underdeveloped, whereas Sindh, which had been administered directly by the British since 1843 had an already westernised capital, Karachi.

We could also think that this divide between the Lohanas and the Sindhis would only reproduce ancient or pre-Partition Lohana social subdivisions, which are unfortunately not well known. However, let us note that, before the partition, this divide was not known in East and South Africa, where immigrant Indian business people were identified as 'Gujarati Banias, Lohanas, Bhatias, Patel, Jains, Memons, Khojas, etc. 'but *not* as 'Sindhis' as they are sometimes known today, in Nigeria for instance.

While persisting after the partition, the existing old subdivisions have also tended to be overshadowed by the Hindu Sindhis who, as a whole, constitute a social entity that has been recently created by, and results from Partition, as Bharadwaj (1988) readily recognizes: 'Sindh has fifty-five centuries of History of wars, invasions... many ethnic groups... different sects of Hindu religions have moulded the Sindhis that was born in turmoil in 1947 (sic)',[34] and Sindhi refugees have been trying to forge a new 'national' identity.

Anand and Bharadwaj are illuminating on this point. Bharadwaj's publications are like a small encyclopaedia of everything that can be, rightly or not, attributed to *the* Sindhis: the ancient history of Sindh from Mohen-jo Daro and Harappa (discovered in 1922) until today, Sindhi literature, folklore, great men and more especially, the Bhaiband merchants and their big firms. Bharadwaj's books aim at shaping a collective answer to the question 'What is a Sindhi?'[35] He does it without academic pretence, and sometimes from a rather personal point of view.[36]

Just after the partition, the young generation of Sindhi intellectuals and literati developed the conception of 'Sindhiat'[37] in order to crystallize the identity of the Sindhis. 'Sindhiat' means all that can be considered as Sindhi culture. Already emotionally loaded, this notion of 'Sindhiat' is exalted by Anand up to the point that it becomes a religious notion by amalgamation with what she considered to be the main Sindhi god, Udero Lal (alias Jhulelal, Daryalal): 'Though the Sindhis are not a religious society in India, they have a distinct cultural religion which is called Sindhiat. Its total and exclusive development in the Indus Valley for hundreds of years has given it a distinctive character. It is the sum total of their cultural heritage including within it the cultural personality of Sindhis… It also represents a language… It further includes all that was brought along by the Sindhis during migration… Thus Sindhiat is the religion of the Sindhis. The god Uderolal is their deity and his birthday is the Sindhiat Day' (Anand, 1996:197). In fact, Udero Lal's birthday has become the 'Sindhiat Day' in Bombay since 1988 at least (Bharadwaj, 1988:217).

Anand suggests also to organize systematically the Sindhi society and religion, to unify the education, to reinforce the common cultural core, to reduce tensions between the Sindhis and the populations among which they are living in India, and to promote the political integration of the Sindhis by creating a Sindhi territory along Pakistan's border and particularly in eastern Kacch, an area which has been culturally, linguistically and socially close to Sindh because of migratory exchanges in both directions.[38] It has a good potential for development for various reasons, and particularly because it includes the Kutchi harbour of Kandla and the near-by town of Gandhidam.[39] However, private enterprises could not develop there as expected because of government regulations,[40] and because the development of infrastructures has been too slow. Anand adds that Kutchis are pressing the Gujarat government to take back the area that was given to the Sindhis. On their side, Sindhi literati and scholars are supporting the project and wish the central government to be in charge of it. According to Anand, who does not mention the Lohana trading community, nor any other Kutchi trading communities: '*There will be no competition with the local population as the Sindhis are neither agriculturists nor artisans. In fact as traders they can complement the farmer.*' For Bharadwaj (1988:234), although 'The Sindhis will continue to be an international trading community,' …[they] are recognized as a positive community whose future lies in recovering the land of their birth and supporting the country as they did in the battle of Hastinapur' (Bharadwaj, 1988:15). According to Anand, 'So a sort of a Zionist enterprise can start here with the lower-middle-class Sindhis settling here, and the rich Sindhis investing in the area' (1996:121, 196, 222-3).

In the actual context of the globalisation of the economy, Non-Resident Indians are invited to invest in India, and the Sindhis living abroad may particularly consider with sympathy the development of the Kandla port and of its Free Trade Zone.

Conclusion

During their forced or voluntary long migrations, Lohanas have subdivided depending on whether, among other factors, they adopted local particularisms or not. This, however, did not prevent some of them, the Kutchi Lohanas in particular, from preserving until today the consciousness of their common Sindhi roots.

In Sindh and in Kacch, Lohanas occupied similar socio-economic positions, and the most notable of them were employed in high administrative posts. In Sindh and in Kutch, up till now, Saraswat Brahmans have been their priests, and their main god has been Daryalal.

Kutchi Lohana ministers and their kinsmen suffered grave setbacks from which, it is said, they could hardly recover, whereas in Sindh their counterpart, the Amils, emerged as a higher status group. Thereafter, under the British who directly administered Sindh, these Amils again enhanced their socio-economic status whereas the Bhaibands, who were mostly issued from among the Lohanas, migrated as petty hawkers of Sindh-works to colonial metropolises of India and the British colonial empire where they started trading companies: today, these Bhaibands are recognized as the 'ancestors' or as the initiators of the Sindhi Diaspora. During the same time, many poor Lohanas from Kutch settled in the Karachi District, while others from Kutch as well as from Saurashtra migrated to continental India and Eastern Africa in order to find better opportunities.

As a matter of fact, Kutchi Lohanas and Sindhis have consciously started separate and diverging processes of identity reformulation after Independence. The Lohanas from Kutch–Saurashtra have built an international network of associations based on older caste relations and linkages, whereas the Sindhis, who avoid referring to or deny their caste subdivisions, tend to assert themselves as a distinct 'national' community and as a transnational mercantile Diaspora.

Reconstruction of a caste identity on one side, assertion of a new 'national identity' on the other; while not forgetting the limits of this work we may provisionally conclude that the divide between the Lohanas from Sindh and those from Kutch–Saurashtra can be attributed, among other reasons, to their incompatible processes of identity reformulation which they started implementing after the partition.

8

COLOUR AND LIGHT: THE TEXTILES OF SINDH BETWEEN SKY AND EARTH

Françoise Cousin

Abstract

This chapter reports data collected more than thirty years ago during fieldwork mainly devoted to cloth dyeing and printing in Sindh. The place of these textiles in the dress and the socio-economic background of the production are presented. Then, patterns and motifs are described and discussed through a comparison with clothes as they are decorated on the other side of the India–Pakistan border in Kutch and Rajasthan. In this way, the original stylistic features of Sindhi textiles, expressed mainly in the use of geometry and symmetry and in the range of shades, are brought to light.

* * * *

Among the crafts which are produced in Sindh, textiles provide, without doubt, a wide field of study, as a recent exhibition made evident (Askari and Crill, 1997). The historical background and the geographical position of this province of Pakistan link the crafts involved with other traditions, either in the east or in the west. The 20th century also brought changes and mutual influences between Pakistan and India, and more especially between Sindh and the Indian states of Gujarat and Rajasthan.

In 1973, I got the opportunity to carry out fieldwork in Sindh, in collaboration with the University of Sindh. Printing and dyeing were the chief topic of this study as they were performed in the main centres of Sindh (Cousin, 1976, 1981). In addition, embroidery, weaving, and techniques used for quilted textiles were studied. A first visit to the Karachi National Museum revealed the variety of patterns, colours, and the range of crafts practised. As soon as the precincts of Karachi were left behind, every person encountered was seen to be dressed in bright colours, and notably, women wore red veils. The landscape, colour of earth, and light create a sensitive link between both sides of the border, strengthened by the picture of their inhabitants. The comparison between costumes and textiles made and worn in Gujarat and Rajasthan, and in Sindh is very fruitful, since it throws light on the common features as well as specific technical processes and designs of these areas (**FIG. 1**). For this reason some comparative data is included in this study. A short description of the costumes for which these textiles are made and decorated, a survey of the conditions of textile production, and a description of motifs and technical data for tie and dye and printing are also given.

Apart from the people of Karachi, the main city of Sindh and the largest in the whole country, most of the inhabitants were engaged in agriculture or were living in a rural area at the time of my survey. Muslim menswear included a loose shirt worn outside wide trousers, which were narrow at the bottom. Both garments were usually made of the same cloth. A small cap, of a specific shape, brightly decorated with embroidery and with small mirrors sewn in, was also worn, sometime with a turban wrapped around it. But, from the point of view of the study, the most important part of this dress was a kerchief which can be placed on the head, as a turban, or thrown over the shoulders to be used in many ways. When printed with specific patterns in a specific way, described later in this chapter, this piece of cloth is known by the name of *ajrak*. Hindu men wore a shirt of the same cloth above the wrapped lower garment known as a *dhoti*, and a turban. In the case of both Hindu and Muslim men, a waistcoat might be added, as well as a coat or a woollen blanket during winter.

Women were also dressed in a shirt and trousers, whose shape was very similar to the men's garments. In addition, they covered their head with a veil called a *dupatta*, which they wound loosely around the neck. But another set of dress, found in Gujarat and Rajasthan, is frequently used in the eastern district. It includes a bareback bodice, a skirt, and a veil which is wider than the dupatta and is wrapped around the body in a different way. What is interesting to note is that the style of dress is not strictly related to the same religious affiliation all over the wide area, but varies more in relation to specific places: in particular the dress in the desert region of Tharparkar and in Kutch and western districts of Rajasthan presents very similar features, and looks different from the dress worn along the Indus.

The socio-economic situation of the family does not lead to a change in the shape of men's and women's daily dress; or if it does, it brings a total change in the form of westernised clothes. Beyond that, what is different is the quality of the textiles used. Garments can be made of silk or cotton, and be embellished with rich adornments. Worthy of mention among the locally produced dress materials is a striped cotton cloth, or a striped satin made of mixed cotton and silk called *mashru*, woven locally for women's trousers. On mill-made cotton, designs are printed and dyed by craftsmen in small workshops, and sometimes embroidered by women on a familial level, as a domestic craft. Most of these textiles are also available in Gujarat or in Rajasthan, with some variants.

As it has been observed all over the world, the work of craftsmen is strongly dependent on their ties with their customers, especially in the area of dress. For, through dress people express themselves and reflect their social situation, their religion, as well as their personal status. Dress distinguishes people according to whether they are Muslim or Hindu; engaged in agriculture, husbandry, craftsmanship; settled in the countryside or living in towns. Some specific patterns also provide information on personal status, especially of women. Married women and unmarried girls do not wear the same dress, nor even the same pattern. Colour combinations and pattern organization are strongly dependent on these social marks. These marks are known and are meaningful inside a large social group; and craftsmen, as a part of this group, can adapt their production to satisfy this demand as well as the desire for change. The same can be said of the domestic crafts, which are probably even more dependent on the social significance of a design, but also on the individual skill and creativity of the craftsmen.

When C.G.H. Fawcett published his monograph on dyeing in what was the Bombay Presidency at the time, craftsmen from Sindh were considered as the best in this part of the British Empire, as far as printing and dyeing were concerned. What was included in Sindh is nowadays shared between Pakistan and India, and the Partition in 1947 has deeply changed the socio-economic situation in textile production. During my visits to Rajasthan I could see Hindu printers from Pakistan starting new productions, and on the other hand, I could see in Pakistan Muslim printers who had come from the Indian side. In both cases, they were separated from the customers for whom they used to work, and they had to adapt themselves to a new situation and try to face an unknown demand. Some of those who, coming generally from UP had settled in Sindh, started to imitate patterns which were locally famous; but they could not reach the quality achieved by local printers. Others were running units on the basis of a completely new organization in the work, using screen-printing, new chemicals for the dyeing process, and so on. They were mainly involved in the production of bedsheets, and only to some extent, in material for skirts.

Printing and Dyeing: The Production

To make clearer what will follow, I will first describe the principle of printing and dyeing crafts in a few words. For printing, the technical steps may change according to the pattern and the colour combination, as we shall see later on, but the principle is the same and combines two different groups of operations: those related to printing and those related to dyeing. Printing means, in this context, the application either of a mordant, or of a resist, sometimes of both, on a white cloth. When a mordant is printed, the dye, once the cloth is put in contact with it, reacts with the mordant and only the printed portions are coloured. When a resist is printed, only the portions which are not protected by this resist are coloured during the dyeing process. In Sindh, mordant and resist are applied on the cloth with the help of small, carved wooden blocks. The pattern is produced by the carving on the block. Generally, a set of several blocks is needed to print one pattern in its different colours.

In tie-dyeing, the principle is to obtain a resist by tying a thread around some portions of a cloth which will protect them when dipped in the dye. The pattern will be different according to the way the thread is tied, the size of the protected places, and the number of colours required.

What are the locally printed and dyed cloths meant to be used for clothes? For men, the main production is *ajrak*, as already mentioned. It is the speciality of the printers living in the Indus valley (Cousin, 1976). Besides this typically Muslim menswear, another headwear is printed for Hindu males of Tharparkar, called *malir;* it is embroidered on its four corners and is worn at wedding ceremonies (**FIG. 2**). The same kind of design also decorates women's veils, and is known as *jimi*. Another print, called *kiriana*, is used for veils as well as a special kind of skirt. It is worn by women of the Khatri community, the community of printers themselves, for their marriages. The pattern is made of regular lines of geometrical designs, white and black on a red ground. And finally, different women's skirt materials are another important product of the Tharparkar printing centres near Umarkot.

As we can see, printing is done for both men's and women's wear. As far as tie and dye is concerned, it is confined to women's dress pieces, and comes in a very similar range of colours and patterns wherever it is produced.

Who are the craftsmen and how is their production organized?

We visited two regions: the lower Indus valley where, in several places around the town of Hyderabad, the dyers'/printers' families were working with them, and Tharparkar. The craftsmen are all Muslim Khatris, except at Umarkot where they are Hindu Khatris. I should add that we find the same situation on the other side of the border, where both Hindu and Muslim communities practise printing and dyeing, with some specialization in the production.

The size of the workshops could be very different. Let us mention for instance Matiari village, north of Hyderabad, where the bigger unit had six craftsmen, all belonging to the Muslim community of Khatri. In Tando Mohammed Khan, in the south of Hyderabad, units were bigger: thirty-five workers, among them twenty-five Khatri, and ten belonging to other communities. In Umarkot, around fifteen families were engaged in printing.

As a rule, only men do printing and dyeing. But it may happen that women help, for instance by crushing some of the raw materials. In Umarkot, however, women may do the printing work along with men, but never the dyeing. And, if the printing and the dyeing are always done by Khatris, generally of the same extended family, other tasks, like the washing of the cloth between two operations, can be the duty of workers belonging to other groups. So, we can tell that a craft is a specialized one by the gender of the workers and by the community they belong to. And finally, the workshop is organized following some hierarchy. We find the master, called *usto*, the craftsman proper, called *karigar* (literally one 'who makes'), and the apprentices, *chokro* (literally boy). Everyone generally works on one given piece of cloth from the beginning to the end. Even in big units where some printers realize a given kind of pattern, they do all the printing for this pattern. The master generally prepares the dye vats himself.

Most of the operations are done in workshops, which are near the habitations but set apart from them. They include covered places where printing is done and courtyards open to the sky where cloth is dried afterwards. Washing and hammering take place in and by the river or some canal. Women work at home. In Umarkot, where women do the printing, they work in the same place as the men of their family (**FIG. 3**).

For tie and dye, each of the two operations may be done by a different group. The tying is often done by women, whether they belong to the Khatri community or not. Sometimes men also do the tying. Afterwards, the dyeing is done by professional dyers, who are always men. I saw exactly the same situation in Kutch, where I returned in 1998, after a first visit nearly twenty-five years earlier.

But let us come to the textiles themselves.

Tie and Dye, as Expression of the Society

As far as tie and dye is concerned, the craft was not very alive in 1973, and it is doubtful if it is in a better state today. The situation is different in the western states of India where this craft has not really lost its importance and could face new markets, besides its traditional one.

The village of Ghulam Nabi Shah was the centre of this craft and the following data were collected there. As already mentioned, the technical principle is to protect some parts of a cloth from the dyeing by tying a thread around small portions of them. With this technical process, a specific pattern is realized on the cloth: some straight lines made of small spots making a frame inside which very stylised vegetal motifs take place. The same three colours are combined on the tied-dyed textiles for wear: black which is in fact a blackish blue, red which is a dark red, and white. The superposition of black and red gives a brownish shade. The operations can be detailed as following:

– First, lines to settle the motifs are drawn with a fugitive pink colour. To do this, wooden blocks are used, as well as strings which are dipped in the colour and pressed on the cloth to print the outlines. This process is called *sutarno*.
– The second step is tying, or *bhindi*: Cotton thread in two colours and two different thicknesses is used to carry on the following processes (**FIG. 4**). Lines with small spots which will leave small white spots when untied, are made with a white thread; for bigger lines which will leave bigger red spots, a thicker black thread is used. The skill of the craftsman is apparent. The thread is tied with the help of a tool called *bhogri*. It is a simple tube from which the thread comes through and can be made in very different materials,

ranging from ivory to plastic taken off a pen top.
- The next step is dyeing the cloth in indigo, *neer*, to achieve the blue shade. After that, the cloth is washed in water, and dried.
- The black thread for knots is removed before dyeing the cloth in the alizarine vat to obtain the red colour. This dyeing, called *bora*, is done by boiling the cloth in the dye, after dipping it in a mordant solution.
- Finally, the remaining knots are removed and the pattern, made of small white spots and bigger red ones, is ready.
- Sometimes, at the end, some portions are dyed yellow and green, only by padding these shades with fugitive colours on the cloth. This is known as *kinjo*.

Three parts of an attire, all made in tied and dyed cotton:

- a small rectangle, called *peti* (stomach), is used in the front part of the bodice worn by women belonging to the different communities living in the desert i.e. Rajar, Mangrio, Samma, Bhil, Mahar, Samejo, Ramdio, Machi, either Muslim or Hindus (**FIG. 5**). According to the groups the women belong to, the *peti* can start from the shoulders or from the breast, before covering the stomach. The central design, which can borrow two different patterns, is framed inside a wide composite border. Very often, the bodice is also embroidered.
- Veils, called *chundri* or *chunri* (in Sindhi), are embellished with a wide central pattern of stylised flowers, inside a frame very similar to the border of the bodice. Veils can be distinguished by the colour of their ground: *rati chunri* for a red-ground veil and *kakrechi chunri* for a black-ground veil. These veils are often embroidered, as are the bodices (**FIG. 6**).
- For cloth used for making skirts, called *paro*, ten yards of material is tied-dyed. There are three varieties of this, according to the colour of their ground: *rato paro* for a red-ground cloth, *kakrechi paro* for a black ground with a central red strip, and *karo udo* for a plain black ground.

We find very similar patterns on both sides of the border. In India, they are used by Hindu as well as Muslim women in the Barmer and Jaisalmer districts of Rajasthan, and specially in the Muslim community of shepherds, known as Sindhhi Sipai. In addition, a wide range of colours and motifs decorate women's veils and men's turbans, and they are used as a non-verbal means of communication to express social differentiation in different situations. Besides the technique described for Sindh, another one is specific to Rajasthan and is mainly used for decorating men's turbans: by rolling the cloth on the bias and tying the rope thus formed, diagonal lines are produced. When the work is done in both the directions, a pattern of two beds of intercrossing lines is obtained.

In Kutch and Gujarat, we find the same technique, but the craft has been developed in another way, often on silk and sometimes on wool, for veils (Cousin, 1975). Patterns are different: either geometrical or figurative and may include lotus flowers, peacocks, scorpions, elephants, and water carriers. The same motifs are nowadays used for saris and other fabrics. Generally, the different colours desired for a pattern are dyed from the lightest to the darkest and the tying is done accordingly. In Sindh, it is different as we have seen: the whole tying is done before the first dyeing, with different kinds of threads to distinguish them. And this first dyeing is the darkest one, in indigo. The shade obtained in such a way is one of the stylistic features of tie and dye in Sindh.

By making a comparison, we can point out some other technical specificities of Sindhi tie and dye and eventually their effect on the designs produced. First, the work is done on cotton cloth, generally of a very good quality. As a consequence, the dots stand out very clearly. A second point to be noted is that the cloth is not folded before tying, as is done very frequently in India. Nevertheless, designs are generally symmetrical, but do not form a radiant composition. And finally, the range of colours, red and blue-black for the ground and white for the drawing, is strongly settled in Sindh and on the border, but not confined to this area, as we can find it in the south-eastern part of Rajasthan as well.

Printing: Process and Designs
While tools and raw materials used in tie and dye are mainly limited to the dyeing process, it is different for printing, and especially for *ajrak* prints for which a very complicated process is employed. As we have seen, printed cloths are the result of two main operations: the printing on the cloth of a mordant or a resist, and the dyeing, either in the alizarine vat or in the indigo vat. In both cases, dyers are nowadays using synthetic dyes in place of the previous vegetable ones (indigo leaves for the blue and madder for the red and the black). According to the nature of the mordant, the colour taken by the cloth after the dyeing in the alizarine vat varies. If the mordant is aluminium sulphate the colour is red, if it is iron sulphate, the colour is black. The indigo bath is cold, and the alizarine one is boiling (**FIG. 7**). All the different kinds of printed textiles made in Sindh in 1973 were combinations of these two main operations, but were applied differently according to the colours and their place in the decorative composition.

Among them the most elaborate textiles are without doubt the *ajrak*, and it would be hardly possible to find such a complicated printing process in another place in the world. The specificity of the technique involved and its close relationship with the motifs it is used to produce make the *ajrak* textiles stand out as symbols of Sindhi culture (**FIG. 8**).

Before presenting them, let us say a few words about other prints. For skirt material, the two mordants are printed, then the cloth is dyed in the alizarine vat. Afterwards, a resist is printed before dipping the cloth in the indigo vat. Some other blocks may be used for adding additional colours like green or yellow to some portions. The Kiriana print with its white and black geometrical designs on a red ground is used, as we saw, on veils and skirts worn by Khatri women at the time of marriage. The first print is the one with the resist. It is followed by a second one, with an iron sulphate mixture, which produces the black. Finally a paste of aluminium sulphate and powdered seeds of the *amli* tree is applied on the whole surface of the cloth. Then the resist is carefully removed and the cloth is dyed in alizarine. After washing, the places without mordants remain white, lines drawn with the iron sulphate are black, and the ground which has been covered with aluminium sulphate is red. In the same way, mordants and resist printings are followed by dyeing for *malir* and *jimi* patterns. *Malir* has the same colour combination as *kiriana*, white and black motifs on a red ground, while *jimi* includes blue.

All *ajrak* is made on blue or red ground; square geometrical patterns for the central field serve for the borders rather than the motifs. The number of the borders around the central field serve to classify the cloth. The names of these motifs are evocative of nature or domestic life, but they are so stylised that the geometrical shape and the repetition produced by the printing are the real decorative principle. A comparison is frequently made with tiles and carved pillars in the mosques and graves of Thatta and shows at least some commonality in the inspiration (Bunting, 1980).

An attempt to give a simple description of the whole process used for one kind of *ajrak* is given below:

– The first step is the preparation of the cloth. The white mill-made cotton cloth, which is bought in big bulk is cut to the appropriate size. Each piece is half the width of a full *ajrak*. Then, the different pieces are washed in boiling water with soda ash. After this the cloth is soaped and oiled, at the same time or in two stages. These operations are made to remove chemicals, and specially starch from the mill cloth, to soften it, and to prepare it for good dyeing. The better these first operations are, the better will be the final result.
– The second step includes three different printings. During the first print, a mixture of *babul* gum and lime in water is applied on the cloth. The printing is done from left to right, starting with transversal borders, followed by the lengthwise border, then the central field. After they are dyed in the alizarine vat, these portions will remain white. Sometimes, a small quantity of alizarine is added to the mixture, which produces a very light red shade after dyeing.

  The second print is done with a solution of iron sulphate, thickened with gum or powdered seeds of the amli tree. This print will produce a black colour after dyeing in the alizarine vat.
  The third print is done with a mixture of clay, flour, gum, aluminium sulphate, and water, and sometimes some molasses is added. Rice waste or powdered cow dung is spread regularly with the help of a sieve to fix this mixture on the cloth. It acts as a resist to protect the cloth from the dyeing in indigo.

– The dyeing in indigo is the third step, and the first dyeing. It is done in cold water in a deep vat dug in the ground and cemented. The pieces of cloth are wrinkled before being dipped in the vat. Then they are dried, and washed in running water. This washing removes the resist, but not the first products applied to them, nor the aluminium sulphate.
– The fourth step is the dyeing in the alizarine vat. In the copper vat, water is boiled on the fire. When it is boiling, alizarine solution and berries of *sakun*, the tamarisk shrub, are added. The cloths are dipped in the dye and kept for about two hours, and regularly moved to obtain a good dye. From time to time, some dye product is added. The cloths are removed, cooled, then dipped in water mixed with fresh camel dung and left for 12 hours. The next day, the cloths are washed in water with soda ash, then in water with caustic soda, finally spread on the bank of the river or the canal and sprinkled with water several times.
– During the fifth step, the cloth is again printed with the same kind of resist, and dyed for a second time in the indigo vat, which gives it a second shade of blue, named after the blue shade of enamel, *mina*. This name is also used for all the shades which are used to brighten a cloth, and specially a pink fugitive colour which is given for the sale and disappears quickly, after washing.
– In the last step the *ajrak* is given its finish. It consists of different washings, then, when the cloth is dry, it is hammered to give it back its smoothness. As the preparation is important for good printing and dyeing, so the finishing helps the colours get their luminosity and the white its brightness.

As we can see, the process is a long one and several days are necessary to produce these cloths with their subtle combination of prints, their light and dark shades of red, two different blues, and black and white lines. A change in the order of the prints will bring a change in the colour combination. A set of several blocks is used for one design; their name is given according to the place, in the manufacture of the design, and of the colour they produce (**FIG. 9**).

A young Muslim woman in a village in Barmer district. Rajasthan, India, 1988 (© F. Cousin)

Detail of a *malir* worn by the Meghwal bridegroom during the marriage ceremonies. The two blocks for printing of round motives can be seen on the picture. The embroidered motives of peacocks and desert flowers symbolize fertility and prosperity. Thar Parkar, Sindh, Pakistan, 20th century. (© Musée du quai Branly, photo Dorine Destable)

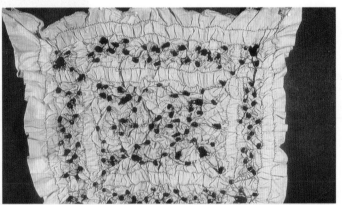

A piece of cloth for the front part of a bodice is ready for dyeing. Thar Parkar, Sindh, Pakistan, Gulab Nabi Shah, 20th century. (© Musée du quai Branly, photo Dorine Destable)

A printing woman in a workshop in Umarkot. Thar Parkar, Sindh, Pakistan, 1973 (© F. Cousin)

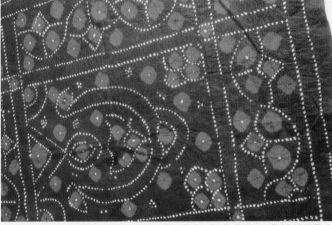

The front part of a bodice ready to be sewn. Thar Parkar, Sindh, Pakistan, Gulab Nabi Shah, 20th century. (© Musée du quai Branly, photo Dorine Destable)

Detail of a red ground veil adorned with embroidery. Pakistan, 20th century. (© Musée du quai Branly, photo Dorine Destable)

Dyeing in the alizarine vat in Matli village. Sindh, Pakistan, 1973 (© F. Cousin)

Detail of the border of an ajrak print. Sindh, Pakistan, 20th century. (© Musée du quai Branly, photo Dorine Destable)

A set of blocks used for printing material for skirts, Thar Parkar, Sindh, Pakistan, 20th century. (© Musée du quai Branly, photo Dorine Destable)

Two printing blocks for ajrak: on the left *badam* pattern, on the right *chalo sarkari* pattern. We can see the iron nails at the corner and in the middle of the sides, Sindh, Pakistan, 20th century. (© Musée du quai Branly, photo Dorine Destable)

But one more difficulty is faced because most of the cloths are printed on both faces. They are called *ajrak bi puri*. To succeed in getting the exact correspondence of the patterns, the blocks have short and thin iron nails at their corners and in the middle of each of their sides. When applied on the cloth, these nails make small hollows which are used as marks when the cloth is turned over to be printed on the other face (**FIG. 10**).

These blocks are the most important of all the tools that are used. But besides these sophisticated implements, very simple tools are also used: they can be simple straw wisps used to measure the appropriate place, or a piece of cloth or paper to mark out the angles in the print.

The whole process is carried out on half a full *ajrak*. To get a finished piece, the two halves, which have been printed one after the other on the same length of cotton, have to be sewn together. When completed, the general decorative composition can be described as follows: at the two ends, there is a border. Selvedge borders are limited by these ends. Inside, there is a rectangular field, surrounded or not by one or several frames. The number of borders and frames, as well as the different patterns generated by the carving of the blocks, serve to distinguish the different varieties of *ajrak* (Cousin, 1976).

Motifs of the central part, made with square blocks of 10 cm, form a network of horizontal, vertical and diagonal lines, produced by repeated printing by one set of blocks. The carving of these blocks is done in such a way that the join is hardly distinguishable and the role of the printing is to enclose each motif inside its own border and at the same time to set it free in an open construction.

We are confronting a very strong techno-aesthetical relationship between a kind of decorative research and the required equipment. The square-based organization, strengthened by the symmetry inside the motif itself, produces a subtle repetition through both the faces of the cloth. The adequacy of tools to such patterns may limit the emergence of new motifs. At least, it seems that the motifs are not different today from what they were twenty-five years ago (Bilgrami, 1990).

Conclusion

The Pakistani province of Sindh is located in a large region of textile production where technical data can be compared. In 1973, the demand from local customers was high enough to maintain an excellent quality of products which were specific in their designs, and to some extent, in their colours. Among them *ajrak* got a special place, and more than other textiles, it was used as a kind of symbol of cultural identity. In the Indian context, *ajrak* is performing the same role among Muslim communities in border districts. Not only printing and dyeing, but also weaving and embroidery from Sindh present common features with Indian production from Rajasthan and Gujarat. In the same way, variations in patterns, in colour combinations, when noticed, are significant and can help to understand the organization of the society and the meaning of its cultural choices.

Probably more than many other items of daily life, dress is an expression of culture and of social organization. It is why changes in clothes are meaningful, and with the modernization of production, the translation of a need in terms of dress can be expressed through new items.

More generally, craftsmen today, all over the world, face a challenge. The quality of craftsmanship pre-supposes a meeting between the offer and the demand, between know-how and appreciation of the skill. Most local customers turn to cheaper industrial products and even with changes in economic conditions of production, or in technical practies, patterns and colours, craftsmen are not always able to face, without assistance, a competitive situation where they can only lose, unless they are able to find new markets for their products. But this does not mean they will be able to maintain the high quality. We can see from the description of the processes involved, especially in printing, how long and difficult they are and how specialized the craftsmen have to be. No doubt customers from abroad cannot imagine when they see the finished cloth how the aesthetical project has been driven from step to final step. They may not be able to distinguish between a cloth that has been worked in the genuine, traditional way and another that is but an ersatz product. Will Sindhi printers and dyers get a chance to enter new markets, without losing their skill, which has given birth to a wonderful sharpness of motifs and brightness of colours?

9

BHOPA'S COSTUMES AND BODY TECHNICAL: THE SHY WOMEN AND THE PROUD MEN

Delphine Maucort

Abstract

This study is based on the first chapter of the PhD defended in the University of Paris X-Nanterre in 2003. The hypothesis is that clothes can be analysed as 'total social facts', to use Marcel Mauss's concept. Among the Bhopas babies go naked up to the sixth day, and no distinction is made between girls and boys until the naming ceremony under the protection of Mataji. Bhopas' clothes are used for resisting the climate and for safeguarding from natural dangers. Their social function is quite important. Of course, the first social role is to distinguish between the sexes: women have their own clothes, and men wear other clothes. Clothes are worn for appearance and also for covering the different parts of the body. In the social field, clothes are used to inform on the status of the wearer according to the rules of the Bhopa society. Finally, clothes show that men are more or less attracted by modernity, while women are the guardians of traditional values.

* * * *

In this chapter, clothes are considered as 'total social facts' (Mauss, 1950) and as artefacts; they are the outcome of different human choices, from the beginning of their conception through their useful life. We want to focus on social aspects which can be ascertained from the choice of raw material and in the different ways of dressing.

We will examine the general shape and aspect of the Bhopas' clothes as finished artefacts and underline the fact that they are worn in different social settings according to gender and social status. We will describe the composition of the costumes as they are worn every day or during rituals, and focus on their functional aspects which are always predominant in the Bhopa discourse. The women wear a woollen veil, first of all, to protect themselves from the morning cold, and men wear a red turban for protection from the sun. From these very pragmatic explanations, we will show the links between mental representations, obligations and prohibitions in the Bhopa community.

Who are the Bhopas?

The word 'Bhopa' literally means 'those of the speaking', and there are numerous men or women who are chosen by the mother goddess (*Mataji*) to be her voice. The Bhopas consider themselves to have this specificity and to be incorporated in the large Rabari nomadic group living between Sindh, Rajasthan and Gujarat.

The Rabaris' origins are a mystery but a few authors like Judy Frater (1975: 47, 1995: 34-38), Jyotindra Jain (1980: 47), and Flavio d'Orazi Flavoni (1990: 16) think they came from further West, perhaps from Arabia. They may have introduced the camel[1] in northwest India in about 500 BC, a time when a lot of migrations and mixing with locals began. They first stayed in the Sindh desert but between the 7th and 11th century, numerous Muslim raids pushed them into Rajasthan. Now, Rabaris are thought to have originated from Jaisalmer and Marwad—between the Arawalli Hills and Udaipur.

Judy Frater (1995: 187) said that in the 15th century, the Bhopas may have split with a Rabari group living in Kutch and called the Kutchi-Dhebaria. They might have migrated into the Dwarka area where they still live in tents or in mud houses. The Bhopas are conscious of their ancient sojourn in Kutch. They speak about old times in the desert and often compare their dresses with those of the Rabaris from Kutch.

In 1995, there were 40,000 Bhopas gathered in multi-caste villages (Frater, 1995: 188) where they were not only grazing camels but also sheep, buffaloes, or goats. Today, some have lands and cohabit with other farmers (Vagheers), Brahmins (Nagars), potters (Kumbhars) and low-caste groups (Vivars) or Muslim wage-earners (Bohras and Khojas).

Children's Costumes

Children upto the Age of Three: Undifferentiated Gender and Nudity

Children start to wear their proper clothes only on the sixth day of their birth called 'day of Chatti' (*Chatti no din*) when Bhopas worship and present the baby to *Chatti Mata*, goddess of the sixth day. Until that event, children are simply wrapped in the mother's clothes—like her woollen veil called *dhabri*—or in a simple square of embroidered textile called *rumal*, which has various general functions: dishcloth, place mat, wall adornment etc. After *Chatti no din,* Bhopas dress the baby in little sets bought in city shops. They may also dress the children in a coloured set of clothes, home sewn or 'ready made', consisting of baggy trousers (*chareno*) and a straight open, long-or-short sleeve shirt (*qamiz*).

It is apparent that gender is not inscribed on the baby's costume. Gender is still indefinite at birth and the baby has no social status. When a child is born, it is not yet a person and is first identified through its biological mother. If children die, they are wrapped in a yellow cloth and buried in a secret place in the jungle. It is the same process that is followed for the umbilical cord. The first social status that children receive disregards their gender but is built on their linkage to the goddess. They are related to *Chatti Mata* who represents the Mother (*Mataji*), the procreative and protective divinity.

Both at home and in the village, babies regularly stay half-naked until they become 'clean' and do not wear any swaddling cloth or nappy. Undergarments are rarely part of the children's apparel. The mother prefers the lack of clothing as it enables her to detect when the children have become 'dirty' and also reduces the amount of washing she needs to do. The children are permitted to stay entirely naked inside the house or just in the doorway.

This very functional explanation also shows the women's desire to get rid of their babies' body impurities as soon as possible. Even if the Bhopas don't speak about 'Manu's laws' (*Manavadharma-shastra*) we can focus on the fact that, in the Hindu context, the twelve body impurities, including urine and excrements, need to be eliminated quickly (V, 135 and IV, 45-52). It could be considered that Bhopa children do not wear a swaddling cloth or nappies so as not to be considered 'impure'.[2]

In Western conceptions, nudity often corresponds to what is considered 'wild' or 'a natural condition' (Descola, in Bonte and Izard, 1991: 651-652). By analogy, we associate 'naked' or 'undressed' people with 'primitives', meaning people without any rules. Colonial administrations seem to have knowingly preserved this image of the people it was ruling, and in India, photographers were still taking photos of 'naked' people after they had been 'dressed' by missionaries (Tarlo, 1996: introduction).

In this study, nudity appears very limited because each worn artefact, scarification, tattoo, or body painting is included in costume definition. From the sixth day after birth the babies wear protective strands and after the bath the mother circles the children's eyes with a black and oily powder composed of zinc oxide called *peteli*. This powder marks a point in the children's forehead that makes them imperfect, protecting them from evil spirits. The mark on the children is to preserve them from the dangers of daily life and this protective function is comparable to those of each element of the children's costume.

Moreover, if we associate the Bhopa children's nudity with a kind of 'natural condition', we can easily make the following objections. First, the babies are wrapped in textiles and the children who start to walk stay without clothes only when they are in their parent's house or in those of their mother's parents or their father's parents, or in extreme proximity to them. Second, wearing no nappy allows the children freedom of movement but sometimes their mothers can also restrain them by tying a muslin veil—called *sal* or *patolu*—round their waist and to the foot of the cradle. What is important for their mothers is that the babies learn as soon as possible the postures to be observed in society and particularly how to sit with their legs always folded under them.

So, the children develop along a strict line defined by society and constantly watched by the mothers who take over their education entirely. Even their simplest movements are guided by social consensus and 'nudity' does not involve more freedom.

Little Girls

When they ask for it, little girls, between three and eight years old, start to wear the costume that corresponds, like those of their elders, to the half-sari type.

This modern, half-English and half-Hindi term, has been introduced by Moti Chandra (Chaturvedi, n.d.: 68) and designates a costume derived from those of the Mughal princesses settled in northern India from the 16th century. This Muslim costume adopted by the Hindu women with the Muslim seclusion (*purdah*) and body covering practices, can be different in the large variety of Indian states and communities. We can find it everywhere in northern rural India and its three components—the top, the skirt, and the veil—can be more or less large and covering.

Little girls wear a straight and closed skirt called *chuniyo* or *ghaghro*. Tight on the waist with a sliding belt, it is pleated low with a few centimetres fluttering (*jhalar*) at the ankles. At the top, they wear a straight, open and more or less long-sleeved shirt called *polko* (**PL. 2A**).

Sometimes, this shirt can be replaced by a little short top called *bherelu kapru*. Cut and adjusted to the chest, it is embroidered on each side and tied with a little strand at the back which is left uncovered.

When they wear this top, the little girls add to their costume a little woollen, cotton, or occasionally polyester veil, respectively called *doriyo* or *patelo* (50-80 x 200 cm). The veil rests unfolded on the top of the head with the two flaps loose on the back (**PL. 2B**) or with a flap wrapped around a shoulder during the winter days (**PL. 5A**).

Generally plaited at the back or worn in bunches with ribbons, a little girl's hair is never cut. The Bhopas think that young girls have to be married with the hair they were born with (*janam muvara*), and as opposed to boys, there is no tonsure ceremony for little girls.

Catherine Weinberger-Thomas says that in all Hindu communities, the birth hair in a girl is as significant as virginity. Even if said to be impure, the young girls keep their birth hair to make sure that marriage will bear more 'fruits' (*phala*) (Weinberger-Thomas, 1996: 141 and 245-246). So hair becomes a sexual, impure, and fecund object at the same time. That is why it will be strictly tied when the young girls become older.

Little Boys

Baby boys wear, for the first time, a costume similar to that of the elders at the first springtime festival (*Holi*) following their birth. That day, their costume called *uhago* is composed of white baggy pants narrowed from the knees to the ankles and a cut, short tunic crossed and folded on the torso to the left. Generally, on this tunic and on the bottom of the pants, women embroider or sew different coloured designs or borders. The little boys may wear a bonnet (*topi*) or a turban (*rumal*) tied on one side (**PL. 3A**).

After *Holi*, the children wear their pants again, notably a pair of tied trousers (*pantalun*) and an open, straight, long-or short-sleeved shirt (*qamiz* or *buscot*) or a sweater for winter (**PL. 2B**). They can also wear a pair of white trousers (*chareno*) matched with a coloured shirt (*qamiz* or *buscot*), but only after the first tonsure ceremony. Literally, the little boys' 'uncut hair' (*bala muvara*) ritual takes place when children are between one and three years old, giving them permission to have a name and to really join the community. Before that, their hair is never cut and is tied up with elastic like a girl's.

Boys and girls slowly begin to look different when they start growing up and wear a costume like that of their elders. Nevertheless, wearing clothes earlier than the girls allows boys to join the Bhopa community sooner. At the springtime festival (*Holi*) and at the first tonsure ritual (*bala muvara*), they are given the 'member of the community' status, which is withheld from the little girls for the time being. Girls will grow up and earn their own social status with the first signs of femininity and fecundity.

Women's Costumes

During puberty, young girls wear a tubular skirt covering the body from the waist to the ankles until they become women, mothers, or grandmothers. Called *pachedo* or *pachedi*, this skirt has different names because its designs can vary, but it always has the same cut and shape.

With this skirt, a young girl or woman does not wear the embroidered top (*kapru*) any longer, but one with the same shape, pleated at the breast level. This top is clinging, and women can easily put a handkerchief (*rumal*) or a few coins in the sleeves without fear of losing them.

Nevertheless, a few women prefer to sew a little inside pocket at the breast level. Others use the *kapru* tie-back strand to hook the house keys (*chabi*) or the chest (*kobat*) keys.

Young girls and women wear a woollen veil folded in two and hanging at the back of the head. Called *dhabri*, it is larger than the little girls' veil (90-130 x 250-300 cm) and can be changed for other lighter fabrics such as cotton or polyester, called *sal* or *patolu*. Knickers (*nikels*, *kahchho*, or *jhangio*), like sandals (*slippers*) or shoes (*mojri*), are more often worn in cities than in the rural areas.

How the Feminine Skirt is worn

Most of the time, the tubular feminine skirt—*pachedo* or *pachedi*—is pleated on the belly with the help of a sliding waistband. It is a twisted woollen strand 50-60 cm long (*nare*) presenting a running knot (*arkayo*) at one tip and a woollen pompom (*phumko*) on the other. This pompom is literally called 'flower' and is linked to women's fertility.

After the skirt is slipped on it is firmly tightened at the waist with a sharp tug. Like this, it is laid flat on the buttocks and the strand will extend the textile to gird all around the waist. It is fixed on the right side with a little coin or a stone placed under the skirt fabric. This creates a relief permitting the running knot to be fixed. Tightened on the belly, the strand is then fixed on the opposite side. The knot is made by simply rolling the tip of the strand around a piece of fabric. When the waist is fixed, the women make pleats (*patli*) between their fingers with the flap of their skirt which is inserted little by little in the waist. They start from one hip to the other patting their hand on the fabric to flatten the pleats at the same time. To finish properly, after fitting and narrowing the skirt, they fix the strand inside with a piece of fabric (PL. 3c).

There is a less formal way of wrapping the feminine skirt which is used when the women are in their own village and are busy. Sometimes, the young girls or the women do not have the time to wrap or pleat their skirt properly. So they wrap it carelessly, simply crossing it on the belly without any waistband (PL. 3b).

We have to point out the fact that the skirt must always be pulled up from below and not pulled down over the head because the jewellery worn around the neck is linked to the dead and to the divinities. Actually, women adorn themselves with pendants and necklaces linked to entities that impose upon them some duties and limitations. Ann Grodzins Gold says that 'you must always step into your skirt (instead of pulling it on over the head), for the proximity of a woman's skirt would be offensive to the deity' worn on the neck (Grodzins Gold, 1988: 71). So, there are what we could call different types of wearing techniques dictated by representations and not only by purely material or functional considerations.

The Different Veil Wrappings

There is only one formal type of veil wrapping used when leaving the village community and on religious or social ceremonial days. The young girls and women wear the veil pleated in two lengthwise, and placed evenly on the top of the head. It hangs freely on the back which is left bare by the fitted top (PL. 3a).

In addition, there are various ways of wearing the veil depending on social and climatic factors. When it is cold, young girls and women wrap their veil like the little girls do throwing the right woollen veil flap on the left shoulder (PL. 4a). When they crouch, while cooking or working in the fields, they bring back the two veil flaps on the thighs and leave their back naked (PL. 4b). Lastly, when they meet specific relatives, married women use their veil to hide their faces. They do this out of a kind of respect that Bhopas call *laj* or *ghumghat*, meaning 'modesty', 'honour' and corresponding to a partial (PL. 4c-a) or complete (PL. 4c-b) body covering.

This 'modesty' is coupled with a few types of avoidance relationships current in Gujarat, which are, however, starting to disappear little by little.[3]

In the Bhopa community, the spouse never pronounces her husband's name and calls him by a periphrasis ('my son's father'—*maru dikro no abo*). On their side, husbands avoid calling their wives by their names to show them respect and affection. In public, married couples keep their distance (never sitting together, never touching each other), and more generally, men and women live separately in symbolic terms while sharing the same space (men eat first—even during big festivals. Men never speak to women who are not from the same consanguinity).

Young married girls must observe 'modesty' (*laj*) in front of all their parents-in-law. During the marriage ceremony, they completely disappear under two superimposed veils (the *sari* and the *dhabri*). They arrive at their in-laws' entirely veiled; then they unveil themselves, and 'show their face' (*moh dekh lo*), only when they are settled inside their new house. Their husband has to be the first to see them and to be seen by them, even if other female and male family members are present. When her face has been shown to the in-laws, the villagers can come to see the young bride. Even then, the brides have to keep their veil on their head and stay still, eyes looking down and without speaking to anyone. During the two or three days just after marriage when they stay in the husband's village, the young married girls must respect this 'modesty' (*laj*) and it is the same thing each time they return to their in-laws during the first year of marriage. The practice is relaxed little by little when they are staying permanently at their husband's place, except in the presence of the husband's father (*abo*), husband's paternal uncle (*kaka*), and husband's elder brother (*jet*).

So, to serve meals on big festival days, women veil themselves, thus carrying on their duties without neglecting their obligation of observing 'modesty'.

To hide their face for casual encounters, they use a pleat of the veil worn conventionally. If they do not see or recognize the passerby, someone informs them that they are about to encounter a parent-in-law, saying 'Your *laj* is coming' (*tumharo laj ave che*). Here, the word *laj* designates at the same time the practice and the person to whom this practice is addressed.

Generally, we find two designations for the practice of hiding the face in order to cry in public without being seen. It depends on the circumstances, usually very ritualised, when the young girls or the women veil themselves. There are circumstances considered auspicious which could be the departure of the new bride to her in-laws. This type of veiling is called *ghumto*, conveying the idea that the person looks like 'something which swells'. She is 'blown up by tears' assisting the departure of a sister or a friend.

The inauspicious occasions to cry under the veil are reduced to the decease of a relative, a villager, or a family member. At this moment, the women have their 'hidden face' (*moh dakiyo*) in order to disappear with their sadness.

Veils used as daily wear can be fixed with the help of a low bun (*ambulo*) to prevent them from slipping. The bun is made by knotting the hair, always very long, and sometimes maintained by a simple or pearled hairnet called *vinil*.

Hair Under the Veil

The young girls' or women's veils hide their long hair, and their back is left bare by the top called *kapru*. Here we have to focus on the fact that according to the Bhopas and other Hindu communities, hair and sexuality have always been considered inter-related. Little by little, the growing girls learn to make their bun, and when they become pubescent, they have to control the technique. Their hair always has to be properly smoothed down, scraped back, and knotted.

Undone only in intimacy, hair was previously shaved for widowhood, signifying the end of sexuality and the end of procreation. Even if the practice has totally disappeared in the Bhopa

Plate 1: Little girls' costumes

1a: A long-sleeved small top (*polko*) and a straight skirt (*chuniyo or ghaghro*).

1b: Apparel similar to that of the elders: *half sari* composed of a skirt (*chuniyo or ghaghro*), a little cut top (*kapru*), and a veil (*doriyo or patelo*).

Plate 2: Little boys' costumes

2a: An *uhago* worn at the first springtime festival day (Holi) following their birth.

2b: Shirt and pants.

Plate 3: Women's costumes

3a: A cut top (*kapru*), tubular skirt (*pachedo or pachedi*), and woollen veil (*dhabri*).

3b and 3c: Different types of skirts and how they are worn.

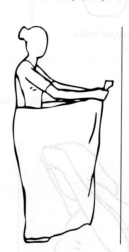
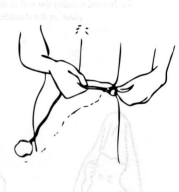

3b: non-formal

3c-a: formal wrapping

3c-b

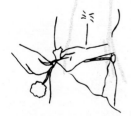

3c-c

3c-d

3c-e

3c-f

Plate 4: The different ways of wrapping the feminine veil

Front   Back

4a: In cold weather the veil is wrapped with a
pleat on the shoulder.

4b: When cooking the back is uncovered.

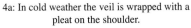

4c Different *laj*.

4c-a The face is hidden when serving a meal.

4c-b Fully covered— the invisible body during
the marriage ceremony.

Plate 5: Masculine costumes

Front Back

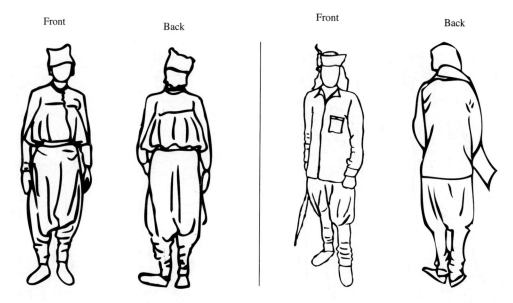

Front Back

5a: Costume with bonnet (*topi*), blouse (*angeli*),
and pant (*chareno*).

5b: Costume with turban (*rumal*), long-sleeved shirt (*qamiz*),
pant (*chareno*), and a shepherd's staff (*lakeda*).

Front Back

5c: A bridegroom's long tunic (*angeli*), turban
(*rumal*), and ceremonial cloth (*chiri*).

5c-b With *chiri* around waist.

Plate 6: Masculine *pachedi* wrapping (A)

Bhet style

6a

6b

6c

6d

6e

Front   Back

Plate 7: Masculine *pachedi* wrapping (B)

Potiyu

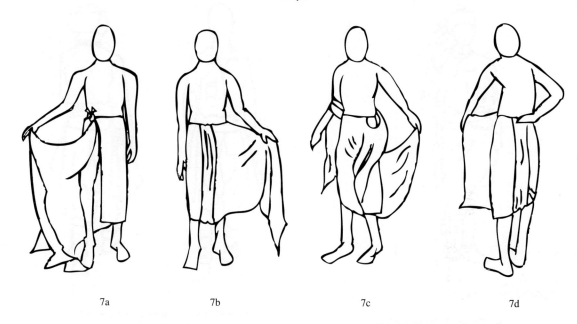

7a   7b   7c   7d

Front   Back

Plate 8: Other *pachedi* types of wrapping

8a: Simply tied on the hip.

8b: Rolled and tied around the waist with two flaps hanging.

8c: Slung over naked shoulders.

community for whom remarriage is possible, young girls or women's hair is always hidden from a man.

To sum up, on a daily basis young girls and women stay entirely covered with the help of their long tubular skirt and their covering veil. In certain circumstances, notably for the *laj* practice, they can totally disappear under the large veil. These circumstances increase as the young girls become wives and cope with new duties and new obligations. So, it is evident that marriage, in accordance with Hindu classical laws, represents the real entrance of the woman into the Bhopa community.[4]

Men's Costumes

The Bhopa costume for men corresponds to the Rajasthani and Gujarati costume. It looks like the set introduced by the Muslim Mughals, which comprises *angarkhi* or the top garment and the *paijama* as the trousers or lower garment (Goswami, 1993).

It is only with the first external signs of puberty, when they begin to sprout a moustache (*mooch*), that the boys give up their shirt and regularly tie their turban like the elders.

They then wear pants (*chareno*) which are larger on the thighs than those of the children, much narrowed on the knees and pleated down to the ankles. With the pants goes a short open and left-crossed blouse (*angeli*) covering entirely the chest, the shoulders, and the arms, with long pleated sleeves and large pleats around the belly (**PL. 5A**). Sometimes a simple white shirt (*qamiz*) (**PL. 5B**) is worn instead of the *angeli*.

The *bandi* worn under the blouse is a narrow, round-collared and sleeveless little top. It is often replaced by a ready-made T-shirt of the same shape.

Sometimes, this costume is completed with a rectangular wrapped cloth called *pachedi*, and in winter days, with a sweater or with a thick woollen veil called *dhabro*.

Some men also wear around the waist a leather or rope sling (*gofan*) which is used to bring back the cattle. It is often replaced by a simple leather belt (*patto*).

Worn daily till fifteen years ago, the Bhopa men's costume is now often abandoned for Western clothes (pants) corresponding to the young boys' 'modern' costume that they do not want to change for the 'old-fashioned' one.

The big leather shoes called *mojri* used in the fields are also forsaken for finer ones. Made of rubber or leather, they are stylised in the Western fashion.

With this new costume, men abandon their specific Gallic moustache for a finer and shorter one, deliberately opposed to the Muslim beard. The hair is often uncombed, and with the moustache, is linked to masculine sexuality. In fact, thick hair is associated with Krishna, the referential Bhopa deity, while Krishna himself is associated with seduction and sexuality and is said to be the One 'with beautiful hair' (Keshava). He seduces numerous cowherds and his love games are famous everywhere in India.

Like the little boys, the bridegrooms wear a costume called *uhago* during the marriage ceremony (*shadi*) and during the first following springtime festival. It is different from the daily costume because of its long tunic called *angeli* and its red cloth called *chiri,* tied on the waist (**PL. 5C-B**) or on the lower back with the two flaps on the shoulders (**PL. 5C**).

With that, bridegrooms wear a *lungi* which is different from the garment of the same name worn all over India. The Indian *lungi* is made of cotton and is worn as a low, Muslim wrap. The Bhopas' lungi is a fine woollen cloth wrapped on the shoulders, under the top tunic.

This wedding costume for men is composed of garments that focus on the importance of the ceremony for the male Bhopa. It signifies the moment when young boys become householders. Everything is organised for them to attain their new status smoothly and with honour. This is true for the wedding itself and also for the following springtime festival day confirming the already contracted alliance.

How to Wrap the *pachedi*

There are two ways of wearing the men's lower wrapping which is a rectangular fabric (about 120 x 300 cm), more often worn over the pants (*chareno*).

When it is wrapped over the pants, it is worn in the *bheth* manner, meaning straight, taken widthwise, rolled and crossed in front on the waist, unfolded but with an internal flap rolled and placed all around the waist. One *pachedi* 'border' (*chedo*) is inserted at one hip in the waist of the pants. The fabric is unfolded and first placed on the belly then the back. The flap is then gathered widthwise, adjusted on the waist at the hip level and carefully twisted. The cloth is taken around the waist and inserted at the hip level (**Pl. 7**).

Worn without pants, this flap is brought back to front between the legs and looks like a pair of trousers from the back and a straight skirt from the front. Called *potiyu* in the Bhopa community. but also *kachcha* or *sakachcha* all over India, this wrapping is generally worn by the field workers or by officiating Brahmins (**Pl. 7**).

These two styles of wearing the *pachedi* correspond respectively to the 'skirt-wrapping' (even if Bhopas add underpants) and to the 'knee breeches-wrapping' described by Anne-Marie Loth (Loth, 1979: 10). So, for Bhopa men the *pachedi* corresponds to the Indian *dhoti* more often worn in the South. Its Muslim version called *lungi* is different because of its geometrical designs. Bhopas believe they do not have another type of wrapping for their lower body.

Nevertheless, less formally, *pachedi* can be pleated in two on the bias before being worn over the pants and tied on the left side (**Pl. 8A**).

Some men wear it rolled on the waist with the decorative borders left hanging outside at each hip. These flaps can disappear when the wrapping is just tied like a large waistband (**Pl. 8B**).

In the evening, men wear a *pachedi* tied on the waist in the *bheth* style but without pants. They stay stripped to the waist when it is very hot but generally wear a towel or cloth—the *rumal* or the *pachedi*—on the shoulders. They can put it on the two shoulders or just on one, lengthwise or pleated in two (**Pl. 8C**). It is a useful type of wrapping, even when they keep the shirt (*qamiz*) on or the short tunic (*angeli*). It permits having at hand a multifunction cloth for mopping one's brow, wrapping stuff they need to carry, using as a pillow for sleeping, or driving away mosquitoes and flies.

Known for its flowing and airy style adjusted for the very hot season (Chatterjee, 1978), the Indian men's wrapping is also, in the Bhopa community, a useful cloth with many functions (floor cloth, towel, pillow, shawl or a spread for eating) and seems not to be linked with questions of purity.

How to Wrap the Turban

The turban (*rumal* or *pageli*) is a square or rectangular piece of fabric (about 100 x 100-900 x 150 cm) wrapped on the head in different styles. We distinguished three types according to the way the cloth was prepared and the surface it covered before it was tied:

1. The 'topee' style covers all the hair and is made with a turban entirely twisted or pleated (**Pl. 9** et **10**).
2. The 'skullcap' or 'headband' style does not cover all the hair and is made with a turban pleated like a long band (**Pl. 11**).

3. The 'long' style covers all the hair with a flap hanging and hiding the nape of the neck. Before it is wrapped, the turban is pleated once on the bias and is placed on the head almost entirely unfolded. Depending on the size of the cloth, this type of wrapping seems different sometimes, but only to the extent of the changing length of the hanging flaps (**PL. 12**).

Men can also wear the turban casually on the shoulders and some do not apply themselves at all, their wrapping appearing like a new variation of the formal one.

Some men wear a woollen bonnet (*topi*) instead of their turban or wrap their turban over the topi, permitting the turban to stay in shape even when it is not worn.

During the day, the turban is used like a casual bag to carry lunch when going to the fields. It is tied to the end of the cowherd stick (*lakedo*) and carried on the shoulder.

Sometimes, little boys play together and transform their turban into a dangerous combative game (*putho*). They do this by twisting the fabric as tightly as possible and holding it folded in two.

Woollen Shawl Wrappings

A *dhabro* is a thick, rectangular woollen fabric (about 120 x 250 cm), worn only in the winter season. It is specially worn during religious and social festivities but is often substituted by a simple sweater. Men can use it lengthwise, placing it on the back and crossing it on the chest with the right flap going over the left shoulder (**PL. 13A** and **13B**). Or, they can place the *dhabro* on the chest with the two flaps wrapping the shoulders, and maintained at the back and fit to the body with the arms (**PL. 13C**).

A *lungi* is a fine woollen fabric (about 120 x 250 cm) worn on the wedding day by the bridegroom. Simply placed on the shoulders, it is adjusted so as to maintain the two hanging flaps at the same level (**PL. 13D**).

When bridegrooms stay in the reception house (*sano*), out of sight of the in-laws, the *lungi* is also worn as a casually wrapped turban. The flaps are simply placed over the head and hang at the back.

According to the general shape of Bhopa costumes, we can clearly distinguish two ways of thinking about the body, depending on the gender. Women's costumes are fitted at the chest and large at the belly in order to emphasize their rounded forms. They accentuate the fullness of the breast and the belly with puffed pleats, focusing on the procreative function of women, who are, in fact, recognised through their maternity.

On the other hand, men's wear is fitted, except around the belly and thighs. Narrowed and pleated at the arms and legs, the costume focuses on the vertical and long male stature.

This visual opposition between Bhopa men and women can be seen at the technical level and in social or religious representations. Not only is gender marked by costume, but also by the way the differences between men and women are perceived.

Costumes and How to Present Oneself in Society

Usually, the large and pleated shape of Bhopa costumes allows the wearer to sit easily in the Indian style. Actually, for the numerous activities in the fields, manual labour, or housework, Indians constantly crouch or sit cross-legged. In the Bhopa community, costumes always allow freedom in these positions called 'sit correctly' (*siddho baith*). In certain circumstances, these postures can also be helpful in relieving pain in tired legs.

From their childhood, Bhopas are used to crouching with the knees high up, thighs coming up to the chest, and heels and buttocks on the ground. Large men's pants and women's skirts allow this position without constraint. Women can easily cook sitting in this position on a short-legged wooded board about 50 cm wide or on a thick piece of wood called *patelo* (**PL. 14c**).

Alternatively, everybody can adopt the cross-legged sitting posture with legs wide open and knees on the ground (**PL. 14a**). When the strain is felt on the thigh, one knee is put up (**PL. 14b**). When the position becomes too painful, men wrap their turban, or their lower wrapping, around their waist and their knees. The cloth holds up the knees and relieves the strain on the aching muscles. The women stretch their skirt on their knees with the same objective (**PL. 14d**).

These seated positions avoid stretching the legs which is considered poor manners in the Bhopa community. This is particularly true when facing an elder or having lunch.

Having lunch is regarded as a vulnerable moment for the people because they can be easily struck down by impurity while eating. On a daily basis, men have lunch isolated in the principal room (*ghar*), seated cross-legged, without looking up from their plate (*tansali*) and wearing at least two garments. When they have taken a bath and do not have time to dress they need to put on a second cloth. With their lower wrapping tied in the straight style (*bheth*), they add a second wrap—the *pachedi* or towel—on a shoulder. Even if Bhopas never speak about it, the ethnographer is reminded of *Manu's Laws* which say that a householder 'mustn't take his food with only one cloth...' (IV, 45).

Women's style is less ritualised but they always have to eat after their husbands. They sit in the kitchen, and like him, eat their lunch with the right hand, while the left hand stays on the folded legs.

During big communal lunches, men and women have food separately but sit crouching in a line outside the house. So, there is a distinction between seating styles during individual lunches and during communal lunches. Being in a group means a special need for organised space, which is met by eating outside and sitting together as close as possible, knees sticking to one's neighbour's. At the same time, it creates a standard which, if not respected, arouses criticism. People who do not sit properly will be considered disrespectful.

Another mark of respect is made when Bhopas receive special guests (*mehman*). They seat them on a blanket (*darki*) or a rope bed (*macho*). This seems to contradict the practice in daily life, when people are always near the soil (*sau*); they often sleep on it, have lunch on it, and work on it. They worship it as a goddess (Bhumi) and those who 'adorn the goddess' give her homage regularly as Earth-World (Gau) and as the female element which is the source of life and nourishment.

At the other end is the cliché of the Hindu woman—respected because of these qualities—who has to keep behind her husband who she must serve as though he were a king (Chambard, 1989), or a god (Leslie, 1991: 199). Working hard for the house and the family, she must nevertheless remain shy and retiring. In the Bhopa community, this attitude is obviously seen to go with 'modesty' (*laj*) which requires covering the face and sometimes the whole body.

Nevertheless, in the townspeople's eyes, Bhopa women have a strong and proud character, which tarnishes their image. This is due to their confident walk and haughty attitude. Constantly with heavy loads on the head and with a veil that slips at each abrupt movement, Bhopa women appear fierce and haughty in the townspeople's eyes. This image is at odds with the obligation to be modest and retiring required of every Hindu woman.

At the same time, Bhopa women's taste for joking and chewing tobacco gives them a masculine image. In India, these habits are often reserved for men to whom almost every pleasure is permitted in society.

Bhopa men have the image of the millet alcohol (*daru*) drinker. This drink is produced on a small scale in the villages, and the townspeople suspect Bhopas of drinking a lot of it because of their wild look. The townspeople also suspect them of being engaged in nasty businesses, and this impression, coupled with that of the haughty women, is in line with the image of a 'tribal' or 'backward' class.[5]

Actually, in India, everyone has to take care of their appearance in order to conform to their social and familial status. We can say that, like in Hindu texts, everything seems to have a costume in accordance with the language, the thinking, the age, the activities, the fortune, the knowledge and the family of the wearer (*Manavadharma-shastra*, 1996: IV, 18). The higher we are in the hierarchy, the stricter are the rules, everyone wanting to attain the householder ideal painted in law texts.

Everything is between being and appearing. The appearance and attitude of someone proclaims his character as being irremediably good or bad. With the adjective *tauko*, Bhopas designate something or someone as being 'right', 'excellent', 'pleasant', 'good', or 'virtuous'. We could say that people who conform to the norm are recognized as beautiful. This beauty, which does not accord with physical character but with general attitude in society, is also associated with kindness. Beauty is linked to morality and people who are of a pleasing appearance are considered beautiful and good. We can see that improving the social status plays a role at this level. Bhopas are more or less conscious of this and want to play the game.

* * * *

Bhopa costumes offer protection against climatic hazards and natural dangers. Woollen veils and shawls are very useful in winter to people who live in the jungle or in the field most of the time.

Daily movements are free and a lot of clothes are multiple-purpose. The male garment called *pachedi* is used as a lower wrapping, over the pants, as a shawl, a sheet, or a bag. The veil, called *dhabri* or *sal,* is also used by women as a blanket, a kitchen cloth, or a baby accessory.

This versatility of a garment is also in keeping with social demands and values. For men, clothes have to cover the shoulders but the chest and calves can be seen bare without shocking anyone. For women, their costume seeks to cover them almost entirely: their long skirt and large veil never allows the naked skin—itself covered with tattoos—to show.

So men and women are distinguished by the shape of their respective costumes, the extent to which the costume covers the body and also by the consistency of its use. Men use more pieces in winter or more occidental elements while women always wear the same costume without addition or subtraction (they can pile up two old veils but they rarely possess more than one because veils are expensive), especially because women must show a certain consistency in their appearance.

The same goes for tattoos, which are indelible anyway and for jewels, which are never taken off. In fact, like the daughters-in-law of Bahadur Shah for whom it would be akin to going out naked if they did not wear jewellery (Seth, 1993: 677), Bhopa women would be indecent if they did not wear some. By analogy, women seem to present themselves as the guardians of morality who strive to push the community higher up in Hindu society.

As Marcel Mauss said, we have to observe social facts, resulting from choices concerning all social levels, in relation with all social matters and we have to understand them from their social use.

In this chapter, we have tried to show how, with woollen masculine scarves and woollen feminine veils wrapped around them in winter or masculine cotton turbans and feminine veils protecting them from the sun, Bhopa costumes offer a protection against climatic risks and natural dangers. They allow freedom of movement and have different uses, which are according to Bhopa social demands and values. The men's costume has to cover the shoulders but the chest and calf can be left bare. Women's costume must cover almost all the body with a long skirt and a large veil, hiding the skin covered with tattoos.

Moreover, Bhopa costumes point at differences between men and women, marking how the little baby boy is more quickly accepted in the community than the baby girl. They also point at differences between social circumstances, between childhood, puberty, adulthood, and old age.

So Bhopa costumes are related to gender, to religion and religious rituals, to seduction, fecundity, and morality. They are a material, but also mental phenomenon. They are entirely concrete or 'global social facts'.

Plate 9: Turban wrappings (A)

'Topee' style with twisted turban

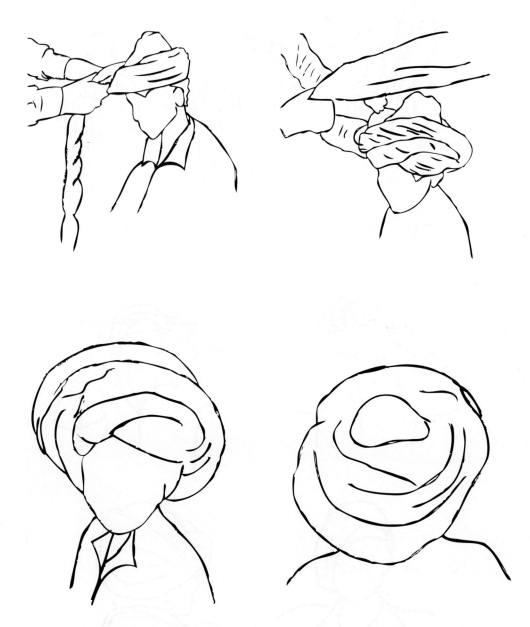

Front   Back

Plate 10: Turban wrappings (B)

'Skullcap' style with pleated turban

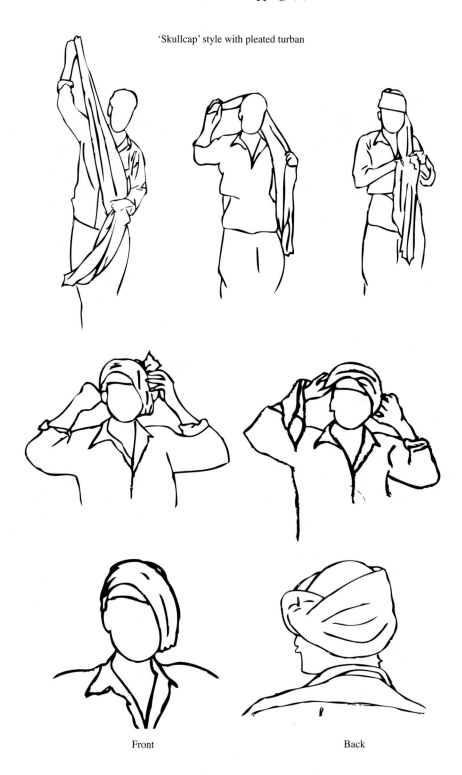

Front   Back

Plate 11: Turban wrappings (C)

'Headband' style

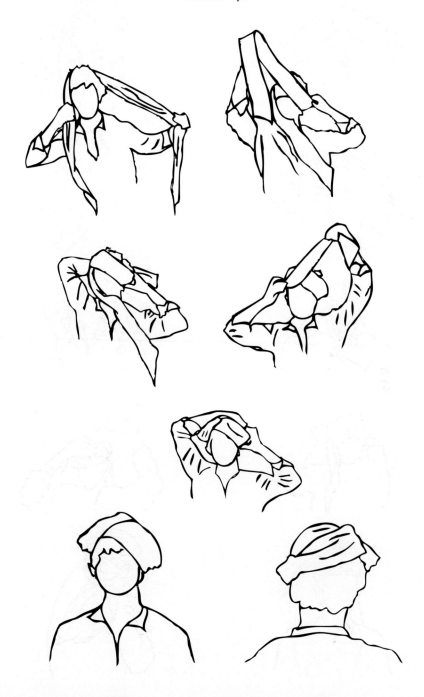

Front   Back

Plate 12: Turban wrappings (D)

'Long' style

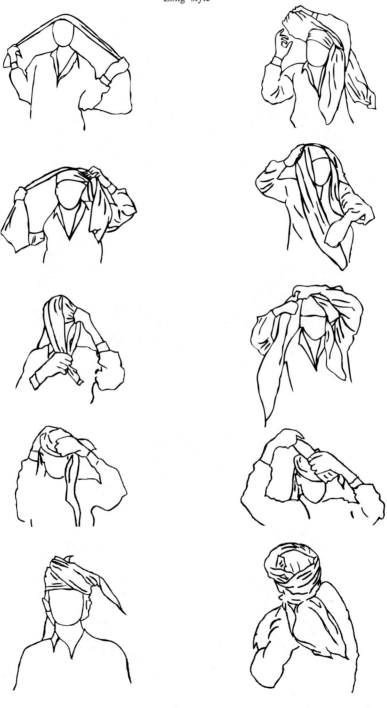

Front   Back

Plate 14 (continued): Different sitting postures

14c: knees up and buttock on the heels

14d: turban or skirt wrapped around the legs or thighs to support posture.

Plate 14: Different sitting postures

14a: cross-legged

14b: cross-legged with a knee up

Plate 13 (continued): *Dhabro* and *lungi* wrappings

13c: *Dhabro* with the two flaps put on the back over the shoulders and fitted to the body by the arms.

Back

Profile

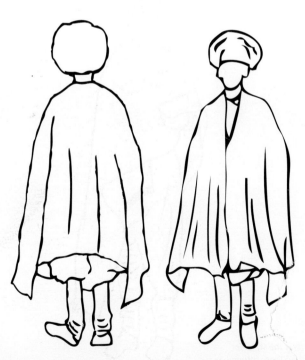

13d: Bridegroom's *lungi*

Plate 13: *Dhabro* and *lungi* wrappings

13a: *Dhabro* with a flap over the shoulder and fitted to the body.

13b: *Dhabro* with a flap over the shoulder and loose fitting.

NOTES

Introduction
Michel Boivin

1. See Michel Boivin (2003), 'An Outline of Pakistan Studies in France', *Pakistan Studies News*, Volume VI, No. 11, 1–7.
2. Nicole Balbir de Tugny, 'De Fort William au hindi littéraire: la transformation de la Khari boli en langue littéraire moderne au XIXe siècle' in F. Mallison, *Littératures médiévales de l'Inde du nord*, EFEO, 1991, pp. 187–204; Annie Montaut, 'Le hindi en 1947: la question de la langue nationale, ses origines et ses conséquences', *Les Cahiers du SAHIB*, Presses universitaires de Rennes, no. 5, 1997, pp. 132–151. For Urdu, see M. Gaborieau, 'Late Persian, Early Urdu: The Case of 'Wahhabi' Literature (1818–1857)', in F.N. Delvoye (ed.), *Confluences of Cultures: French Contributions to Indo-Persian Studies*, Delhi, Manohar/Centre for Human Sciences/Institut Français de Recherche en Iran, 1994, pp. 170–196. For the teaching of Urdu in France, see *Langues'O 1795–1995: deux siècles d'histoire de l'Ecole des langues orientales*, textes réunis par Pierre Labrousse, Editions Hervras, pp. 203–215 et 220–222.
3. Gopal Advani (1926), *Etude sur la vie rurale dans le Sind (Inde)* [*Study on Rural Life in Sind (India)*], thèse de lettres, université de Montpellier.
4. See Monique Kervran (2005), 'Pakistan: mission archéologique française au Sud-Sind' [Pakistan: French Archaeological Mission in South Sindh], *Archéologies, 20 ans de recherches françaises dans le monde*, Ministère des Affaires Etrangères, Maisonneuve et Larose/ADFP-ERC, pp. 595–598.
5. The reader can visit the following site; http:/ceias.ehess.fr/document.php?id=640

CHAPTER 1
Annabelle Collinet

1. This chapter is based on a lecture given to the Sindh Workshop, AFEMAM 18th Congress, Lyon, 2 July 2004. I thank warmly Alastair Northedge, (Art et Archéologie Islamiques, Université de Paris I Panthéon-Sorbonne), who was patient enough to correct my English for this chapter.
2. Kervran, 2005. Dr Monique Kervran, Director of Research at CNRS, Paris, founded the Mission of Sindh in 1989, under the patronage of the Department of Archaeology and Museums, Government of Pakistan, and Ministry of Foreign Affairs, France. From 1989 to 1996, this Mission surveyed the deltaic area, from the West coast to Badin, and made excavations at Ratto Kot and Juna Shah Bandar. From 1996 to 2002, the Mission explored the site of Sehwan Sharif and opened a large stratigraphical sounding in order to provide a reference for the medieval ceramic of Sindh. The Mission is very grateful to the Secretary for Culture, Government of Sindh, for providing us with a perfect house for working on this site. I warmly thank Dr Kervran who entrusted me with the study of the ceramic material collected during her surveys and excavations in Sindh.

3. Collinet, 2001.

4. Translation of Kalichbeg Fredunbeg, 1900, pp. 92-95. This source is the most detailed one on the Arab conquest of Sindh and is widely corroborated by al-Baladuri (Chapter *Futuh al-Sind* in the *Futuh al-Buldan*). The *Chach Nama* is a Persian translation (AH 613 [AD 1216]) by Ali ibn Muhammad Kufi, from Uchch (Punjab), of an Arabic source found by the translator in al-Rur (Upper Sindh). He got it from the Qazi of the city, descendant and heir of the al-Taqafi family (Ibid., pp. 5-7).

5. For terms related to Buddhists and their part during the conquest, see Maclean, 1989, and p. 5 for the words Samani/Samaniyan/Sumaniyah.

6. Kalichbeg Fredunbeg, 1900, pp. 114-116.

7. Reinaud, 1845, p.170.

8. The coins and *ostraca* are currently studied (from pictures). The first numismatic results were kindly given to me by Dr Joe Cribb, Keeper of Coins and Medals, London, British Museum, who I very warmly thank for his precious help.

9. Structure no. 1150.

10. Structure no. 1147.

11. The Islamic ceramic material of the site was drawn by V. Bernard, R. Dehghan and A. Péli and inked by the author. The pictures of the ceramics used for the colour plates were all taken by Dr M. Kervran.

12. Very few sherds of grey ware—obtained by firing the pots in a reduced atmosphere—were found in Levels IVa and IVb.

13. EU 407.

14. EU 416, 413 and 406.

15. Al-Yaqubi, *Ta'rikh al-Yaqubi*, quoted by Pathan, 1974, (p. 50 and p. 57).

16. In EU 407, 411 and 428.

17. In EU 406, 439, 411, 428 and 416.

18. Al-Yaqubi says that Umar b. Hafs and then Hisham b. Amr were sent to Sindh (Pathan, 1974, pp. 59-60). According to al-Baladuri, Hisham b. Amr al-Taghlibi exerted a real power over Sindh and was named by al-Mansur before Umar b. Hafs Hazarmard (Reinaud, 1845, pp. 185-187). But Tabari (*Tarikh al-Rusul wa'l Muluk*) says that Umar b. Hafs ruled Sindh before Hisham b. Amr (Ibid., note 3, p. 186).

19. The *ostraca* of Sehwan are studied (for pictures) by Dr Frederic Imbert, Lecturer in Arabic Epigraphy and Language Universite de Provence - IREMAM (Aix-en-Provence), Directeur du Departement d'Enseignement de l'Arabe Contemporain (Cairo), who I warmly thank for giving me his first paleographical results.

20. Anon., 1964, pl. XXII and Khan, 1976, p. 37, with plate of painted sherds. The second publication deals with the excavations conducted on the site between 1958 and 1965.

21. Khan, 1981, p. 116 describes the painted ceramics of the first Islamic phase (a). He mentions the fine quality of the red pastes, the ducks, birds, long petaled flowers, and also circles and sun motifs painted in black and red slips. See also Khan, 1990, pl. 36 and 39. The site was excavated by F.A. Khan between 1966 and 1980.

22. This type of handle with a serpentine motif is very common on pitchers with incised ornaments found in several sites roughly in ancient Mesopotamia (Susa, Samarra, al-Hira, al-Kufa, Tulul al-Uhaydir, Kish, Ctesiphon, and al-Raqqa). It is datable between c. AD 650-800 in Susa according to M. Rosen-Ayalon, 1974 (pp. 76-77) and before the 'Samarra Horizon' (from AD 836) according to A. Northedge, see Rousset, 1994, pp. 30-34.

23. Quoted by Pathan, 1974, p.62 and reference of Panhwar, 1983, p. 184.

24. EU 335.
25. Sehwan local information, from an ancient ethnographical movie, Bangladesh, where necklaces were linked with the quantity of milk given by the animals. (Oral communication, Monique Kervran, 2005).
26. Khan, 1981, p. 116.
27. For Banbhore see Khan, 1976, p. 35 and picture p. 39 and 40; for al-Mansura see Khan, 1990, pl. 46.
28. Hobson, 1928-1930, p. 22. The sherds come from excavations in 1854 by Bellasis and Richardson and are in the British Museum London. Khan, 1990, pl. 37 shows three sherds of this type coming from al-Mansura.
29. Khan, 1976, p. 41.
30. Northedge and Kennet, 1994, p. 29.
31. *Les Prairies d'Or* (*Muruj al-Dahab*), Pellat, 1962.
32. *Kitab al-Aqalim*, Elliot & Dowson, 1976, pp. 26-30.
33. Kramers and Wiet, 1964.
34. Pellat, 1962, p. 152; Elliot & Dowson, 1976, p. 28; Kramers and Wiet, vol. II, p. 316.
35. Al-Muqaddasi (c. AH 375 [AD 985]) went to southern Sindh only. Following al-Istakhri, he only mentions Sadusan, but he saw al-Mansura, the capital of the *quraysh* that is to say the Habbarid emir (Collins, 1994, pp. 419-420).
36. In EU 333, 382, 384, 328.
37. EU 328.
38. Panhwar, 1983, p.193 et 196.
39. EU 382.
40. Hobson, 1928-30, pp. 21, 22 and pl. VIII.
41. Ibid., p. 22.
42. Khan, 1976, p. 17.
43. This text has not been translated. Pathan, 1978 (pp. 240-242) used a Teheran edition (AH 1311 [AD 1894]). Later historians like Ibn al-Atir and Ibn Khaldun attribute the fall of the Habbarids to Mahmud of Ghazna (Ibid).
44. EU 321 and 312.
45. EU 312.
46. Size of a complete brick, 33x20x4.5 cm.
47. Structure no. 1128. Size of a complete brick, 20x22x4-5 cm.
48. Sizes of complete bricks, 22x12x5 and 22x16x4 cm.
49. Structure no. 1141-1142-1143.
50. This very particular production is still known in Pakistan (NWFP) and was studied during 1970 (see Rye and Evans, 1990) and by J. Husain more recently (Husain, 1992).
51. Khan, 1981, pp. 113 and 117.
52. Wilkinson, 1973.
53. Gardin, 1957, p. 92 and pp. 96-97.
54. Gardin, 1963, pp. 140-145.
55. Pellat, 1962, p. 142.
56. Khan, 1990, pl. 37, 38 and 51.
57. Anonymous, 1968, pl. LXXIIIb.
58. Whitehouse, 1968, especially p. 15.
59. Khan, 1976, p. 17.
60. Anonymous, 1964, pl. XXIII.
61. Bosworth, 1963, p. 1075.

62. The author of the *Adab al-Harb wa Shuja* lived at the time of the Ghurid Muizz al-Din Muhammad (r. AH 569-602 [AD 1173-1206]) and dedicated his work to Iletmish (r. AH 607-633 [AD 1211-1236]) (Shafi, 1938, pp. 191-192). His text gives some anecdotes on the Ghaznawids and was partially translated by I. Shafi.

63. Shafi, 1938, p. 201.

64. Raverty, 1881-1899, pp. 449 and 452.

65. Panhwar, 1983, p. 243.

66. Raverty, 1881-1899, vol. I, p. 532.

67. Ibid., pp. 294-295.

68. Ibid., vol. II, p. 609 and p. 1074.

69. Ibid., vol. I, p. 143.

70. Ibid., pp. 539-541.

71. Ibid., note pp. 240-241 and pp. 232-233.

72. EU 222, 207, 193.

73. Size of complete bricks, 21x23x5 cm and 23x36x5 cm.

74. Structures no. 1114, 1115, 1118, 1109 and 1110.

75. Size of complete bricks, 22x23x5 cm, 22x34x4 cm and 20x24x5 cm.

76. Structures no. 1096, 1090, 1091, 1099, 1105 and 1100, 1044 and 1063.

77. Mehta, 1975, p. 20. The puzzling fact is that according to Mehta, the black wares appear later in Baroda (see infra.). I thank warmly Dr E. Lambourn who gave me this article.

78. Sounding Asma Lower West, EU363 (Level Vf).

79. Wilkinson, 1973, pp. 3-53.

80. Gardin, 1963, pp. 139-144 for the chronology of types between c. AD 1000-1220.

81. Scerrato, 1959.

82. Gardin, 1957, pl. XVIII, no. 1 and 2.

83. Gardin, 1957, p. 92.

84. See for instance Gardin, 1963, pp. 142-144.

85. Scerrato, 1962.

86. Ibn Battuta, vol. II, pp. 329-331.

87. EU 177-243 and EU 172.

88. Raverty, 1881-1899, vol. II, p. 614.

89. Ibid., p. 628.

90. Ibid., pp. 1153-1154.

91. *Ta'rikh-i Masumi*, Kalichbeg Fredunbeg, 1902, p. 12.

92. Ibid., pp. 15-16.

93. Panhwar, 1983, pp. 272-73 and Kalichbeg Fredunbeg, 1902, p. 17.

94. Ibid., pp. 269-270.

95. Kalichbeg Fredunbeg, 1902, p. 18.

96. Ibid., p. 19.

97. Ibn Battuta, vol. II, pp. 331-333.

98. *Futuh al-Salatin* quoted by Blayac, 2004, p. 36. According to Mir Masum, the sultan Firuz Shah Tughluq named Malik Ali Shir and Taj al-Din Kafur in charge of Sehwan when he was in the city (Kalichbeg Fredunbeg, 1902, p. 20).

99. Panhwar, 1983, p. 315, using Muhammad Shafi's *Banadid-e Sindh* (in Urdu), edited Lahore, 1970.

100. EU 235.

101. Structures no. 1089-1090-1091 and 1014-1075.

102. Structure no. 1033-1034.

103. Waddington, 1946.

104. Mehta, 1949, pp. 9-10.

105. Waddington, 1946, fig. 6 and pl. XIX-XX.

106. Kalichbeg Fredunbeg, 1902, p. 42.

107. Panhwar, 1983, Samma Jams chart.

108. Kalichbeg Fredunbeg, 1902, pp. 47-48.

109. Quoted by Panhwar, 1983, p. 350.

110. Written before AD 1434 by al-Sarhindi, quoted by Panhwar, 1977, pp. 413-414 and Panhwar, 1983, p. 345.

111. Kalichbeg Fredunbeg, 1902, pp. 52-53.

112. Panhwar, 1983, p. 348 et pp. 354-55.

113. Ibid., p. 348, from the *Marat-i Sikandari*.

114. Structures no. 1089-1090-1091.

115. Structures 1014-1075 and 1019.

116. Pillar no. 1076 in structure 1014-1075.

117. Waddington, 1946, fig.7, no. 36 and 22.

118. Mehta, 1949, pp. 5-6 and Mehta, 1950, p. 47. Great thanks are due to Dr Elizabth Lambourn (Senior Research Fellow, De Montfort University & Honorary Research Associate, Centre for South East Asian Studies, SOAS) who gave me these articles.

119. Hasan, 1995, p. 86.

120. Mehta, 1949, p. 6.

121. Mehta, 1949, pp. 8-9, fig. E.

122. Translated by Siddiqi, 1972.

123. Siddiqi, 1972, p. 26.

124. Ibid., pp. 32-33. His inspection of the defences of the fort can be understood as a rebuilding of the walls.

125. Ibid., 1972, p. 78 and p. 83.

126. Ibid., 1972, pp. 87-89 and p. 94.

127. Ibid., 1972, p. 100.

128. Ibid., 1972, p. 116, p. 126 and p. 133.

129. Ibid., 1972, pp. 134-136.

130. For this episode and the different dates given by Mir Masum, Abul Fazl, and other sources, see Siddiqi, 1972, pp. 186-188.

131. Siddiqi, 1972, p. 194 and p. 203.

132. Structure 1014-1075.

133. Structure 1011.

134. Mehta, 1949, p. 7.

135. Akhtar, 1990, p. 76 and p. 137. The only other city of Sindh with this status of *Khalisa-i Sharifa* was the Indus Delta port of Lahori Bandar.

136. Khan, 1980, p. 113.

137. Akhtar, 1990, pp. 76-77.

138. Ibid., pp. 139-161.

139. Ibid., chapter 4, section I of the text.

140. He wrote the Tuhfat al-Kiram in AH 1180 (AD 1766-67). The text was partly translated by Kalichbeg Fredunbeg, 1902.

141. Ibid., Kalichbeg Fredunbeg, 1902, p. 130.

142. Ibid., p. 134.

143. Structure no. 1013 (c.40.58-41.29 m).

144. Péli, 2002, p. 84.
145. The site was surveyed by M. Kervran in 1989-1991 and excavated in 1993-94. The ceramic material from that site and others in the Indus Delta will be included, in addition to Sehwan's ceramic wares, in my forthcoming PhD dealing with the Islamic ceramics from Sindh.
146. Péli, 2002, p. 86.

CHAPTER 2
Michel Boivin

1. Carl Ernst's contribution is to be noted for the theoretical reflection he develops. See especially the introduction in his last paper on the topic (Ernst 2005).
2. In the Puranas, the *devadasi*s are nevertheless devoted to Sun temples. Hiuen Tsang referred to the hordes of dancing girls at the notorious temple of Sûrya at Multan (Hiuen Tsang 1884, II: 274).
3. Note the reservations of Lorenzen, arguing that the similarities between the two schools are common to the whole of the tantric tradition (Lorenzen 1972: 38).
4. The *guru-mantra* is the secret formula the *guru* reveals to the disciple during initiation. The meaning of *alakh niranjan* is 'Supreme Being without attributes'.
5. On the Kanphatas disciples of Ratannath, see V. Bouiller (1998), *Ascètes et rois. Un monastère de Kanphata Yogis au Népal*, Paris, Editions du CNRS.
6. Thanks to Derryl MacLean for informing me on these points; email dated 28 June 2004.
7. See the sharp discussion of the question by MacLean (MacLean 1989: 116). It is beyond the scope here to reappraise it.
8. Schimmel gives the date of 905 for Hallaj's visit to Sindh. See Schimmel 1986: 96.
9. The place was surveyed by Monik Kervran and her team in 1989. I warmly thank her for giving me these precious details.
10. The only exception is Shaykh Tahir also known as Udero Lal, who belongs to the prior period, the time of the ascetics.
11. Briggs mentions several times that he has got data on Pir Patho from G.E.L. Carter.
12. I am not sure of the meaning of this apparent *laqab* Shaykh Laqah. In Persian, the word designates 'souls', or a male camel....
13. See his *Shah-jo-Risalo* 1951, especially *Sur Ramkali* III, 4-8. It is to be noted that in Gujarat, although Kutchi is a Sindhi dialect, the interpolation between r and d is very common. The Kaparis mentioned by Shah Latif should be the Kapadis of Mata-no-Madh.
14. For a more detailed study of Lal Shahbaz Qalandar, see Boivin 2003 and 2005b.
15. Other places claim to be Bhartrhari's *samadh*, for example Chunar fort, near Mirzapur in India. Bhartrhari is sometimes introduced as the patron saint of the Jogis.
16. The author has devoted a small paper to the topic of dance in the Sindhi area. See Boivin 2005a.
17. The name Laki can be found with different spellings: Laki, Lakhi etc. Laki is nevertheless the most common.
18. Udero Lal's connexion was expounded in the first part of the present paper, as was Shah Abdul Latif's, whose mausoleum is located in Bhit Shah. Tando Allahyar is the place

where the biggest temple devoted to Ramdeo Pir, another local saint with strong connexions with the Nathpanth, is located.

CHAPTER 3
Claude Markovits

1. In 1937, there were only 83 'large' (i.e. employing more than 20 workers) perennial establishments (including railway workshops) in the province, employing a total of 9934 persons, and 132 seasonal establishments (mostly cotton gins and presses), employing a total of 16,807 people. See *Large Industrial Establishments in India, 1937,* Delhi, 1939.
2. In 1917, Hindus, almost exclusively *Amils*, accounted for 56 per cent of Deputy Collectors and 79 per cent of *Mukhtiyarkars* in the Revenue Department, 82 per cent of Sub-Judges in the Judicial Department, 74 per cent of those employed in the Educational Department, and 77 per cent of those employed in the Public Works Department. Political File No. 349 (1917), vol. II, Commissioner-in-Sind Records, Karachi, quoted in S.F.D. Ansari, *Sufi Saints and State Power: The pirs of Sind 1843-1947,* Cambridge, 1992, note 29, p. 109.

CHAPTER 4
Laurent Gayer

1. R. Bhattacharya, *Pundits from Pakistan. On Tour with India, 2003-04,* New Delhi, Picador, 2005, p. 77.
2. The first known historical reference to Karachi was made by an emissary of Nader Shah, Muzafar Ali Khan, who mentions his stay in the city in his *Tuhfat-ul Kirram*, written in 1742. Karachi was founded 13 years earlier by a certain Bhojumal, who had its ramparts built by Arabian workers paid in dates imported from Bahrain and Muscat; *cf.* S. K.H. Katrak, *Karachi. That was the Capital of Sindh*, Lahore, 1963.
3. The notion of 'proto-globalisation' was coined by world historians 'to refer two interacting political and economic developments that became especially prominent between about 1600 and 1800 in Europe, Asia and parts of Africa: the reconfiguration of state systems, and the growth of finance, services and pre-industrial manufacturing'; *cf.* A.G. Hopkins, 'Introduction: globalisation—an agenda for historians', in A.G. Hopkins (ed.), *Globalisation in World History*, Londres, Pimlico, 2002, p. 5.
4. A. F. Baillie, *Kurrachee. Past, Present and Future*, Karachi, Oxford University Press, 1997 (1st edition in 1890), p. 12.
5. For a remarkable history of the Sindhi trade diaspora, which played a decisive role in the rise of Karachi, *cf.* C. Markovits, *The Global World of Indian Merchants, 1750-1947: Traders of Sindh from Bukhara to Panama*, Cambridge, Cambridge University Press, 2000.
6. Karachi's occupation resulted from the first Anglo-Afghan war. The first British expedition anchored off Manora on 1 February 1839.
7. Although the construction of Karachi's port docks started in 1882, it was only completed in 1944.
8. In the 1860s, the American civil war led to a dramatic decline of cotton production.
9. A.F. Baillie, *Kurrachee, op. cit.*, p. 4.

10. Y. Lari and M. S. Lari, *The Dual City*, op. cit., p. 130.

11. S.K.H. Katrak, *Karachi*, op. cit., p. 27.

12. Z.A. Nizami, *Karachi Through the Centuries*, Karachi, Karachi Development Authority, 198[?].

13. 900,000 Mohajirs settled in Karachi between 1947 and 1951; *cf.* L. Gayer, *Les politiques internationales de l'identité. Significations internationales des mobilisations identitaires des Sikhs (Inde) et des Mohajirs (Pakistan)*, Ph.D Dissertation, Paris, Sciences Po, 2004, annexure 2.4, p. 839.

14. T.Y. Tan & G. Kudaisya, *The Aftermath of Partition in South Asia*, London/New York, Routledge, 2000, p. 179.

15. Ibid., p. 181.

16. The Karachi Municipal Corporation (KMC) was established in 1832 to counter epidemics affecting the city as a whole.

17. T.Y. Tan & G. Kudaisya, *The Aftermath of Partition*, op. cit., p. 181.

18. S.F.D. Ansari, 'Partition, migration and refugees: responses to the arrival of Muhajirs in Sindh during 1947-48', in D.A. Low & H. Brasted (eds.), *Freedom, Trauma, Continuities: Northern India and Independence*, Delhi, Sage, 1998.

19. R. Bhattacharya, *Pundits from Pakistan*, op. cit., p. 78.

20. M. Abou-Zahab & O. Roy, *Islamic Networks: The Pakistan-Afghan Connection*, London, Hurst, 2003; L. Goodson, *The Talibanization of Pakistan*, New York/Basingstoke, Palgrave-Macmillan, 2002.

21. Y. Lari and M. S. Lari, *The Dual City*, op. cit.

22. Only the notables, big landowners and merchants lived in the 'clean' part of Karachi, east of the old centre, which had much more and much better educational, health and recreational facilities than the 'black' part of the city. In this way, 'the dominating position of the rulers was reflected in the spatial structure of the city in which separation was the main element'; H. Meyerink, 'Karachi's growth in historical perspective', in J.W. Schoorl, J.J. van der Linden & K.S. Yap (eds.), *Between Basti Dwellers and Bureaucrats: Lessons in Squatter Settlement Upgrading in Karachi*, Oxford, Pergamon Press, 1983, p. 8.

23. A. Hasan, *Understanding Karachi. Planning and Reform for the Future*, Karachi, City Press, 1999, Appendix 2, p. 166.

24. *Bastis* are 'spontaneous settlements that came about without official government planning'; J.J. Van der Linden, 'The Bastis of Karachi: the functioning of an informal housing system', in J.W. Schoorl, J.J. van der Linden & K.S. Yap (eds.), *Between Basti Dwellers and Bureaucrats*, op. cit., p. 43.

25. T. Y. Tan & G. Kudaisya, *The Aftermath of Partition*, op. cit., p. 185.

26. 'Katcha' houses are temporary structures made of mud and thatch; in the subcontinent, the notion of 'katcha' has a deeply pejorative connotation, as it implies impurity. 'Katcha' housing is opposed to 'pakka' housing, which relates to permanent buildings made of cement.

27. M. Waseem, 'Ethnic conflict in Pakistan: the case of MQM', *The Pakistan Development Review*, 35 (4), Winter 1996, p. 620; S F.D. Ansari, 'The Movement of Indian Muslims', art. quoted, p. 159.

28. J.V.D. Linden, E. Meijer & P. Nientied, 'Informal housing in Karachi', in J.V.D. Linden & F. Selier (eds.), *Karachi. Migrants, Housing and Housing Policy*, Lahore, Vanguard, 1991, pp. 67-68.

29. S. Tambiah, *Leveling Crowds. Ethnonationalist Conflicts and Collective Violence in South Asia*, New Delhi, Vistaar, 1996, pp. 84-185.

30. Ninety per cent of Karachi's minibuses belonged to policemen; *cf.* 'Traffic in death', *The Herald* (Karachi), May 1985, p. 43.

31. Mohajirs and Pathans each constituted 25 per cent of Orangi's population, the remaining 50 per cent of the population being a mixture of Punjabis, Sindhis, Baluchis, Bengalis and Afghan refugees.

32. Karachi saw anti-Ahmedi 'riots' in the early fifties, anti-Pathan 'riots' in the late 1950s and again in 1965, anti-Ahmedi 'riots' again in 1969-70 and Sindhi-Mohajir riots in 1972-73. However, the ethnic clashes which occurred in the second half of the 1980s in the city were unprecedented in their scale and brutality. Clashes have occurred between Pathans and Biharis in April 1985, October and December 1986, and February and July 1987, and between Mohajirs and Sindhis in May, September, and October 1988, and again in May-June 1990.

33. Approximately 250,000 of the estimated 1.5 million Pathans of Karachi were living in Orangi.

34. Interview, Montreal, 4 April 2000.

35. A. Hussain, 'The Karachi riots of December 1986: Crisis of State and Civil Society in Pakistan', in V. Das (ed.), *Mirrors of Violence. Communities, Riots and Survivors in South Asia*, New Delhi, 1990, p. 188.

36. 'Traffic in death', *The Herald*, May 1985, p. 44.

37. J.J. Richards, *Mohajir Subnationalism and the Mohajir Qaumi Movement in Sindh Province, Pakistan*, PhD dissertation, Cambridge, Cambridge University, 1993.

38. A. Feldman, *Formations of Violence. The Narrative of the Body and Political Terror in Northern Ireland*, Chicago, University of Chicago Press, 1991, p. 28.

39. S. Tambiah, *Levelling Crowds*, op. cit., p. 188.

40. Ibid., p. 186.

41. A. Hasan, 'A generation comes of age', *The Herald*, October 1987, pp. 52-53.

42. Ibid., p. 53.

43. Oskar Verkaaik, *Inside the Citadel. Fun, Violence and Religious Nationalism in Hyderabad, Pakistan*, PhD dissertation, University of Amsterdam, 1999, p. 56.

44. Hussein Haqqani was an IJT activist who later became Nawaz Sharif's councillor; *cf.* J.J. Richards, *Mohajir Subnationalism,* op. cit., p. 249.

45. 'The campus mafias', *The Herald*, October 1988, pp. 52-65.

46. O. Verkaaik, *Inside the Citadel,* op. cit., p. 151.

47. M. Anif, 'The gun-runners of Karachi', *Newsline*, October 1989, p. 23.

48. E. Picard, 'Liban, la matrice historique', *in* François Jean, Jean-Christophe Rufin (dir.), *Economie des guerres civiles*, Paris, Hachette, 1996, p. 92.

49. M. Anif, 'The gun-runners of Karachi', art. quoted, p. 22.

50. Quoted by ibid., p. 23.

51. Ibid., p. 22.

52. Ibid.

53. On the contribution of ultra-violence to the construction of a Mohajir identity in Hyderabad, see O. Verkaaik, *Inside the Citadel,* op. cit.

54. B.K. Axel, *The Nation's Tortured Body. Violence, Representation and the Formation of a Sikh 'Diaspora'*, London/Durham, Duke University Press, 2001, p. 31.

55. D. Pécaut, 'De la banalité de la violence à la terreur', *Cultures & Conflicts*, no. 24-25, Winter 1995, p. 162, where the author suggests that by offering armed protection to the residents of their zones of influence, militias contribute to the fragmentation of urban space and to 'the transformation of territory into a patchwork of micro-territories'. An

English version of this paper was published in K. Koonings & D. Krujit (eds.), *Societies of Fear: The Legacy of War, Violence and Terror in Latin America*, London , Zed Books, 1999.

56. 'The anatomy of violence', *Newsline*, October 1989, pp. 17-18.

57. A. Mouzoune, *Les transformations du paysage spatio-communautaire de Beyrouth, 1975-1996*, Paris, published, 1999, p. 108.

58. H. Arendt, *Condition de l'homme moderne* [*The Human Condition*], Paris, Calmann-Lévy, 1983, p. 92.

59. 'The Hong Kong factor', *The Herald Annual*, January 1995, pp. 58-59.

60. At the end of the 1990s, Karachi was still generating 25 per cent of state revenues and 23.2 per cent of the GNP. Thirty-three per cent of the country's activities in the industrial sector were taking place in the city, as well as 61.6 per cent of the activities in the banking sector and 37.6 per cent of the activities in the tertiary sector. The income per inhabitant is the highest in the country; in 1997, at 900 dollars, it was more than twice the amount of the GNP per inhabitant. Half the vehicles registered in the country belong to Karachiites, who also possess 35 per cent of the country's televisions; see M. Boivin, 'Karachi et ses territoires en conflits: pour une relecture de la question communautaire', *Hérodote*, no. 101, 2001, p. 186.

61. In face-to-face interviews, MQM leaders are often more outspoken; an American diplomat who met unofficially with Altaf Hussain in London was even told that Karachi might separate from Sindh in the future, following Singapore's example; interview at the American consulate in Karachi, April 2001.

62. Muhammad Anwar, who was at that time the Joint-Chief Organizer for the MQM UK and Europe.

63. In July 2001, Imran Farooq told me that he never left Karachi during these seven years; he also told me that a few weeks before the rebellion, he had finally received the fake British visa he had been waiting for and that it was merely a 'coincidence' if he had reappeared in London at a time when his colleagues were 'very upset'. His arguments obviously failed to convince me.

64. Interview with Farooq Sattar, Karachi, 20 February 2005.

65. H. Mansoor, 'Has MQM struck a deal with the government?', *The Friday Times*, 30 August –5 September 2002, p. 4.

66. Interview with Farooq Sattar, Karachi, 20 February 2005.

67. The MQM is committed to the separation of politics and religion, breaking away from the fundamentalist past of the Mohajirs, who supported the Jama'at-e Islami before shifting their loyalty to the MQM. The party cannot be described as perfectly 'secular', though, as it enjoys playing with religious symbols and feelings when it suits the interests of its leaders.

68. Interview, Toronto, 15 August 1999.

69. On the contribution of the Internet to the redefinition of identity politics, *cf.* P. Jeganathan, 'Eelam.com: Place, nation and imagination in cyber-space', *Public culture*, 10 (3), 1998; H. Nazeri, 'Imagined Cyber Communities: Iranians and the Internet', *Middle East Studies Association Bulletin*, 30 (2), December 1996.

70. One could for instance have a look at Sufi web pages at [http://www.luarisharif.com/] and [ttp://world.std.com/~habib/sufi.html].

71. Transcription of Altaf Hussain's online chat with *India Times*, 5 2001 July, available at [http://www.indiatimes.com/chatevents/altaf.htm].

72. Interview with Dr Christophe Jaffrelot, Karachi, 31 January 1999. With his courteous authorization.

73. A. Baillie, *Kurrachee*, op. cit., p. 1.

74. Karachi is the financial capital of Pakistan and 50 per cent of the bank assets in the country are concentrated there; all the major Pakistani banks have their head office in the city and most foreign banks operating in Pakistan have set up their main branch here as well. The development of Karachi's banking sector predates independence; in the 1860s, several banks started operating in the city, such as the Agra and Masterman Bank, the Agra and United Service Bank and the Oriental Cooperation Bank. The Bank of Kurrachee was founded in 1861 and several other banks opened branches in the city in the following years, such as the Chartered Bank of India, Australia and China, the Sindh, Punjab and Delhi Ltd. and the Bank of Bombay.

75. K. Khan, 'Government's options limited in dealing with militancy', *The News International*, 2002, quoted by W. John, *Karachi. A Terror Capital in the Making*, Delhi, Rupa Co., 2003, p. 16.

76. The *Dar-ul Uloom Islamia Binori* has 8000 students from all around the world. In Sindh at large, 20 *madrassas* and 30 'Model Schools' (as defined by the Education Department after *madrassas* were accused of training *jihadis*) and run by the Jama'at-ud Dawa (the parent organization of the Lashkar-e Taiba). In Karachi, the JuD's bastion is the *Ahl-e Hadith Jamia al-Darshat-ul-Islamia* university.

77. The foundation of this jihadist organization, which is organically linked to the sectarian Sipah-e Sahaba Pakistan (SSP), was announced by Masood Azhar at the Masjid-e Falal, in Karachi, on 3 February 2000. Masood Azhar is a former student of the *Dar-ul Uloom Islamia Binori*, where he taught before joining jihadists in East Africa and later in Kashmir. Two other 'Binory Town' professors played a key role in the foundation of the JeM: Mufti Nizamuddin Shamzai and Maulana Yusuf Ludhyanvi (the latter was the commander-in-chief of the Sipah-e Shahaba Pakistan in Karachi). In May 2000, both of them left for Afghanistan, where they tried to convince the Taliban to extradite Usama Bin Laden. On 18 May 2000, two days after his return from Afghanistan, Ludhyanvi was assassinated in Karachi. Nizamuddin Shamzai was also murdered in Karachi in May 2004.

78. Four thousand people have been killed in terrorist-related violence in Karachi since 1994, but 'only' a few hundred have fallen to the bullets of sectarian terrorists. On the presence of sectarian groups in Karachi, see N.S. Ali, 'Doctors under fire', *Newsline*, August 2001; M. Ansari, 'Moving target', *Newsline*, February 2002; N.S. Ali, 'The Jihad within', *Newsline*, May 2002. On the events of May 2004, see 'Bloody May', *The Herald*, June 2004.

79. M. Hanif, 'In the name of religion', *Newsline*, August 1994, p. 27.

80. M. Abou-Zahab, 'Sectarian groups after 9/11', working paper presented at CERI, 18 November 2005.

81. M. Qureshi is the first Haqiqi candidate to have won a seat in the national assembly. However, he died shortly after his victory and the MQM (A) won his seat back.

82. The first results released by the Electoral Commission were attributing 13 NA seats to the MQM, but when the new Assembly opened its first session, the number of MQM representatives had somehow mysteriously risen to 17.

83. The MMA is a coalition of Sunni and Shiite religious parties, which was formed in Fall 2002 to contest the first general elections held in Pakistan since General Musharraf's coup.

84. H. Mansoor, 'Karachi electioneering becomes violent', *The Friday Times*, 27 September-3 October 2002.

85. S.S. Hasan, 'APMSO-IJT standoff forebodes trouble in local bodies elections', *The Herald*, March 2005.

86. See http://www.mqm.org/English-News/Sep-2001/news010913.htm

87. M. Boivin, 'Karachi et ses territoires en conflit', art. quoted, p. 197.

88. A. Schimmel, *Mystical Dimensions of Islam*, Chapel Hill, University of North Carolina University Press, 1975, p. 366.

89. For O. Verkaaik, Altaf Hussain is 'a human icon that *absorbs* rather than *expresses* meaning'; see Oskar Verkaaik, *Inside the Citadel*, op. cit., p. 52.

90. P. Werbner & H. Basu (eds.), *Embodying Charisma. Modernity, Locality and the Performance of Emotion in Sufi Cults*, London, Routledge, 1998, p. 5.

91. On the ambivalence of popular representations of *pirs* in Pakistan, see L. Werth, 'The saints who disappeared: saints of the wilderness in Pakistani village shrines', in ibid., p. 89.

CHAPTER 5

Françoise Mallison

1. Françoise Mallison, 'Saints and Sacred Places ...', p. 348 note 12 on the etymology of Nakalanki/Niskalanki, especially the popular etymology in reaction against the misinterpretation of *Kalki* as *Kalanki*: one 'with a mark or a stigma' and *Na* or *Niskalanki* as one 'without stain, pure'.

2. Dominique-Sila Khan, 'The Coming of Nikalank Avatar ...'.

3. Mohan Devraj Thontya, 'History of Barmati Panth', p. 16.

4. Twelve days after death: *barehi bara* (Interview with Mr V.T.Mangalia, Bhuj, 18 January 2001).

5. Mohan Devraj Thontya, 'History of Barmati Panth'.

6. I thank Dr Michel Boivin for information and the location of the sites on a map drawn by him, and reproduced here.

7. Ed. Kavi Kanji Khenga Kocara.

8. Ed. Matang Malsi Ladha Bhagavant.

9. Matang, *Matanga Purana*, pp. 391-4.

10. Cf. Rosa Maria Perez, *Kings and Untouchables: A Study of the Caste System in Western India*, New Delhi: Chronicle Books, DC Publishers, 2004, chapter 8, pp.148-58 and Harald Tambs-Lyche, 'Koli, Rajput, Kanbi et Pattidar: revendications identitaires au Gujarat hier et aujourd'hui', in *Tribus et basses castes, Résistance et autonomie dans la société indienne*, ed. M.Carrin et C.Jaffrelot, Paris: Editions de l'EHESS, 2003, pp. 265-95.

11. Cf. Harald Tambs-Lyche, *Power, Profit and Poetry. Traditional Society in Kathiawar, Western India*, New Delhi: Manohar, 1997.

12. Mohan Devraj Thontya, 'History of Barmati Panth', pp. 89-91.

13. Ginan of Mamaïdev: *Ali bhadaji cala*, 'The Desire of Ali the Brave', unpublished manuscript. I thank Mr Mohan Devraj Thontya for having sent me a copy taken from his own collection of Barmati Panthi Ginans.

14. 'Pancorath' means 'fifth' and is consistent but there is no explanation for the name of the *avatar*: 'Muro Raja'. Might it be possible to link it with one of the names of Vishnu/ Krishna 'Murari' meaning the enemy (*ari*) of the demon 'Mura'?

15. Dominique-Sila Khan, 'The Coming of Nikalank Avatar ...'.
16. Mohan Devraj Thontya, 'History of Barmati Panth', p. 102.
17. Françoise Mallison, 'Saints and Sacred Places ...', p. 342.
18. Unpublished manuscript, a copy of which was handed to me by Mr Mohan Devraj Thontya whom I thank.
19. A sacred mountain near Junagadh in Saurashtra, abode of holy men of all sects, famous for its Shaiva, Shakta and Jain shrines as well as Sufi tombs.
20. Not yet edited, orally transmitted by the lineage of the descendants of Mamaidev, these approximately one thousand Ginans have an utterly confused transmission. They were committed to writing for the first time by Mr Gaba Bhanji Lala (who died in 1995), a descendant of Mamaidev's youngest son, and several copies are with the Matangs (Barmati Panthi priests). According to Mr Mohan Devraj Thontya, there are several substantially different versions. The edition he is working on will therefore be very welcome.
21. A community very close to the Barmati Panthis would be for instance the followers of Pithoro Pir (or Pir Panthis) whom one finds among Untouchables and Rajputs from Sindh and Kutch. They are studied by Michel Boivin: 'Pithoro Pir et les Pirpanthis: matériaux pour une tradition méconnue entre Sindh et Kutch', Paper read at the research group 'Etudes Gujarati: Société, langue, culture', Paris, on 17 May 2005.
22. The Sindh Archives Department launched a project entitled 'Identification of the Shrines of Maheswari Meghwar Saints in Sindh', on which Mr Mohan Devraj Thontya is currently working.

CHAPTER 6
Dominique-Sila Khan

1. See for example the article published in *Sindhu Dhara Times,* 10 September 1995, pp. 29-31, by Y. Wadhwani Shah: 'Victim of History and Neglect: Sindhi Language and Culture'.
2. Many young Sindhis still speak Sindhi at home but very few are able to read or write it. Various publications and institutions are now attempting to prompt them to learn the Sindhi alphabet and awaken their interest in the rich literary heritage associated with Sindh.
3. This song beginning with the words *'damadam mast Qalandar...'* was originally composed in the Siraikhi language, but a Sindhi version was created which became still more popular thanks to the famous Sindhi singer Bhagwanti Nawani.
4. According to a famous myth, Lohanas would be the descendants of one of Rama's sons, Lava.
5. The importance of Jainism can be illustrated by the presence of a Sindhi Jain temple in Adarsh Nagar, a mohalla of Jaipur where Sindhis are particularly numerous.
6. According to a version of the legend the saint would have disappeared in the water, taking his *jal samadhi,* while the other version claims that he vanished under the earth.
7. Like *dharamsala* and *gurudvara* the word *darbar* refers to a Sikh shrine. For example, the golden temple of Amritsar is known as 'Darbar Sahib'.
8. I am indebted to Claude Markovits for this precious information.

CHAPTER 7
Pierre Lachaier

1. This is a modified version of 'Lohana and Sindhi Networks', Proceedings of the EFEO Seminar *The Resources of History: Tradition, Narration and Nation in South Asia*, held on 15-16 January 1997 in Pondicherry, ed. J. Assayag, *EFEO-IFP*, Pondicherry, 1999. Some more details about the Lohanas are to be found in my book reviews of: 'Markovits, Claude: *The Global World of Indian Merchants, 1750-1947, Traders of Sind from Bukhara to Panama*, Cambridge University Press, 2000, in the *BEFEO*, 2001, no. 88, pp. 373-376; Levi Scott, C.: *The Indian Diaspora in Central Asia and its Trade, 1550-1900*, Brill, Leiden, 2002, Paris, 2004, in the *BEFEO,* 2003-2004, no. 90-91, pp. 523-28; Bharadwaj, Prakash, ed., Worldwide Publishing Company, Hong Kong, Bombay: *Sindhis Through The Ages (Far East and South East)*, Vol. I & II, 1988, *Sindhis' International Year Book, Glimpses of Sindhis, 1841-1990*, *150 Years around The World*, 1990' in the *BEFEO* 1997.
2. Burton, R.F.: *Scinde or the Unhappy Valley*, Vol. I & II 1851, and *Scinde Revisited*, 1877, could not be consulted. *Sindh and the Races that inhabit the Valley of the Indus*, 1851, Asian Educational Services, Madras, reprint 1992.
3. Tod, James: *Annals and Antiquities of Rajasthan*, Vol. I & II, 1899. Could not be consulted.
4. Thakur, U.T., *Sindhi Culture*, 1959. According to Schimmel, 1974, Part of Vol. VIII, Note 171: '*a book which is strictly anti-Muslim and advocates the acceptance of Devanagari letters.*'
5. Histories of the origin of the Lohanas are given in the publications of the Shri kacchi lohana mahajan, Mulunda, 1967-68, of the Shri kacchi lohana mahajan, Puna, 1984, and of the Shri dakshina bharata lohana samaja, 1989. They are of variable quality and value. We refer here mostly to the history of the Pune Kutchi Lohana Mahajan, see Lachaier, 1999:67-71.
6. Regarding the exploitation of the Ramayana, see: Thapar, 1995.
7. Thakur, 1959:56-57. J.M. Campbell, 1880: 54-56, note no. 2. Information about Lohanas often came from colonial sources, mainly from R.F. Burton, and from Elliot H.M., *The History of India*, Vol. I, 1867.
8. *Imperial Gazetteer of India*, 1908:106. 'Though legend attributes the founding of Lahore or Lohawarana to Lava, the son of Rama, it is not probable that Lahore was founded before the first century A.D.'
9. Campbell, 1880:55, note 2, who quotes Burton.
10. Enthoven, ibid. Vol. II, p. 381, quoted by Thakur, 1959:59.
11. Thakur, 1959:57, quotes Aitken, *Gazetteer of the Province of Sind*, p. 88 and refers to Narsain, J.J., *The Amil Community of Sindh Hyderabad*, unpublished thesis of the University of Bombay, 1932, p. 26.
12. All sources I have quoted mention it except Rushbrook, 1958. See Thakur, 1959:20-1, 129-31; Anand, 1996:13-14, 196-99; Bharadwaj, 1988:56, 1990:40.
13. Rushbrook, 1958:163-64. 'There is little doubt that he [Maharao god, ruler of Kutch] found the money to sustain his large army by murdering, and confiscating the fortune of Diwan after Diwan—more than twenty of them in all—during his reign... the Diwans, by the nature of their duties, were drawn mostly from the Lohana or Bania castes. The authority which they wielded, and the fortunes which they amassed caused them to be despised by the nobles and hated by the masses. Thus their fall excited no protest...'.

Devkaran: pp. 129-134, murdered in 1738; his son Punja Sheth, poisoned in 1765: pp. 142-158; their disciple Jivan Sheth: pp. 147-154, killed in the 2nd battle of Jhara; Dev Sheth, son of Punja: p. 160, poisoned.

14. Anand follows Thakur explicitly, p. 6, or not; according to Burton, Lohanas in Sindh had some 50 subdivisions, in Campbell, 1880:55. Following Thakur, authors generally underline that the caste system was very weak in Sindh.

15. Thakur, 1959:23, 60. Anand, 1996, follows Thakur, U.T., and quotes Burton, p. 7. See also Bharadwaj, 1990:69.

16. Thakur, 1959:37. Bharadwaj, 1988:256. Anand, 1996:16, 'The Lohana Bhaiband Sindhi workers spread their network throughout the world and from hawkers they became owners of big business empires.'

17. See a description of these Sindhi networks in Markovits, 2000.

18. Others are civil servants and professionals; the percentage of farmers was very small.

19. Thakur, 1959:36-7. For Thakur, Bhaibands, or 'Sindh Works' are 'the leading community of Lohana traders'. However, there is no question of the Bhaibands being Lohanas in Bharadwaj who should know them well particularly in Hong Kong.

20. Grierson, 1919: Sindhi dialects are: the Siraikai (north of Shikarpur), the Vicholi (Hyderabad), the Lari (Thatta), the Tharili (Rajasthan border), and the Kutchi spoken in the south-east in Kutch, and in the western part of Saurashtra. Kutchi is spoken in the Karachi District and in the north of it (50,000 speakers), in Khatiavar or Saurashtra (76,214 speakers), in Bombay and in its area (45,000 speakers). Schimmel, A., ibid., 1974, 'Kutchi is used in some comparatively early Ismaili works', p. 3.

21. Bhanusalis are often to be found in the vicinity of the Kutchi Lohana in Bombay, Mulund, Nasik and Pune.

22. Rushbrook, 1958:6. 'For immemorial times they have gone forth, as they do today, to East Africa, Arabia, and the Persian Gulf. They have long been established in Zanzibar and Tanganyika. Their courage and enterprise, which is shared, if perhaps in lesser measure, by their kinsmen in Saurashtra and Gujarat, mark them out from the mercantile and trading classes in most other parts of India.'

23. *Imperial Gazetteer of India*, Vol. XV, 1908:14, 'Even before the period of British rule, the commerce of Karachi had attained some importance'. See the maps of the port establishments of the Bay of Gvatar, of the Makran coast and of the Khambat Gulf in: Deloches, 1980: 50-63.

24. Those I have met used to live in Kutch. From Kutch, they soon came to Bombay or Pune. They do not identify themselves as refugees, even less as Sindhis.

25. Bharadwaj, 1990: Schools and Dharamshala pp. 124-141; Colleges p. 121; Cultural associations pp. 162-169 and following, Hospitals pp. 122-3.

26. Bharadwaj, 1990:11, 266-7, 'Sindhi Population Around the World'. Lists pp. 266-7 are less detailed and may give different figures from these on the map p.11. There are many mistakes and no references at all. Census data of 1951 are in Anand, 1996:63, and in Thakur, 1959.

27. Bharadwaj, 1990:161, 'Awards for Export'. See also p. 149. No reference for the given data.

28. Bharadwaj, 1988:149-151, for the cinema, pp. 204-6.

29. While not mentioning the Sindhi Indian Chhabria M.R. group based in Dubai, and the Chhabria P.P. group based in Pune, which are both among the largest groups in India, Bharadwaj is over enthusiastic about the business achievement of the Sindhis; the fact

is that the Parsi, the Natukottai Chettyar and the Punjabi business communities each globally control much bigger assets than the Sindhis.

30. According to Bharadwaj, 1990:52, Bhatias from Thatta were smart businessmen who travelled to the Middle East (Dubai, Bahrain, etc). Under the title 'Tribes of Sind' are listed in alphabetical order: Amils, Bhatias, Kutchis, Khatris, Khojas, p. 48. Lohanas are mentioned only once: they organized a meeting in Karachi in 1912, p. 96.

31. Anand, 1996:10. 'A leading community of Lohana traders were the Sindh workies who came to be characterised as such after the British conquest of Sindh and rose to high positions from their original state of Hawkers'.

32. The word '*jati*' is used by the Lohanas.

33. See for instance, the case of the Nadar, Tamil Nadu, in Tempelman, Dennis, *The Northern Nadars of Tamil Nadu*, Oxford University Press, Delhi, 1996.

34. Bharadwaj, 1988, on the back side of the cover of the book.

35. Bharadwaj, 1988:6, 'The questions posed here are deceptively simple, what does it feel like to be a Sindhi? What is the flavour, texture, smell of the Sindhis?'

36. Bharadwaj was honoured with the 'Ambedkar Award' in 1990-91 and with the National Award as 'Best Historian of Sindhi Community' in 1990. Bharadwaj, 1990:230-1.

37. Prof. Kalyan B. Advani in his preface to Bharadwaj, 1988:11. Bharadwaj, 1988:162. Also to be seen on cars: a sticker 'Sindhuja', which sounds a bit like 'Hinduja'. The President of the BJP, L.K. Advani, gives in the book *Sindhis Through the Ages* his appreciation of it, 1988:13.

38. The author says also 'Thus the people of Kutch and border Rajasthan never went back and got assimilated into the Sindhi population', p. 206. K.R. Malkani, in his preface, underlines: 'A goodly percentage of the Sindhi Hindus who migrated from Sindh in 1947 had gone to Sindh only about three centuries earlier', p. vi.

39. Kandla port, which has been developed to replace Karachi, has become the 6th in importance in India, and Gandhidam is a new township created with the support of the Sindhi Resettlement Corporation for the Sindhi refugees.

40. See 'Dreamland of the Sindhis', Bharadwaj, 1990.

CHAPTER 9
Delphine Maucort

1. *Camelus dromedaries*.
2. It is quite the same aversion we can find with female periods that have to flow outside the body contaminating the dress. Moreover, they are so impure that they bring numerous prohibitions like cooking and worshipping.
3. We take the avoidance relationships definition in Ghasarian: 'Avoidance relationships with someone can take different forms: it can be on the fact to pronounce their name, to have a physical contact with them, to be under the same roof, to cross them on the road, etc. Extremely formal, this relationship, shows respect, shyness, sometimes fear' (Ghasarian, 1996: 190).
4. Altekar says that, in ancient India, girls were not married before the age of sixteen and received an education. Little by little, this female education has been neglected in favour of marriage. During Vedic times, unmarried women start to be rejected and at about 300 BC, 'if upanayana was an obligation for boy, marriage, that was its counterpart, has to be absolutely binding on girls' (Altekar, 1991: 33).
5. O.B.C. means 'Other Backward Classes'

GLOSSARY*

Boivin

linga: the erected stone symbolizing a phallus under which Shiva is worshipped

yoni: a symbolic womb representing a form of the Devi, Shakti, when it is associated with the *linga*.

*devadasi*s: women who were dedicated to temple service; professional dancers, often kept as temple prostitutes.

panjra: short five line poems dedicated to Udero Lal.

mahdi: name given to the one who will restore peace and justice before the end of the world.

tazkira: biography or biographical dictionary of Muslim mystics

qalandar: wandering *be-shar'a* dervish

be-shar'a: a mystic who does not observe the Islamic law

Markovits

banias: name given to a group of Hindu merchants or traders

shroff: a money-changer; a banker

haris: cultivators; mostly working for a landlord

wadero: head of a village or a tribe; honorific title given to the landlords

pir: Sufi master

syed: member of an upper Muslim class in South Asia who traces his ancestry back to the Prophet Muhammad.

murid: follower of a Sufi master

mullah: Muslim cleric

Gayer

*Basti*s: informal neighborhoods developed in unplanned urban areas.

Katcha: impure, raw; when related to housing, it refers to 'soft' habitats, made out of mud, wood, thatch, or corrugated iron.

Dallal: broker ; local 'big man'

Mohalla: neighborhood.

Izzatdar: man of honor ; respectable man.

Ajrak: Sindhi shawl.

Bhatta: protection money.

Suhbat: spiritual conversation between master and disciple, in the Sufi tradition.

Tawajjuh: concentration of master and disciple on each other, in the Sufi tradition.

Cousin

ajrak: piece of cotton cloth used by men either as headgear or as a shawl. It sports red, blue, black and white geometrical patterns.

ajrak bi puri: *ajrak* printed on both sides

alizarine: formerly dye from the madder plant, nowadays synthetic dye producing the same colors: red and black according to the mordant used.

amli: local name for tamarind, *Tamarindus indica*, Linn.
babul: local name for the local acacia, *Acacia nilotica*.
bhindi: tying process in tie-and-dye.
bhogri: small tube through which the thread is directed during the tying process in tie and dye.
bora: dyeing in alizarine vat (for red and black)
chokro: apprentice in a workshop
chundri, chunri: woman's veil, especially among Hindus; *Rati chunri*: red-ground veil;
kakrechi chunri: black-ground veil
dhoti: piece of cotton cloth, generally white, worn wrapped around the lower part of the body by Hindu men.
dupatta: veil worn by women along with the shalwar and kameez.
jimi: block printed woman's veil decorated with white and black patterns, sometimes blue, on a red ground.
karigar: worker in a workshop
kinjo: padding with fugitive colors, as a finishing.
kiriana: small geometrical designs in black and white on a red ground for women's dress of the Khatri community of printers.
malir: block-printed cloth with white and black patterns on a red ground for men's and women's dress; with embroidery on the four corners, used as headgear worn by Hindu men during wedding ceremonies.
mashru: piece of satin made of silk for the warp and cotton for the weft, often with stripped pattern.
mina: blue shade on ajrak named after the blue shade of enamel.
mordant: chemical product which lets a dye produce a given color.
neer: indigo dye.
odhani: woman's veil
paro: woman's skirt
rato paro: red-ground skirt
kakrecho paro: black- and red-ground skirt
karo udo: plain black-ground skirt
peti: front part of a woman's bodice, covering the stomach.
resist: any process to protect a given space on a textile from the dye. It can be a paste or wax in printing, or a tied thread in tie and dye.
sakun: local name for tamarisk, *Tamarisk articula*, Vahl. or *Tamarix gallica*, Linn.
sutarno: process used in tie and dye to mark the lines where the cloth is tied.
usto: master in a workshop

Khan
chilla: A Sufi practice consisting of a forty-day period of meditation; a shrine built in the memory of a Muslim saint.
jati: caste.
kshatrya: The second socio-religious category among Hindus, *varnas* comprising rulers and noble warriors.
mohalla: neighborthood.
panth: Lit. 'path'; a sectarian tradition.
samadhi: A stage of meditation in the yoga tradition. Hindu funerary monument.
sampraday: A religious tradition or movement.

shakti:	Lit. 'Energy'; the great goddess in Hindu tradition.
shuddhi:	Purification ritual initiated by the Arya Samaj.
shudra:	The fourth socio-religious category comprising menial castes.
varna:	Any of the four socio-religious categories defined in the Brahmanical treatises.

Maucort

angeli:	bridegroom's long tunic
chareno:	men's large trousers
chatti:	A Hindu ceremony which takes place on the sixth day after the birth of a child, when the baby is named.
chiri:	red cloth tied on bridegroom's waist
chuniyo or *ghaghro*:	straight skirt
dhabri:	woollen veil wora by women
doriyo or *patelo*:	cotton or polyester veil for little girls
ghughat or *laj*:	'modesty' or 'honour'
kapru:	women's short top
lungi:	men's woollen or linen cloth wrapped around the waist.
mojri:	big leather shoes
pachedo or pachedi:	tubular skirt worn by women
polko:	long-sleeved top for little girls
qamiz or *buscot*:	long-sleeved shirt
rumal:	turban
topi:	bonnet

Editor's Note:

*The glossary does not attempt to be exhaustive. It only includes the most important non-English words used in the various chapters.

Bibliography

Chapter 1: *Chronology of Sehwan Sharif Through Ceramics (The Islamic Period)*
Annabelle Collinet

Abu Umar-i-Usman, Maulana Minhajuddin, *Tabaqat-i Nasiri, A General History of the Muhammadan Dynasties of Asia, including Hindustan; from AH 194 (AD 810) to AH 658 (AD 1260)*, translated by H.G. Raverty, 2 volumes, London.

Akhtar, M.S., 1990, *An introduction to Sind under the Mughuls, Translation of and Commentary on the Mazhar-i Shahjahani of Yusuf Mirak (1044/1634)*, Islamabad/Karachi, National Institute of Historical and Cultural Research, Department of Culture, Government of Sindh.

Al-Mas'udi, 1962, *Les prairies d'Or*, translated into French by Barbier de Meynard and Pavet de Courteille, reviewed and edited by Ch.Pellat, Vol. I Paris.

Al-Muqaddasi, 1994, *The Best Divisions for Knowledge of the Regions, Ahsan al-Taqasim fi Ma'rifat al-Aqalim*, translated by B.A. Collins, reviewed by M.H. Alta'i, London.

Anonymous, 1964, 'Excavations at Banbhore', *Pakistan Archaeology*, 1, pp. 49-55.

Anonymous, 1968, 'Banbhore', *Pakistan Archaeology*, 5, pp. 176-185.

Blayac, Johanna, 2004. *La dynastie tughlukide, etat des recherches*, Master's thesis under the direction of L. Kalus, University of Paris IV Sorbonne, unpublished.

Bosworth, C.E., 1963, 'Ghaznavides', *Encyclopédie de l'Islam*, 2nd edition, vol. II, pp. 1074-1079.

Collinet, Annabelle, 2001, *La céramique islamique du site de Sehwan Sharif, Sind, VIIIe-XVIe siècles (Résultats de la campagne 1999-2000)*, DEA thesis under the direction of A. Northedge and M. Kervran, Paris I Panthéon-Sorbonne, unpublished.

Edwards, H.F., 1990, *The Genesis Of Islamic Architecture In The Indus Valley*, Ph.D., New York University, unpublished.

Elliot, H.M., and J. Dowson, 1867, *The History of Sind as told by its own historians. The Muhammadan Period*, Vol. I reprinted Karachi, Allied Book Company, 1985.

Gardin, J.C., 1957, *Céramiques de Bactres,* Mémoires de la DAFI, T.XV, Paris.

_____, *Lashkari Bazar II, les trouvailles,* Mémoires de la DAFA, T.XVIII, Paris.

Hasan, T., 1995, 'Ceramics of Sultanate India', *South Asian Studies*, 11, pp. 83-106.

Hobson, L., 1928-1930, 'Potsherds from Brahminabad', *Transactions of the Oriental Ceramic Society*, VIII, pp. 21-23.

Husain, J., 1992, 'Potter's craft at Shaikhan Dheri, an ethnoarchaeological reconstruction', *Pakistan Archaeology*, 27, pp. 171-195.

Ibn Batutta, 1858, *Voyages,* vol. II, *De la Mecque aux steppes russes et à l'Inde* et vol. III, *Inde, Extrême-Orient, Espagne et Soudan*, translated from Arabic by C. Defremery and B.R. Sanguinetti (1858), Introduction and notes by Stéphane Yerasimos, Paris, 1982, reprinted 1997.

Ibn Hauqal, 1964, *Configuration de la Terre (Kitab Surat al-Ard)*, introduction and translation by J.H. Kramers and G.Wiet, Beirut and Paris, Vol. II.

Kalichbeg Fredunbeg, 1900, *The Chach Namah, An Ancient History of Sind, giving the Hindu period down to the Arab Conquest,* translated from Persian by Mirza Kalichbeg Fredunbeg, reprinted Karachi, 1990.

————, 1902, *History of Sind, vol. II, part I, Giving the Musulman period from the Arab Conquest to the beginning of the reign of the Kalhorahs, Part II, Giving the reigns of the Kalhorahs and the Talpurs down to the British Conquest*, translated from Persian by Mirza Kalichbeg Fredunbeg, re-printed Karachi, 1982.

Kervran, Monique, 2005, 'Mission archéologique française au Sud-Sind', Archéologies, 20 ans de recherches françaises dans le monde, Ministère des Affaires Etrangères, Maisonneuve et Larose/ADPF-ERC, pp. 595–598.

Khan, A.N., 1990, *Al-Mansurah, A Forgotten Arab Metropolis in Pakistan*, Karachi, 1990.

Khan, F.A., 1976, *Banbhore, a Preliminary Report on the Recent Archaeological Excavations at Banbhore*, Karachi.

————, 1981, 'Debal and Mansura, the Historical Cities of the Early Islamic Period', *Pakistan Journal Of History and Culture*, II, no. 1, pp. 103–122.

Maclean, Derryl, 1989, *Religion and Society in Arab Sind*, Monographs and Theoretical Studies in Sociology and Anthropology in Honour of Nels Anderson, Leiden & New York, Brill.

Mehta, R.N., 1949, 'Some archaeological remains from Baroda', *Bulletin of the Baroda State Museum and Picture Gallery,* IV, pp. 3–16.

————, 1950, 'Some glimpses into Muslim material culture in Gujarat, archaeological finds at Baroda', *Islamic Culture*, pp. 45–49.

————, 1975, 'Khambat (Cambay): Topographical, archaeological and toponymical perspective', *Journal of the M.S. University of Baroda*, 24, 1, pp. 17–29.

Northedge, A. and D. Kennet, 1994, 'The Samarra Horizon', *Cobalt and Lustre, Naser D. Khalili Collection of Islamic Art*, vol. IX, dir. E.J. Grube, London, pp. 21–35.

Panhwar, M.H., 1977, *Source Material on Sind*, Institute of Sindhology, University of Sindh, Jamshoro.

————, 1983, *Chronological dictionary of Sind*, Institute of Sindhology, University of Sindh, Jamshoro.

Pathan, M.H., 1974, *Arab Kingdom of al-Mansurah in Sind*, Institute of Sindhology, University of Sindh, Hyderabad.

————, 1978, *Sind, Arab Period,* Sindhi Adabi Board, Hyderabad.

Péli, Audrey, 2002, *Les carreaux islamiques à décor peint sous glaçure de Kalan Kot, de Lahori Bandar et de Sehwan, Sind (Pakistan): datation et attribution*, Master's thesis under the direction of A. Northedge and M. Kervran, Paris I-Panthéon Sorbonne, unpublished.

Reinaud, J.T., 1845, 'Fragments Arabes et Persans relatifs à l'Inde', *Journal Asiatique*, V, 4th série, pp. 121–192.

Rosen-Ayalon, M., 1974. *Ville Royale de Suse IV, Poterie Islamique*, Mémoire de la DAFI, T.L, Paris.

Rousset, M.O., 1994, 'Quelques précisions sur le matériel de Hira (céramique et verre)', *Archéologie Islamique*, 4, pp. 19–55.

Rye, O.S. and C. Evans, 1974. *Traditional Pottery Techniques of Pakistan*. Smithsonian Institution Press, Washington D.C., reprinted Islamabad, 1990.

Scerrato, U., 1959, 'The first two excavation campaigns at Ghazni, 1957-58, Summary Report of the Italian Archaeological Mission in Afghanistan', *East and West*, 10, pp. 23–55.

————, 1962, 'Islamic glazed tiles with moulded decoration from Ghazni', *East and West*, 13, pp. 263-287.

Shafi, I., 1938, 'Fresh light on the Ghaznavids', *Islamic Culture*, 12, pp. 189-234.

Siddiqi, M.H., 1972, *History of the Arghuns and Tarkhans of Sind (1507-1593), an annotated translation of the relevant parts of Mir Masum's Ta'rikh-i-Sind with an Introduction and Appendices*, Karachi.

Waddington, H., 1946, 'Adilabad', *Ancient India*, I, pp. 60–76.

Whitehouse, D., 1968, 'Excavations at Siraf, First Interim Report', *Iran*, 6, pp. 1–22.

Wilkinson, C.K., 1973, *Nishapur: Pottery of the Early Islamic Period*, New York.

Chapter 2: *Shivaite Cults and Sufi Centres: A Reappraisal of the Medieval Legacy in Sindh*
Michel Boivin

Aitken, H.T. *Gazetteer of the Province of Sind* 1907. Reprint, Karachi: Indus Publications, 1986.

Allana, Ghulam Ali. *Ginans of Ismaili Pirs*. Karachi: His Highness Prince Aga Khan Shia Imami Ismailia Association for Pakistan, 1984.

Allana, Khwaja Ghulam Ali. *Lar ji adabi ain thaqafati tarikh*. Hyderabad: Institute of Sindhology, Sindh University, 1977.

Ansari, Sarah. *Sufi Saints and State Power: The Pirs of Sind, 1843-1947*. Lahore: Vanguard Books, 1992.

Boivin, Michel. 'Reflections on La`l Shahbaz Qalandar and the Management of his Spiritual Authority in Sehwan Sharif.' *Journal of the Pakistan Historical Society LI, no. 4*, (2003): 41–74.

———, 'The Renunciant in the Ismaili *Ginan*s and in Sindhi Devotional Literature', in *Second International Conference on the Ginans, Rajkot, November 2004*, Rajkot: Saurashtra University, 2004. Unpublished Paper.

———, 'Note Sur la Danse Dans les Cultes Musulmans du Domaine Sindhi.' *Journal d'Histoire du Soufisme* 4, pp. 179–187.

———, 2005b, 'Le pèlerinage de Sehwan Sharif dans le Sindh (Pakistan): territoires, protagonistes et rituels', in S. Chiffoleau and A. Madoeuf (éds.), *Les pèlerinages au Maghreb et au Moyen-Orient. Espaces publics, espaces du public*, Damascus, Institut Français du Proche-Orient, pp. 311–346.

Briggs, George, 1938, *Gorakhnath and the Kanphata Yogis*, reprinted Delhi, Motilal Barnarsidass, 1998.

Burton, Richard, 1851, *Sind and the races that inhabit the valley of the Indus*, reprinted Karachi, Indus Publications, 1988.

———, 1877, *Sindh Revisited*, vols I & II, reprinted Karachi, Department of Culture and Tourism, Government of Sindh, 1993.

Carter, G.E.L., 1917, 'Religion in Sind', *Indian Antiquary*, September, pp. 205–208.

———, 1932, 'Old sites on the lower Indus. Thambhanwaro Masjid and some other sites', *Indian Antiquary*, May, pp. 86–90.

Chach Nama (ca 3rd/9th century), Tr. From Arabic into Persian in the year 613/1216 by Ali b. Hamid al-Kufi, ed. by Umar b. Muhammad Da'udpotah, Delhi, Matba'at Latifi.

Cousens, Henry, 1929, *The Antiquities of Sind*, rprinted Karachi, Department of Culture, Government of Sindh, 3rd ed. 1998.

Digby, Simon, 1970, 'Encounters with Jogis in Indian Sûfi Hagiography', Seminar on Aspects of Religion in South Asia, SOAS, London, Unpublished Paper.

———, 2000, *Wonder-Tales of South Asia*, Jersey, Orient Monographs.

Elliott, H.M. & John Dowson, 1867, *The History of Sind as Told by its own Historians*, reprinted Karachi, Allied Book Company, 1985.

Ernst, Carl, 2005, 'Situating Sufism and Yoga', *Journal of the Royal Asiatic Society*, Series 3, 15: 1, pp. 15–43.

Grodzins Gold, Ann, 1992, *A Carnival of Parting. The Tales of Bharthari and King Gopichand as Sung and Told by Madhu Natisar Nath of Ghatiyali, Rajasthan*, Berkeley, University of California Press.

Haig, M.R., 1894, *The Indus Delta Country*, reprinted Karachi, Indus Publications, 1972.

Huien Tsang (7th century), *Si-yu-ki: Buddhist Records of the Western World*, tr. by Samuel Beal, 2 vols, London, Kegan Paul, Trench, Trübner & Co., 1884.

Hughes, A.W., 1876, *Gazetteer of the Province of Sindh*, reprinted Karachi, Indus Publications, 1995.

Kervran, Monique, 1989 and 1994, *Indus Delta Survey*, Unpublished Manuscript.

———, 2005, 'Pakistan: mission archéologique française au Sud-Sind', *Archéologies, 20 ans de recherches françaises dans le monde*, Ministère des Affaires Etrangères, Maisonneuve et Larose/ADFP-ERC, pp. 595–598.

Khan, Ansar Zahid, 1980, *History and Culture of Sind. A Study of Socio-Economic Organization and Institutions during the 16th and 17th centuries*, Karachi, Royal Book Company.

Khan, G.M., 1976, 'Naqshbandi Saints of Sindh', *Journal of the Royal Society of Punjab*, vol. XII-2.

Lari, Suhail Zaheer, 1994, *History of Sindh*, Karachi, Oxford University Press.

Lari, Suhail Z. & Yasmeen, Lari, 1997, *The Jewels of Sindh. Samma Monuments on Makli Hill*, Karachi, Heritage Foundation and Oxford University Press.

Lohuizen, J.E. van, 1981, 'The pre-Muslim Antiquities of Sind' in H. Khuhro (ed.), *Sind Through Centuries*, Karachi, Oxford University Press, pp. 43–58.

Lorenzen, David N., 1972, *The Kapalikas and Kalamukhas. Two lost Shivaite sects*, Delhi, Motilal Banarsidass.

MacLean, Derryl, 1989, *Religion and Society in Arab Sind*, Leiden, E.J. Brill.

———, 2000, 'La sociologie de l'engagement politique: le Mahdawiya indien et l'Etat', *Revue du Monde Musulman et de la Méditerranée*, 91-92-93-94, pp. 239–256.

Majumdar, N.C., 1934, *Explorations in Sind. Being a report of the exploratory survey carried out during the years 1927-28, 1929-30 and 1930-31*, reprinted Karachi, Indus Publications, 1981.

Marshall, Sir John, 1931, *Mohenjo Daro and the Indus civilization*, 3 vols, London, Arthur Probsthain.

Matringe, Denis, 1992, 'Krisnaite and Nath Elements in the Poetry of the Eighteenth Century Panjabi Sufi Bullhe Sah', in R. McGregor (ed.), *Devotional Literature in South Asia: Current Research*, Cambridge, Cambridge University Press, pp. 190–206.

Naimi, Mawlana Qazi Muhammad Iqbal Husayn Saheb, 1997, *Tazkirah-ye awliya'-ye Sindh*, Karachi, Ilmi Kitab Ghar.

Shah-jo Risalo, 1951, ed. Ghulam Mustafa Qasmi, Shikarpûr, Mehran Akedemi.

Rizvi, S.A.A., 1970, 'Sufis and Natha Yogis in Medieval Northern India (XII to XVI Centuries)', *Journal of the Oriental Society of Australia*, 7, pp. 119-133.

———, 1978, *A History of Sufism in India*, 2 vols, New Delhi, Munshiram ManoharLal Publishers.

Ross, David, 1883, *The land of the five rivers and Sindh. Sketches Historical and Descriptive*, reprinted Karachi, Allied Books Co., 1990.

Rushbrook-Williams, L.F., 1958, *The Black Hills. Kutch in History and Legend*, London, Weidenfeld and Nicholson.

Schimmel, Annemarie, 1986, *Pearls from the Indus. Studies in Sindhi culture*, Jamshoro/Hyderabad, Sindhi Adabi Board.

Smyth, J. W., 1919-20, *Gazetteer of the Province of Sindh*, B, 7 vols, Bombay, Government Central Press (2nd ed. 1926-1929).

Thakur, U.T., 1959, *Sindhi culture*, Bombay, University of Bombay.

Walker, Benjamin, 1968, *Hindu World: An Encyclopedic Survey of Hinduism*, 2 vols, reprinted New Delhi, Munshiram ManoharLal Publishers, 1983.

Chapter 3: *Urban Society in Colonial Sindh (1843-1947)*
Claude Markovits

Advani, A.B., 1940, 'Hyderabad. A Brief Historical Sketch', *Sindhian World*, vol. I, no 6, pp. 356-369.

Ansari, S.F.D., 1992, *Sufi Saints and State Power: The Pirs of Sind 1843-1947*, Cambridge.

_____, 1998, 'Partition, Migration and Refugees: Responses to the Arrival of Muhajirs in Sind during 1947-48', in D.A. Low and H. Brasted (eds.), *Freedom, Trauma, Continuities: Northern India and Independence*, New Delhi, pp. 91–103.

Askari, N. and R. Crill, 1997, *Colours of the Indus: Costume and Textiles of Pakistan*, London.

Banga, I., 1992, 'Karachi and its Hinterland under Colonial Rule', in Banga (ed.), *Ports and their Hinterlands in India*, Delhi, pp. 337–358.

Burton, R.F., 1851, *Sindh and the races that inhabit the Valley of the Indus, with Notices of the Topography and History of the Province*, London.

Census of India 1891, vol. VIII, *Bombay and its Feudatories*, part I, *Report*, W.W. Drew, Bombay.

Census of India 1941, vol. XII, *Sind*, H.T. Lambrick, Karachi.

Cheesman, D., 1997, *Landlord Power and Peasant Indebtedness in Colonial Sind 1865-1901*, London.

Gankovsky, Yu., 1981, 'The Durrani Empire', in USSR Academy of Sciences, *Afghanistan Past and Present*, Moscow, pp. 76–98.

Gommans J.L.L., 1995, *The Rise of the Indo-Afghan Empire, c. 1710-1780*, Leiden, New York, Köln.

Habib, I., 1982, 'Population', in I. Habib and T. Raychaudhuri, *The Cambridge Economic History of India, Volume I, c. 1200-c. 1750*, Cambridge, pp. 163–171.

Haider A., 1974, *A History of Karachi, with special reference to Educational, Demographical and Commercial Developments, 1839-1900*, Karachi.

Hasan, K.S., 1992, *Sindh's fight for Pakistan*, Karachi.

Indian Statutory Commission, 1930, vol. XVI, Selections from Memoranda and oral evidence by non-officials (Part I), London.

Khuhro, H., 1978, *The Making of Modern Sind: British Policy and Social Change in the Nineteenth Century*, Karachi.

_____, 1982, (ed.), *Documents on Separation of Sind from Bombay Presidency*, Islamabad.

_____, 1998, 'Masjid Manzilgah, 1939-40. Test Case for Hindu-Muslim Relations in Sind', *Modern Asian Studies*, vol. 32, 1, pp. 49–89.

Kirpalani, S.K., 1993, *Fifty Years with the British*, Bombay.

Lari, S.Z., 1994, *A History of Sindh*, Karachi.

Levi, S.C., 2002, *The Indian Diaspora in Central Asia and its Trade, 1550-1900*, Leiden, Boston, Köln.

Mariwalla, C.L., 1981, *History of the Commerce of Sind (From Early Times to 1526 AD)*, Jamshoro.

Markovits, C., 2000, *The Global World of Indian Merchants: Traders of Sind from Bukhara to Panama*, Cambridge.

Masson, Charles, 1842, *Narrative of Various Journeys in Baloochistan, Afghanistan and the Panjab. Including a Residence in these Countries from 1826 to 1838*, London.

Memoirs of Seth Naomul Hotchand, C.S.I., A Forgotten Chapter of Indian History 1982, Karachi, (1st ed., Exeter, 1915).

Narsain, S.J. 1932, 'The Amil Community of Hyderabad (Sind)', Unpublished thesis, University of Bombay.

Schimmel, A., 1974, *Sindhi Literature*, Wiesbaden.

Talbot, I., 1988, *Provincial Politics and the Pakistan Movement: The Growth of the Muslim League in North-West and North-East India 1937-1947*, Karachi.

Chapter 4: *A History Of Violence: Ethnic And Sectarian Conflicts In Karachi (1985-2005)*
Laurent Gayer

Abbas, M., 2002, 'The MQM's new reality', *Newsline*, November.

Abou-Zahab, M. & O. Roy, 2003, *Islamic Networks. The Pakistan-Afghan Connection*, London, Hurst.

Ali, N.S., 2001, 'Doctors under fire', *Newsline*, August.

————, 2002, 'The Jihad within', *Newsline*, May.

————, 2002, 'Highway to hell', *Newsline*, August.

————, 2002, 'Doctors under fire', *Newsline*, August 2001; M. Ansari, 'Moving target', *Newsline*, February.

————, 2002, 'The Jihad within', *Newsline*, 2002.

Anderson, B., 1998, *The Spectre of Comparisons. Nationalism, Southeast Asia and the World*, London, Verso.

Anif, M., 1989, 'The gun-runners of Karachi', *Newsline*, October.

Ansari, M., 2002, 'Moving target', *Newsline*, February.

Ansari, S.F.D., 1998, 'Partition, migration and refugees: responses to the arrival of Muhajirs in Sind during 1947-48', *in* D. A. Low & H. Brasted (eds.), *Freedom, Trauma, Continuities. Northern India and Independence*, Delhi, Sage.

Arendt, Hannah, 1983, *Condition de l'homme moderne* [*The Human Condition*], Paris, Calmann-Lévy.

Axel, B.K., 2001, *The Nation's Tortured Body. Violence, Representation and the Formation of a Sikh 'Diaspora'*, London/Durham, Duke University Press.

Boivin, M. 2001, 'Karachi et ses territoires en conflits: pour une relecture de la question communautaire', *Hérodote*, no. 101.

Dawn, 2003, 'MMA conspiring to destroy peace: Altaf', *Dawn*, internet edition, 18/01.

Feldman, A., 1991, *Formations of Violence. The Narrative of the Body and Political Terror in Northern Ireland*, Chicago, University of Chicago Press.

Friday Times, The (Lahore), 2003, 'Having a raving good time', February 7-13.Gayer, L., 2004, *Les politiques internationales de l'identité: Significations internationals des mobilisations identitaires des Sikhs (Inde) et des Mohajirs (Pakistan)*, Ph. Dissertation, Paris, Sciences Politiques.

Goodson, L., 2002, *The Talibanization of Pakistan*, New York/Basingstoke, Palgrave-Macmillan.

Hanif, M., 1995, 'Cry, my Karachi', *Newsline*, March.

Hasan, A., 1987, 'A generation comes of age', *The Herald*, October.

_____, 1999, *Understanding Karachi. Planning and Reform for the Future*, Karachi, City Press.

Hasan, S.S., 2005, 'APMSO-IJT standoff forebodes trouble in local bodies elections', *The Herald*, March.

Hasnain, G., 1997, "For us, Altaf Hussain was like a God', *Newsline* (Karachi), May.

Herald, The 1988, 'The campus mafias', *The Herald*, October, pp. 52–65.

Herald, The, 1985, 'Traffic in death', *The Herald*, May.

Herald, The, 2004, 'Bloody May', June.

Herald, The, 2004, 'Bloody May', *The Herald*, June.

Herald Annual, The, 1995, 'The Hong Kong factor', January.

Hopkins, A.G. (ed.), 2002, *Globalization in World History*, London, Pimlico.

Hussain, A., 1990, 'The Karachi riots of December 1986: crisis of state and civil society in Pakistan', *in* V. Das (ed.), *Mirrors of Violence. Communities, Riots and Survivors in South Asia*, New Delhi.

Katrak, S. K.H., 1963, *Karachi. That was the Capital of Sindh*, Lahore.

Lari, Y. and M. S. Lari, 1996, *The Dual City. Karachi During the Raj*, Karachi, Oxford University Press.

Linden, J. Van Der, E. Meijer & P. Nientied, 1991, 'Informal housing in Karachi', *in* J. V. D. Linden & F. Selier (eds.), *Karach. Migrants, Housing and Housing Policy*, Lahore, Vanguard.

Mansoor, H., 2002, 'Has MQM struck a deal with the government?', *The Friday Times*, August 30-September 5.

_____, 2002, 'MQM shake-up will test Altaf's control', *The Friday Times*, November 15-21.

_____, 2002, 'Karachi electioneering becomes violent', *The Friday Times*, September 27-October 3.

_____, 2003, 'Islamicising Pakistan's secular centre', *The Friday Times*, January 17-23.

_____, 2003, 'An eerie sense of déjà vu', *The Friday Times*, 24-30/01.

Markovits, C., 2000, *The Global World of Indian Merchants, 1750-1947. Traders of Sindh from Bukhara to Panama*, Cambridge, Cambridge University Press.

Meyerink, H., 1983, 'Karachi's growth in historical perspective', *in* J.W. Schoorl, J.J. van der Linden & K.S. Yap (eds.), *Between Basti Dwellers and Bureaucrats. Lessons in Squatter Settlement Upgrading in Karachi*, Oxford, Pergamon Press, 1983.

Mouzoune, A., 1999, *Les transformations du paysage spatio-communautaire de Beyrouth, 1975-1996*, Paris, Publisud.

Naqvi, M., 1998, *Mass Transit*, Karachi, Oxford University Press.

Newsline, 1989, 'The anatomy of violence', October.

Nizami, Z.A., 198? *Karachi Through the Centuries*, Karachi, Karachi Development Authority.

Pécaut, D., 1995, 'De la banalité de la violence à la terreur', *Cultures & Conflits*, no. 24-25, Winter; An English version of this paper was published in K. Koonings & D. Krujit (eds.), *Societies of Fear. The Legacy of War, Violence and Terror in Latin America*, London , Zed Books, 1999

Picard, E., 1996, 'Liban, la matrice historique', *in* François Jean, Jean-Christophe Rufin (dir.), *Economie des guerres civiles*, Paris, Hachette.

Rana, A., 2003, 'Jehad Inc -back in business', *The Friday Times*, January 17-23.

Richards, J.J., 1993, *Mohajir Subnationalism and the Mohajir Qaumi Movement in Sindh Province, Pakistan*, Ph.D dissertation, Cambridge, Cambridge University.

Scheff, T.J., 1994, *Bloody Revenge. Emotions, Nationalism and War*, Boulder, Westview Press.

Schimmel, A., 1975, *Mystical Dimensions of Islam*, Chapel Hill, University of North Carolina University Press.

Secretariat Karachi Port Trust, 1980, *History of Karachi Port*, Karachi.

Tan, T.Y. & G. Kudaisya, 2000, *The Aftermath of Partition in South Asia*, London/New York, Routledge.

Tambiah, S., 1996, *Leveling Crowds. Ethnonationalist Conflicts and Collective Violence in South Asia*, New Delhi, Vistaar

Verkaaik, O., 1999, *Inside the Citadel. Fun, Violence and Religious Nationalism in Hyderabad, Pakistan*, Ph.D dissertation, University of Amsterdam.

Waseem, M., 1996, 'Ethnic conflict in Pakistan: the case of MQM', *The Pakistan Development Review*, 35 (4), Winter.

Werbner, P. & H. Basu (eds.), 1998, *Embodying Charisma: Modernity, Locality and the Performance of Emotion in Sufi Cults*, London, Routledge.

Werth, L., 'The saints who disappeared: saints of the wilderness in Pakistani village shrines', in *ibid*, p. 89.

Yusufzai, R., 1989, 'The Frontier connection', *Newsline*, October.

Chapter 5: *Barmati Panth: A Messianic Sect established in Sindh, Kutch and Saurashtra Françoise Mallison*

Devraj, Mohan Thontya 'History of Barmati Panth', Forthcoming, Karachi (Typescript of the author).

Gohil, Nathalal, *Baramati sampradaya (kaccha-saurastrana meghavala samajamam calati baramati upasana)*, Ahmadaba, Shri Meghani Lokvidya Sanshodan Bhavan, 2002.

Jani, Balvant, ed., *Santvani, tattva ane tantra*, Gandhinagar, Gujarati Sahitya Akadami, 1996.

Khan, Dominique-Sila, *Conversions and Shifting Identities, Ramdev Pir and the Ismailis of Rajasthan,* New Delhi, Manohar and Centre de Sciences Humaines, 1997.

————, 'The Coming of Nikalank Avatar, A Messianic Theme in Some Sectarian Traditions in North Western India', in *Journal of Indian Philosophy*, Vol. 25, 1997, pp. 401–26.

Maclean, Derryl N., *Religion and Society in Arab Sind*, Leiden, B.J. Brill, 1989.

Mallison, Françoise, 'Saant-vani and Harijan, Mahamargi Bhajan and Ismaili ginan. A New Appraisal of Popular Devotion in Saurashtra' in *The Banyan Tree*, *Essays on Early Literature in New Indo-Aryan Languages*, ed. Mariola Offredi, vol. 1, New Delhi, Manohar, 2000, pp. 235–43.

————, 'Saints and Sacred Places in Saurashtra and Kutch, The Case of the Naklamki Cult and the Jakhs' in *Pilgrims, Partons, and Place. Localizing Sanctity inn Asian Religions*, ed. Phyllis Granoff and Loichi Sinohara, Vancouver, UBC Press, 2003, pp. 332-49.

Mamaidev, *Mamaideva Purana*, ed. Kavi Kanji Khenga Locara, Gandhidham, 1974.

Matang, *Matanga Purana*, ed. Matang Malsi Ladha Bhagavant, Gandhidham, Matang Jatashankar Malsi, 1992.

Rushbrooke Williams, L.F., *The Black Hills: Kutch in History and Legend: A Study in Indian Local Loyalties*, London, Weidenfield and Nicolson, 1958.

Chapter 6: *Jhulelal and the Identity of Indian Sindhis*
Dominique-Sila Khan

Allana G., 1984, *Ginans of Ismaili Pirs rendered in English verses*, Karachi, Shia Imami
  Ismaili Association for Pakistan.
Ansari S., 1992, *Sufi Saints and State Power, The Pirs of Sindh 1843-1947*, Cambridge,
  CUP.
Briggs G.W., 1938, *Gorakhnath and the Kanphata Yogis*, reprinted Delhi, Motilal Banarsidass,
  1990.
Carter G.E.L., 1917-1918, 'Religion in Sind' *Indian Antiquary*, vol. XLVI, September 1917,
  pp. 205-8 and August 1918, pp. 197–208.
Israney S., 1994, 'Roohani Rohri' *Aseen Sindhi*, August 1994, vol. 2, no. 1, pp. 34.
Jaffrelot C., 1994, 'Les (re)conversions à l'hindouisme (1885-1990): politisation et diffusion
  d'une 'invention de la tradition'' in *Archives de Sciences sociales des religions*, July-
  September, pp. 73–98.
Jotwani M., 1995, 'The Sindhis through the centuries' *Sahyog Times International*, October-
  December 95, pp. 17–19.
Khan A.Z., 1975, *History and Culture of Sind*, Karachi, Royal Book Company.
Khan D.S., 1997, *Conversions and Shifting Identities: Ramdev Pir and the Ismailis in
  Rajasthan*, Delhi, Manohar, CSH.
Mayaram S., 1997, *Resisting Regimes: Myth, Memory and the Shaping of a Muslim Identity*,
  Delhi, OUP.
Maclean D.N., 1989, *Religion and Society in Arab Sind*, Leiden, E.J. Brill.
Nanji A., 1978, *The Nizari Ismaili Tradition in the Indo-Pakistan Subcontinent*, Delamar-New-
  York, Caravan Books.
Oberoi H., 1994, *The Construction of Religious Boundaries*, Delhi, OUP.
Rajpal S.,1996, '*Kya sindhi samaj dharam, jati, panth ya sampraday hai?*', *Sindhu Dhara
  Times* May-June 1996, pp. 11–12.
Shackle C. and Z. Moir,1992, *Ismaili Hymns from South-Asia - An Introduction to the ginans*,
  London, SOAS.
Thomas RH., 1855, *Memoirs on Sind*, 2 vol; reprinted Delhi, Low Price Publication, 1993.

Chapter 7: *Lohana and Sindhi Networks*
Pierre Lachaier

Anand, Shubadra, 1996, *National Integration of Sindhis*, Delhi, Vikas Pub. House Pvt. Ltd.
Bharadwaj, Prakash (ed.), 1988, *Sindhis Through The Ages*, Vol. I & II, 1988, Hong Kong,
  Bombay. Worldwide Publishing Company.
————, (ed.), 1990, *Sindhis'International Year Book, Glimpses of Sindhis, 1841-1990, 150
  Years around The World*, Hong Kong, Bombay Worldwide Publishing Company.
Deloches, Jean, 1980, *La circulation en Inde avant la révolution des transports,* Tome II*, la
  voie d'eau*, pp. 50–63, Paris, Ecole Française d'Extrême Orient.
Enthoven, R.E., 1920, *The Tribes and Castes of Bombay*, Vol. I & III, reprinted Delhi, Cosmos
  Pub. 1975.
Hughes, A.W., 1876, *Gazetteer of the Province of Sindh*, 2d.ed., London.
Campbell M. James, 1880, *Gazetteer of the Bombay Presidency*, Vol. V, Cutch, Palanpur, and
  Mahi Kantha, Bombay.
Aitken, E. H., 1907, Gazetteer of the Province of Sind.

(The) Imperial Gazetteer of India, New Ed. Oxford, Clarendon Press, 1908.

Patel, G.D. ed., 1971, *Gazetteer of India, Gujarat, Kutch District*, Ahmedabad.

Grierson, G.A., 1919, *Linguistic Survey of India*, Vol. VIII, Part I, *Indo-Aryan Family North-Western Group, Sindhi & Lahnda*, reprinted Delhi, Motilal Banarsidass, 1963.

Lachaier, P., 1993, 'Le capitalisme lignager assigné aujourd'hui: les marchands Kutchi Lohana, Inde', *Annales E.S.C.*, July-October 1993.

————, 1997, 'The Merchant Lineage Firm and the Non-invisible Hand', in Cadene, Philippe & Denis, Vidal, (eds.), *Webs of Trade, Dynamics of Business Communities in Western India*, Manohar-Centre de Sciences Humaines, p. 23–52.

————, 1999, *Firmes et entreprises en Inde, La firme lignagère dans ses réseaux*, IFP-Karthala-E.F.E.O., 1999.

Markovits, Claude, 2000, *The Global World of Indian Merchants, 1750-1947, Traders of Sind from Bukhara to Panama*, Cambridge University Press.

Rushbrook, Williams, L.F., 1958 *Kutch in History and Legend: A study in Indian local loyalties*, London, Weidenfeld and Nicolson.

Schimmel, Annemarie, 'Sindhi Literature', ed. Jan Gonda, Otto Harrassowitz, Wiesbaden, 1974, *A History of Indian Literature*, Part of Vol. VIII.

Shri dakshina bharata lohana samaja, *Dvitiya Parivara paricaya grantha 1988-89*, 1989.

Shri kacchi lohana mahajan, Mulunda, *Vasti patraka, samvat 2024* (1967-68).

Shri kacchi lohana mahajan, Mulunda, *Parivara paricaya grantha, sam. 2042* (1986).

Shri kacchi lohana mahajan, Puna *Bamdharan ane samajik dhorano tatha vasti patraka, avrtti trji samvat 2040* (1984).

Shri puna lohana mahajan, Puna, *Bandharan, Vasti-patrak, samvat 2042, [sam.] 1986*, prakashan 24 September 1987, Puna 411002.

Shree Lohana Mahaparishadanun Mukhpatra, *Pratam Varsha, Dvitiya Patrika, 15 August 1994*.

Thakur U.T., 1959, *Sindhi Culture*, University of Bombay Pub. Sociology Series, No. 9, University of Bombay.

Thapar, Romila, 1995, 'L'histoire de Rama, L'élaboration continue d'une tradition écrite', *Enquête, Sociologie, Histoire, AnthropologieNQUÊTE*, No. 2, pp: 143–70 (English version: 'Tradition, Dissent and politics in India', *Past and Present*, no. 125, Oxford, 1989, p. 1–26.).

Chapter 8. *Colour and Light: The Textiles of Sindh between Sky and Earth*
Françoise Cousin

Askari, Nasreen and Rosemary Crill, 1997, *Colours of the Indus. Costume and Textiles of Pakistan*, Merrell Holberton and Victoria and Albert Museum.

Bilgrami, Noorjehan, 1990, *Sindh jo Ajrak*, Karachi.

Bunting, Ethel-Jane W., 1980, *Sindhi Tombs and Textiles. The persistance of Pattern*, The Maxwell Museum of Anthropology and University of New Mexico Press.

Cousin, Françoise, 1975, 'Teinture à réserves ligaturées et décor de voiles dans le Kutch', *Objets et Mondes*, XV 47-56.

————, 1976, Lumière et ombre, bleu et rouge: les azrak du Sind', *Objets et Mondes*, XVI: 65-78.

————, 1981, 'Some data on block-printing in Sind', in *Sind through the centuries*, Proceedings of the International Seminar 1975, Hamida Khuhro (eds.), Karachi, Oxford University Press.

————, 1999, 'Noeuds de la vie, couleurs du temps', in *Dans le sillage des techniques, Hommage à Robert Cresswell*, J.-L. Jamard, A. Montigny, F.-R. Picon (eds.), L'Harmattan, Paris,: 127–151.

Fawcett, C.G.H., 1896, *Monograph on dyes and dyeing in the Bombay Presidency*, Bombay.

Chapter 9: *Bhopa's Costumes and Body Technical: The Shy Women and the Proud Men Delphine Maucort*

Bonte P. and M. Izard (eds.), 1991, *Dictionnaire de l'ethnologie et de l'anthropologie*, Paris, P. U. F.

Chambard J-L., 1989, 'La chanson de Nehru: de Râm à Nehru. Ce que pensent de leurs rois les femmes d'un village indien', *Nehru, l'homme et le visionnaire*, seminar held at Unesco from 27 au 29 September 1989 (typed document).

Chatterjee S. K., 1978, 'The Pattern of Indian Clothing in Relation to Tropical Climate', *Journal of Human Evolution*, VII, 95–99.

Chaturvedi B. K., n. d., *Dresses and costumes of India*, Delhi, Diamond Pocket Books.

d'Orazi Flavoni F., 1990, *Rabari: a Pastoral Community of Kutch*, New Delhi, Indira Gandhi Centre of the Arts and Brij Printer Private Limited.

Frater J., 1975, 'The Meaning of Folk Art in Rabari Life', *Textile Museum Journal*, IV, 2, 47–60.

————, 1985, 'The Rabari Lodi, Creating a Fabric Through Social Alliance', *The Weavers Journal*, X, 1, 28–31.

————, 1989, 'Living Textile Arts of the Bhopa rabari', *Arts of Asia*, XIX, 4, 90–98.

————, 1993, 'Elements of Style: The Artisan reflected in Embroideries of western India', in *Mud, Mirror and Thread: Folk Tradition of Rural India*, Ahmedabad, Mapin.

————, 1993, 'Rabari Dress: Adornment that Tells of Tradition', in *Mud, Mirror and Thread: Folk Tradition of Rural India*, Ahmedabad, Mapin.

————, 1995, *Threads of Identity. Embroidery and Adornment of the Nomadic Rabaris*, Middletown and Ahmedabad, Grantha Corporation and Mapin Publishing.

Goswami B. N., 1993, *Indian Costume in the Collection of the Calico Museum of Textiles*, Ahmedabad, Calico Museum of Textile.

Grodzins Gold A., 1988, 'Spirit Possession Perceived and Performed in Rural Rajasthan', *Contributions to Indian Sociology*, n. s. XXII, 1, 35–63.

————, 1992, *Fruitful Journeys. The Ways of Rajasthani Pilgrims*, University of California Press.

Jain J., 1994, 'Rabari', *Shreyas Museum*, Catalogue of museum Shreyas, Ahmedabad.

Leslie J., 1991, 'The significance of Dress for the Orthodox Hindu Woman', in Barnes R. and Eicher J. B., *Dress and Gender. Making and Meaning*, New York, St Martin's Press, 198–213.

Loth A-M., 1979, *La vie publique et privée dans l'Inde ancienne*, Vols. I & II, Paris, Musée Guimet.

Mauss M., 1950, *Sociologie et anthropologie*, Paris, P. U. F.

————, 1950, 'Les techniques du corps', in *Sociologie et anthropologie*, Paris, P. U. F., 365–386.

Seth V., 1993, *Un garçon convenable*, Paris, Grasset.

Tarlo E., 1991, 'A Stitch in Time Revives an Old Skill', *The India Magazine*, February, 19–27.

Tarlo E, 1996, *Clothing Matters. Dress and Identity in India*, New Delhi, Viking–Penguin.

Weinberger-Thomas C., 1996, *Cendres d'immortalité. La crémation des veuves en Inde*, Seuil, Paris.

CONTRIBUTORS

Michel Boivin is Research Fellow at the Centre of Indian and South Asian Studies (EHESS/ CNRS), and teaches contemporary South Asian history at the University of Savoie. He did extensive fieldwork in interior Sindh (Pakistan). After focusing on the Ismaili communities, he is doing research on Sufism and related cults in the same area. With other European and Pakistani scholars and advanced students, he is launching a research project based on an interdisciplinary approach to the monuments of Sehwan Sharif. He is also studying other artistic expressions related to Sufism. Michel Boivin is currently editing two collective books on Sindhi studies.

Annabelle Collinet is a Ph.D. candidate in the University of Paris I – Panthéon Sorbonne. Her research deals with the ceramics of Sindh between the medieval and late Islamic period (2nd–12th centuries AH/8th–18th centuries AD). She is Studies Engineer in the Musée du Louvre, Department of the Arts of Islam, where she was involved in several exhibitions. She is working on the publication of the metal wares collection of the Department. She graduated from the Ecole du Louvre and the Sorbonne University, and teaches Islamic Art History in the Ecole du Louvre.

Françoise Cousin, Ph.D. Musée de l'Homme, is in charge of the comparative technology department and is a specialist of textiles. She is mainly involved, as an anthropologist, in studies on material culture in Rajasthan, India. She has several publications: the book *Tissus imprimés du Rajasthan*, exhibition catalogues, and papers on different topics related to textiles and food.

Laurent Gayer received a Ph.D. in political science from the Institute of Political Studies (Sciences Po) in 2004. His doctoral dissertation, which dealt with the international dimensions of Sikh and Mohajir identity politics, was entitled 'Les politiques internationales de l'identité. Significations internationales des mobilisations identitaires des sikhs (Inde) et des Mohajirs (Pakistan)' [The Globalisation of Identity Politics. International Dimensions of Sikh and Mohajir Ethnic Movements]. He is currently a lecturer in political science/international relations at Sciences Po, Paris and at the Institut National des Langues et Civilisations Orientales (INALCO). He is preparing a book on the contribution of disorder and violence to state formation in Pakistan.

Dominique-Sila Khan obtained her first doctorate in literature in 1981 at the Sorbonne University and completed a second Ph.D. in social anthropology in 1993. Since 1987 she has been settled in Jaipur, India, where she is currently working as an independent researcher, associated with the Institute of Rajasthan Studies. She has chosen to specialize in Hindu-Muslim interactions in South Asia, and in particular in the study of the forgotten branches of Nizari Ismailism in India. Her first book *Conversions and Shifting identities: Ramdev Pir and the Ismailis in Rajasthan* was published in 1997 (Delhi, Manohar). In 2004 her second book *Crossing the Threshold: Understanding Religious Identities in South Asia* appeared in London

(I.B. Tauris – The Institute of Ismaili Studies). She has contributed a number of articles to various publications and volumes in India and abroad.

Pierre Lachaier is Senior Lecturer and researcher in Social Anthropology at the Ecole Française d'Extrême-Orient, Paris. He is teaching and doing research about Indian merchants and industrialists, and more particularly about the Gujarati Lohanas. He has published *Firmes et entreprises en Inde, La firme lignagère dans ses réseaux* (EFEO-IFP-Karthala, Paris, 1999), as well as many articles.

Françoise Mallison is Emeritus Professor (Directeur d'Etudes) at the Ecole Pratique des Hautes Etudes. Her research focuses on Gujarat, Sindh, and the religious culture of medieval India. She edited a collective volume on *Constructions hagiographiques dans le monde indien: Entre mythe et histoire* (Bibliothèque de l'Ecole des Hautes Etudes, Sciences Historiques et Philologiques, vol. 338, Paris, Honoré Champion, 2001, 475 pages). She is currently editing another book with Tazim Kassam, *Ginans: Texts and Contexts. Essays on Ismaili Hymns from South Asia in Honour of Zawahir Moir* (New Delhi).

Claude Markovits is a Directeur de Recherche (Senior Research Fellow) at the Centre National de la Recherche Scientifique, Paris. He is the author of *Indian Business and Nationalist Politics 1931–1939* (Cambridge University Press, 1985), *The Global World of Indian Merchants 1750–1947* (Cambridge University Press, 2000), which was awarded the A.K. Coomaraswamy Book Prize by the American Association of Asian Studies in 2002, and *The Un-Gandhian Gandhi* (Delhi, Permanent Black, 2003). He edited *A History of Modern India 1480–1950* (London, Anthem Press, 2002), and co-edited (with J. Pouchepadass and S. Subrahmanyam) *Society and Circulation: Mobile People and Itinerant Cultures in South Asia 1750–1950* (Delhi, Permanent Black, 2003).

Delphine Maucort has worked on Indian clothes and costumes for more than ten years. She collaborated with the Musée de l'Homme, in Paris, to inventory and highlight the collection of Indian saris. She has also visited India several times to research Gujarati costumes, especially in Ahmedabad and in Jamnagar district. In 2003, she received her doctorate for her research on the Bhopas' clothing, underlining all the technical processes of making, using or re-using clothes.

INDEX